T0222324

Flame Game Development

Your Guide to Creating Cross-Platform Games in 2D Using Flame Engine in Flutter 3

Andrés Cruz Yoris

Apress®

Flame Game Development: Your Guide to Creating Cross-Platform Games in 2D Using Flame Engine in Flutter 3

Andrés Cruz Yoris
Caracas, Venezuela

ISBN-13 (pbk): 979-8-8688-0062-7
https://doi.org/10.1007/979-8-8688-0063-4

ISBN-13 (electronic): 979-8-8688-0063-4

Managing Director, Apress Media LLC: Welmoed Spahr
Acquisitions Editor: Jessica Vakili
Development Editor: James Markham
Coordinating Editor: Spandana Chatterjee

Distributed to the book trade worldwide by Apress Media, LLC, 1 New York Plaza, New York, NY 10004, U.S.A. Phone 1-800-SPRINGER, fax (201) 348-4505, e-mail orders-ny@springer-sbm.com, or visit www.springeronline.com. Apress Media, LLC is a California LLC and the sole member (owner) is Springer Science + Business Media Finance Inc (SSBM Finance Inc). SSBM Finance Inc is a **Delaware** corporation.

For information on translations, please e-mail booktranslations@springernature.com; for reprint, paperback, or audio rights, please e-mail bookpermissions@springernature.com.

Apress titles may be purchased in bulk for academic, corporate, or promotional use. eBook versions and licenses are also available for most titles. For more information, reference our Print and eBook Bulk Sales web page at http://www.apress.com/bulk-sales.

Any source code or other supplementary material referenced by the author in this book is available to readers on GitHub (https://github.com/Apress/Flame-Game-Development). For more detailed information, please visit https://www.apress.com/gp/services/source-code.

Paper in this product is recyclable

Table of Contents

About the Author

Andrés Cruz Yoris has more than ten years' experience in the development of web applications. He works with PHP, Python, and client-side technologies like HTML, JavaScript, CSS, and Vue among others and server-side technologies like Laravel, Flask, Django, and CodeIgniter. I am also a developer in Android Studio, Xcode, and Flutter with which he creates native applications for Android and iOS.

About the Technical Reviewer

 **Lukas Klingsbo (spydon)** is part of the Blue Fire open source collective and is the top contributor and maintainer of the Flame game engine.

When not improving Flame, you can see him giving talks and holding workshops on Flutter all over the world.

Acknowledgments

Thanks to everyone on my publishing team. Thanks to my father, who was always there for me. And thanks to my mom for her support.

Introduction

This book is intended to get you started with Flame using Flutter; with this, we are going to clarify two things:

1. It is not a book which provides 100% knowledge of Flame or takes you from being a beginner to an expert, since it would be too big an objective for the scope of this book. What it offers is knowledge about the main aspects of Flame, such as sprites, collision systems, tiled inputs, and much more, and how to apply them to 2D game development.

2. It is assumed that you have at least basic knowledge of Flutter and its basic technologies such as Dart.

Flame is a very interesting package to create our first multiplatform 2D games. Being implemented in Flutter, with a single project, we can have the same game for mobile, desktop, and web without much problem. Flame contains all the basic elements to create 2D games provided by similar game engines like collision handling, events, sprite loading, sprite sheet, and of course interacting with all these elements.

This book applies a practical approach, from knowing the key aspects of the technology to putting them into practice, gradually implementing small features and functionalities that can be adapted to a real game.

To follow this book, you need to have a computer running Windows, Linux, or MacOS.

CHAPTER 1

Create a Project in Flutter and Add Flame

In this chapter, we are going to learn how to create a Flutter project and add the necessary base library to develop our 2D games using Flutter; therefore, it is a chapter that you should refer to every time we create a new project in later chapters.

Let's start by creating the project that we will use to create the application:

```
$ flutter create <ProjectName>
```

Once the project is created in Flutter, we change to the project folder:

```
$ cd <ProjectName>
```

And we add the Flame library:

```
$ flutter pub add flame
```

Finally, we open VSC or the editor you use to develop in Flutter; for this, you can do the manual process (open the project we created earlier from VSC) or use the VSC command (in case you have it configured):

```
$ code .
```

© Andrés Cruz Yoris 2024
A. Cruz Yoris, *Flame Game Development*, https://doi.org/10.1007/979-8-8688-0063-4_1

CHAPTER 2

Flame Basics

In this chapter we will know the key elements of Flame and its organization, components, and key structures. This chapter purely acts as a reference; do not worry if you do not understand all the terms explained. The following chapters offer a more practical scheme in which we build an application step-by-step, and when you encounter one of the classes and functions introduced in this chapter, you can return to this chapter to review what was explained about it.

You can create a project called "testsflame" following the process shown in the previous chapter.

Game Class and Components

A project in Flame can be divided into two parts:

1. The main class, which is the one that allows all the modules of the application to communicate and uses Flame's own processes such as the collision and input system (keyboard, gestures, etc.)

2. The components, which are the elements of our game, such as a background, a player, an enemy, etc.

To make the idea easier to understand, you can see Flame's **Game** class as Flutter's **MaterialApp** and the Flame components as each of the pages that make up a Flutter application.

© Andrés Cruz Yoris 2024
A. Cruz Yoris, *Flame Game Development*, https://doi.org/10.1007/979-8-8688-0063-4_2

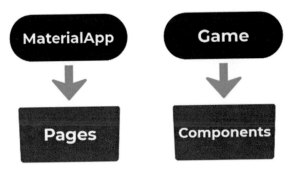

Figure 2-1. *Widgets in Flutter vs. components in Flame*

Let's get to know each of these Flame elements in more detail.

Components

One of the great aspects of Flame is that we can use the different features of Flame with the help of its component system. A component can be many things like a player, an enemy, a background, particle effects, texts, or a joystick, among others, with which we can incorporate more features such as the use of collisions, updates, and interactions with keys, like drag and drop, tap, etc. As you can see, Flame has a very similar approach to Flutter, but in this case with components instead of widgets and based on games.

In essence, a game entity, such as a player, is represented by a component, which is a class. Through the **Game** class of our application, which is a Game-type class, the components can communicate with each other, for example, in entries or collisions, which gives us a very modular and scalable environment for the application.

We have many types of components. In this book, we will see some like

- SpriteComponent

- SpriteAnimationComponent

- PositionComponent

- TextComponent

You can see the complete list at `https://docs.flame-engine.org/latest/flame/components.html`.

Game Classes: Game and FlameGame

As we do in any project, it is important to have a base structure that we can easily maintain and scale. Flame is designed for modularity. Globally, we have a **Game** class that gives us a lot of control over each of the components that make up the application. This Game class is global to the entire application and can be represented by many types of classes; **FlameGame** is the most widely used Game class in Flame, and it's the one we'll mainly be looking at in this book. Any component we add in the **FlameGame** class can be used for collision detection, providing an easy way for components to communicate in Flame.

Thanks to the **FlameGame** class, which is a Game-type class of the application, it is possible to divide our game into components (classes) that represent each entity in our game, such as a player, a background, enemies, a setting, etc.

You can find more information in `https://docs.flame-engine.org/latest/flame/game.html`.

Regarding the class itself called **Game**, it is a low-level class. Like the **FlameGame** class, we can use it as the main class or the Game-type class for the game, but unlike FlameGame, it offers a more basic approach with which to create the game; for example, we do not have access to adding components in separate classes, and we must implement the **update()** and **render()** methods, which we will talk about later.

In this book, when referring to the term "**Game**-type class," it refers to any of this type of classes, which allow the creation of a global instance of the game; as we indicated before, the **FlameGame** class is the one that we are going to use throughout the book to develop the applications, since it allows us to use the typical Flame functionalities, such as collision handling and managing components in classes.

Example 1: Draw a Sprite

In the following code, you can see the basic structure of an application in Flame, in which we have the FlameGame class with its definition and subsequent addition of a component:

```
import 'package:flame/components.dart';
import 'package:flame/game.dart';
import 'package:flutter/material.dart';
```

```
class MySprite extends SpriteComponent {
  MySprite() : super(size: Vector2.all(16));

  @override
  void onLoad() async {
    sprite = await Sprite.load('image.png');
  }
}
class MyGame extends FlameGame {
  @override
  void onLoad() async {
    await add(MySprite());
  }
}
main() {
  runApp(GameWidget(game: MyGame()));
}
```

For the preceding implementation, we load an image:

```
sprite = await Sprite.load('image.png');
```

This image must exist in the following path:

```
assets/images/image.png
```

And register the image in the app:

```
pubspec.yaml
  assets:
    - assets/images/image.png
```

And the sprite will have a size of 16 pixels as specified in the class's constructor:

```
size: Vector2.all(16)
```

Then we add it from the global instance:

```
add(MySprite());
```

Once an image is registered in your project, you will see a result like the following.

Figure 2-2. *Example sprite*

Example 2: Draw a Circle

In this example, we'll see how to draw a circle with the **FlameGame** class:

lib/main.dart

```
import 'package:flame/components.dart';
import 'package:flame/game.dart';
import 'package:flame/palette.dart';
import 'package:flutter/material.dart';

class MyCircle extends PositionComponent {
  MyCircle() : super();

  @override
  void onLoad() async {}

  @override
  void render(Canvas canvas) {
    canvas.drawCircle(const Offset(10, 10), 10, BasicPalette.red.paint());

    // canvas.drawRect(Rect.fromCircle(center: const Offset(0, 0),
    radius: 20),
    //      BasicPalette.red.paint());
  }
}
```

```
class MyGame extends FlameGame {
  @override
  void onLoad() async {
    await add(MyCircle());
  }
}

main() {
  runApp(GameWidget(game: MyGame()));
}
```

In this other example, we have the same application, but using the **Game** class instead:

lib/main.dart

```
import 'package:flame/palette.dart';
import 'package:flutter/material.dart';
import 'package:flame/game.dart';

void main() async {
  runApp(GameWidget(game: MyCircle()));
}

class MyCircle with Game {
  @override
  void onLoad() async {
    super.onLoad();
    // init
  }

  @override
  void render(Canvas canvas) {
    canvas.drawCircle(const Offset(10, 10), 10, BasicPalette.red.paint());

    // canvas.drawRect(Rect.fromCircle(center: const Offset(0, 0),
    radius: 20),
    //     BasicPalette.red.paint());
  }
```

```
  @override
  void update(double deltaTime) {}
}
```

If you run either program with the **Game** or **FlameGame** class, you will see an output like the following.

Figure 2-3. *Circle drawn with Flame*

As you can conclude, this approach of organizing the code in classes allows us to reuse the components more easily, as well as extend them or create others; therefore, these examples reinforce the reason it is used. Apart from that, with the **FlameGame class**, we have access to other features of the Flame API.

The **FlameGame** class maintains a list of all game components, and these can be dynamically added to the game as needed; for example, we could add many enemy **SpriteComponents** to the game and then remove them from the game as the player kills the enemies. The **FlameGame** class will then iterate over these components telling each component to update and render itself.

The **GameWidget** class represents the constructor we usually use to instantiate the game in Flame and set it to the widget tree in Flutter.

As a recommendation, Ctrl/Command-click the **FlameGame, Game, PositionComponent, SpriteComponent**, and the rest of the classes to see their details and what properties they implement, as in the following:

```
class PositionComponent extends Component
    implements
        AnchorProvider,
        AngleProvider,
        PositionProvider,
```

```
        ScaleProvider,
        CoordinateTransform {
  PositionComponent({
    Vector2? position,
    Vector2? size,
    Vector2? scale,
    double? angle,
    this.nativeAngle = 0,
    Anchor? anchor,
    super.children,
```
***

You can also see the functions that you can implement and what parameters you can send and their type, as in the case of **Canvas**, and test them and evaluate the result.

For example, to draw a rectangle, we can do it by defining two points on the screen:

```
canvas.drawRect(Rect.fromPoints(const Offset(10,10), const
Offset(500,500)), BasicPalette.purple.paint());
```

Or instead of drawing a circle with **canvas.drawCircle()**, we draw a rectangle using a circle:

```
canvas.drawRect(Rect.fromCircle(center: const Offset(100, 100), radius:
50.0),BasicPalette.brown.paint());
```

Example 3: Update the Circle Position

Another example, a little more elaborate in which additional functions are used to update the game, is creating a circle that we move from left to right until it disappears from the screen in a few seconds. Let's look at both implementations, first, with the **FlameGame** class:

```
import 'package:flame/components.dart';
import 'package:flame/game.dart';
import 'package:flame/palette.dart';
import 'package:flutter/material.dart';

class MyCircle extends PositionComponent {
  MyCircle() : super();
```

```
  double circlePos = 10;
  final Paint _paint = BasicPalette.red.paint();

  @override
  void onLoad() async {}

  @override
  void render(Canvas canvas) {
    canvas.drawCircle(
      Offset(circlePos, circlePos),
      10,
      _paint
    );

    // canvas.drawRect(Rect.fromCircle(center: const Offset(0, 0),
    radius: 20),
    //     _paint );
  }

  @override
  void update(double dt) {
    super.update(dt);
    circlePos++;
  }
}

class MyGame extends FlameGame {
  @override
  void onLoad() async {
    await add(MyCircle());
  }
}

main() {
  runApp(GameWidget(game: MyGame()));
}
```

And here's with the **Game** class:

```dart
import 'package:flame/palette.dart';
import 'package:flutter/material.dart';
import 'package:flame/game.dart';

void main() async {
  runApp(GameWidget(game: MyCircle()));
}

class MyCircle with Game {
  double circlePos = 10;

  @override
  void onLoad() async {
    super.onLoad();
    // init
  }

  @override
  void render(Canvas canvas) {
    canvas.drawCircle(
        Offset(circlePos, circlePos), 10, BasicPalette.red.paint());

    // canvas.drawRect(Rect.fromCircle(center: const Offset(0, 0),
    radius: 20),
    //     _paint);
  }

  @override
  void update(double dt) {
    circlePos++;
  }
}
```

In the **Game** class, the game component, in this case the circle, is implemented directly in the **Game** class, while for the implementation with the **FlameGame** class, we can make use of a separate class (component) in which we handle all the logic of said component, in this case moving the circle, which leaves us with a much cleaner implementation. Additionally, in the **Game** class, it is mandatory to implement the **render()** method (to draw on the canvas, in this case, the circle) and **update()** method (to make updates to the game), which we will explain in the next section.

At the moment we will not go into detail about what each of the lines of code allows to carry out. The important thing is to note the implementations of both **Game**-type classes and compare them. In the next chapter, we'll go into detail and explain what each line of code in the preceding examples carries out.

In the Flame API, there is also a component called **CircleComponent** that we could also use in a similar way:

https://docs.flame-engine.org/latest/flame/components.html#circlecomponent

Or if you want to draw a rectangle, you can uncomment this code shown previously:

```
canvas.drawRect(Rect.fromCircle(center: const Offset(0, 0), radius: 20,
_paint);
```

Key Processes and Methods in Flame

In this section, we will get to know the basic cycle of a game and, with this, its key functions. Every existing game, regardless of the engine used to create it, consists of two defined processes:

1. A process that allows us to draw on a canvas, that is, we can draw figures and images on the canvas to display them on the screen. Its use is very similar to what we can handle in the HTML API.

2. Another process that updates the elements of the game. For example, suppose we have a player. Then, by clicking buttons on the screen or pressing keys, the player moves; by receiving damage from the enemy, the player moves. You can implement this same logic in other types of components and scenarios. To give another example, we can have a grass component, which, when a character steps on it, becomes deformed, and this said deformation in this case is done by the interaction between the components: the grass and the player.

These two processes are known as the **game loop**, which is explained in the following.

Game Loop

Flame's module called **GameLoop** or the game loop is nothing more than a simple abstraction of the game loop concept. Basically, most of the video games are based on two methods:

- The render method takes the canvas to draw the current state of the game.

- The update method receives the time (delta) since the last update and allows the game to go to the next state, that is, updates the game state.

That is, we have a method to initialize the game and another to perform updates. Flame follows these principles, and we have a couple of methods that allow us to perform such operations.

Render Method

The **render()** function receives an object-type parameter that refers to the canvas:

```
@override
void render(Canvas canvas) {
  canvas.drawRect(squarePos, squarePaint);
}
```

This is just like with other technologies like HTML5; it's nothing more than a blank canvas to draw on. Here, we can draw anything, for example, a circle:

```
@override
void render(Canvas canvas) {
  canvas.drawCircle(const Offset(10, 10), 10, BasicPalette.red.paint());
}
```

Update Method

The elements that are in the game need to be constantly redrawn according to the current state of the game; to understand this more clearly, let's see an example.

Suppose that a game element is represented by a sprite (an image), which in this example we will call as a "player." When the user clicks a button, then the player must update its position; this update is applied in-game via a function called **update()**.

As we saw in the example of the moving circle, it is this function that is responsible for updating the position of the circle on the screen.

The **update() method** is, as its name indicates, an update function, which receives a parameter called "delta time" (dt) that tells us **the time that has elapsed since the previous frame was drawn**. You should use this variable to make your component move at the same speed on all devices.

Devices work at different speeds, depending on the processing power (i.e., depending on what processor the device has, specifically the frequency at which the processor works), so if **we ignore the delta value and just run everything at the maximum speed the processor can run it**, the game might have speed issues to control your character properly as it would be too fast or too slow.
By using the deltaTime parameter in our motion calculation, we can guarantee that our sprites will move at whatever speed we want on devices with different processor speeds.

When updating any aspect of the game through the **update()** function, it is automatically reflected through the **render()** function, and with this, the game updates at a graphical level.

The game loop is used by all implementations of Game classes and their components:

https://docs.flame-engine.org/latest/flame/game.html

Other Important Functions in Flame

The preceding functions have an equivalent in the use of components. We have an **update()** function to perform updates; like the one in **Game-type** classes, it receives the **delta time** parameter. We also have a function to initialize the components; in this case, it is called **onLoad()**, which is used to only initialize data and not to render as it is in the case of the **render()** function. We can use this method to, for example, to draw figures or sprites on the screen.

Of course, there are many more functions in Flame, which we will see as they are necessary to advance in the different examples that we will see in this book; however, the functions that we saw in this chapter are key and the most important in Flame. Remember that this chapter acts as a reference, which you can consult later when you see the implementations of our games.

CHAPTER 3

Flame Fundamentals

In this chapter, the main elements that we must know to work with Flame will be discussed. We will see how to create the components, which are the key pieces or elements of our game. We will look at the basic structure of a game with Flame and the use of inputs (keyboard, joystick, etc.), which is the way in which the user can interact with the application.

SpriteComponent: Components for Rendering Images

One of the fundamental components that we have is the **SpriteComponent**. A sprite sheet is a series of images joined in the same file next to each other.

Figure 3-1. *Sprite sheet for the player, who can walk in all directions (https://pipoya.itch.io/pipoya-free-rpg-character-sprites-nekonin)*

© Andrés Cruz Yoris 2024
A. Cruz Yoris, *Flame Game Development*, https://doi.org/10.1007/979-8-8688-0063-4_3

Figure 3-2. *Sprite sheet for the player, who can move horizontally or up by jumping (www.gameart2d.com/free-dino-sprites.html)*

A sprite is nothing more than an image that graphically represents an object, character, or element of the game (like the tiger sprite shown before).

A sprite sheet is nothing more than a collection of images put into a single image, and they are widely used in any game engine such as Unity. In video game development, a sprite sheet is an image where all the movements (states) of a character or object are included; therefore, it is common for a 2D game to have multiple images for each animable object.

In conclusion, a sprite sheet is an image, for example, a PNG image that we can upload to render somewhere on the screen.

In Flutter with Flame, we can create our sprites using the **SpriteComponent** class and, with this, implement all the necessary logic for some elements of our game, such as a player, an enemy, non-playable characters, etc.

The **SpriteComponent** class implements the **PositionComponent** class that we will discuss later, in which we must implement three mandatory properties:

1. *position*: position is simply a **Vector2** that represents the position of the component relative to its parent; if the parent is a **FlameGame**, it is relative to the viewport.

2. *size*: The size of the component when the camera zoom level is 1.0.

3. *sprite*: The sprite handled in the component.

You can see the full reference at `https://docs.flame-engine.org/latest/flame/components.html#positioncomponent`.

In this book, we will use the properties we need; the preceding link refers to the **PositionComponent**, which is implemented by the **SpriteComponent** class.

Practical Case: Single-Image Sprite

Let's start by adding some images to our project to start learning how Flame works; to do this, we will use an icon like the following:

`www.flaticon.com/free-icon/tiger_6457888`

We must download and incorporate this into our project:

`pubspec.yaml`

`assets/images/tiger.png`

We add the image asset:

`pubspec.yaml`

```
assets:
  - assets/images/tiger.png
```

And we are going to create a new file to handle this image, which will have the following structure:

`lib/components/player_image_sprite_component.dart`

```
import 'package:flame/components.dart';
import 'package:flutter/material.dart';

class PlayerImageSpriteComponent  extends SpriteComponent{

  late double screenWidth;
  late double screenHeight;
```

```
late double centerX;
late double centerY;

final double spriteWidth = 512.0;
final double spriteHeight = 512.0;

@override
void onLoad() async {

  sprite = await Sprite.load('tiger.png');

  screenWidth = MediaQueryData.fromWindow(window).size.width;
  screenHeight = MediaQueryData.fromWindow(window).size.height;

  size = Vector2(spriteWidth, spriteHeight);

  centerX = (screenWidth/2) - (spriteWidth/2);
  centerY = (screenHeight/2) - (spriteHeight/2);

  position = Vector2(centerX, centerY);
  }
}
```

Explanation of the preceding **code**

We define the size of the image. In this example, it is a 512-pixel image, but you can place a different scale, for example, 48 pixels:

```
final double spriteWidth = 512.0;
final double spriteHeight = 512.0;
```

We obtain the size of the window, both its width and height. With this, we have all the space that we can use to draw:

```
MediaQueryData.fromWindow(window).size
```

And we set the sizes, specifically the width and the height:

```
screenWidth = MediaQueryData.fromWindow(window).size.width;
screenHeight = MediaQueryData.fromWindow(window).size.height;
```

Currently, getting the size this way is deprecated, which means that its use is discouraged. In case you have access to the application context, you can get the window size with

```
screenWidth = MediaQueryData.fromView(View.of(context)).size.width;
screenHeight = MediaQueryData.fromView(View.of(context)).size.height;
```

Or if you're in a Flame component, where we don't have access to the context, you can use Flame's game object that we can get as an import reference in the component, for example:

```
class PlayerImageSpriteComponent extends SpriteComponent with
HasGameReference {
}
```

And with this, we have access to an object **game**:

```
game
```

And with this object, we have the size:

```
game.size
```

Therefore, an equivalent to obtain the size would be

```
screenWidth = game.size.x;
screenHeight = game.size.y;
```

We are going to want to place the image in the middle of the window. To do this, we calculate the middle of the window:

```
(screenWidth/2)
(screenHeight/2)
```

Regardless of the scheme you want to use, we calculate the space occupied by the image. Therefore, we subtract half the size of the image; with this, the image will appear centered:

```
centerX = (screenWidth/2) - (spriteWidth/2);
centerY = (screenHeight/2) - (spriteHeight/2);
```

And with this, we can calculate the position, to set it in the **position** property of the **SpriteComponent** class. We need to indicate the position by means of a 2D vector in which it is specified, the position that was previously calculated through the **centerX** and **centerY** properties:

```
position = Vector2(centerX, centerY);
```

We indicate the total size of the image. As with the position, it is indicated by a two-dimensional vector:

```
size = Vector2(spriteWidth, spriteHeight);
```

Finally, we load the image, the sprite:

```
sprite = await Sprite.load('tiger.png');
```

Remember that all the processes that require access to the storage memory of the device are asynchronous processes; in this case, it is necessary to access the storage memory, which is where the image we want to load is located.

To use the previously created component, we add it to the scene from main:

```
lib/main.dart

import 'package:flame/game.dart';
import 'package:flutter/material.dart';
import 'package:testsflame/components/player_image_sprite_component.dart';

class MyGame extends FlameGame with KeyboardEvents {
  @override
  void onLoad() {
    add(PlayerImageSpriteComponent());
  }
}

void main() async {
  runApp(GameWidget(game: MyGame()));
}
```

Because we added the component called "PlayerImageSpriteComponent" in the **onLoad()** function of the **FlameGame** class, **FlameGame** is now tracking that component.

From the component, its own **onLoad()** function is called to initialize the sprite; we could also use additional processes to render additional objects via the **render()** function and update the sprite via the **update()** function as we'll see later.

Finally, we will see the following on the screen.

Figure 3-3. *Draw a sprite in Flame*

The image is in the specified size, which would be about 512 pixels; for a little challenge, you can try resizing the image and placing it in different positions on the screen.

This small example that we created is a base case that we must understand since any Flame component has a logic similar to this; that is, create a component class with the structure and logic and add it to the **Game** class to be able to use it in the application.

Going back to our application, we are going to update the position vector using the **update()** function. For this example, we will not use the delta time:

```
@override
void update(double dt) {
  // TODO: implement update

  position = Vector2(centerX++, centerY);

  super.update(dt);
}
```

This results in the constant movement of the image when executing the application.

With this, the next step that we have pending is to add interactivity with the user, that is, the user can somehow interact with the application (the game) and something happens, such as moving the sprite.

Here's the code if we wanted to update the position of the sprite:

```
class PlayerImageSpriteComponent extends SpriteComponent {
  ***
  @override
  void update(double dt) {
    position = Vector2(centerX++, centerY++);
    super.update(dt);
  }
}
```

Practical Case: Sprite Sheet

Now, we are interested in not only processing a single image but several of them. For this, we will use an image that consists of several images, like the one presented in the following.

Figure 3-4. *Player sprite*

This sprite sheet simulates a walking motion for our player.
For this example, we have individual images for the walk.

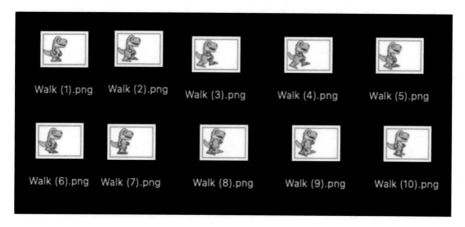

Figure 3-5. *Player sprite generated individually*

To avoid loading an image one by one in the project, managing them independently, and, with this, increasing the consumption of resources (since, at the project level, each image should be loaded individually), we are going to do all these steps at once; this format is known as a "sprite sheet." For this task, you can use any image editing program, but, to facilitate the process, it is recommended to use programs such as the following:

`www.codeandweb.com/texturepacker`

The preceding program called **TexturePacker** allows us to create a sprite sheet for the images; you can install the program on Linux, Windows, and MacOS. For this process, you can download any image kit you want, although on the website `www.gameart2d.com/freebies.html`, you will find several sprites that you can use for free.

Once the program is installed and your image kit has been downloaded, we are going to create the sprite sheet. To do this, we drag and drop the images we want to work with into the area shown in the following figure; in this book, they are the images shown previously.

Figure 3-6. *Drag-and-drop section for TexturePacker folders or sprites*

And we will have the following.

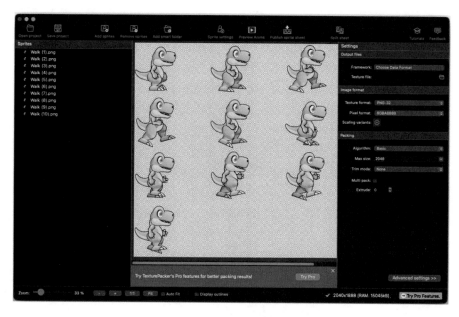

Figure 3-7. *Display of the player sprite in TexturePacker*

You can use the "Zoom" option located in the lower-left corner to fully view the sprite sheet.

Figure 3-8. *Zoom in TexturePacker*

You can preview the scene.

Figure 3-9. *Preview animation*

You can indicate the FPS (speed) of the animation (remember to select all loaded sprites).

Figure 3-10. *Movement test of a sprite sheet in TexturePacker*

And finally, export our sprite sheet.

Figure 3-11. *Publish the sprite sheet*

And we will have our sprite sheet that we will call **dino.png**.

Figure 3-12. *Sprite sheet generated in TexturePacker*

Then, we will copy the sprite sheet into the project in Flutter and reference it at the project level to be able to use it:

pubspec.yaml

```
assets:
  - assets/images/dino.png
```

Finally, at the level of our code, we will create the following class:

lib/components/player_sprite_sheet_component.dart

```
import 'package:flame/sprite.dart';
import 'package:flutter/material.dart';

import 'package:flame/flame.dart';
import 'package:flame/components.dart';
```

```
class PlayerSpriteSheetComponent extends SpriteComponent with
HasGameReference {
  late double screenWidth;
  late double screenHeight;
  late double centerX;
  late double centerY;
  final double spriteSheetWidth = 680;
  final double spriteSheetHeight = 472;

  @override
  void onLoad() async {
    //sprite = await Sprite.load('tiger.png');

    final spriteImage = await Flame.images.load('dino.png');
    final spriteSheet = SpriteSheet(image: spriteImage, srcSize:
    Vector2(spriteSheetWidth, spriteSheetHeight));

    sprite = spriteSheet.getSprite(2, 1);

    screenWidth = game.size.x;
    screenHeight = game.size.y;

    size = Vector2(spriteSheetWidth, spriteSheetHeight);

    centerX = (screenWidth / 2) - (spriteSheetWidth / 2);
    centerY = (screenHeight / 2) - (spriteSheetHeight / 2);

    position = Vector2(centerX, centerY);
  }
}
```

Explanation of the preceding code

As you can see in the preceding code, we define the size for each sprite in our sprite sheet; for the image we select, it would be 680 pixels × 472 pixels.

Figure 3-13. *Properties of the sprite sheet generated in TexturePacker*

To do this, we use a couple of properties:

```
late double spriteSheetWidth = 680.0, spriteSheetHeight = 472.0;
```

It is important to note that you must specify the size according to the sprite you are using.

We load the sprite sheet:

```
var spriteImages = await Flame.images.load('dino.png');
```

And we define the sprite sheet so that it can be manipulated through a property; it is in this step that we use the individual dimensions of each state:

```
final spriteSheet = SpriteSheet(image: spriteImages, srcSize:
Vector2(spriteSheetWidth, spriteSheetHeight));
```

Finally, it is now possible to consult the position of each step of the sprite sheet individually:

```
sprite = spriteSheet.getSprite(1, 1);
```

You can try other positions.

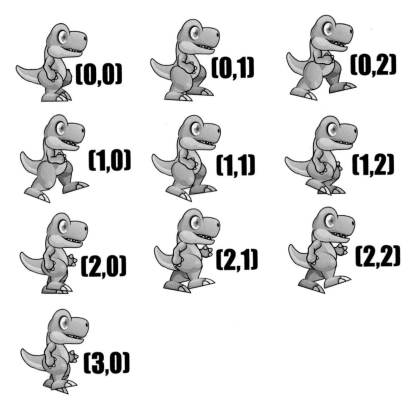

Figure 3-14. *Possible values for the sprite sheet using spriteSheet.getSprite*

To be able to visualize the corresponding step on the screen, at the Game class level, we use the preceding component:

lib/main.dart

```
import 'package:testsflame/components/player_image_sprite_component.dart';
import 'package:testsflame/components/player_sprite_sheet_component.dart';

@override
void onLoad() async {
  super.onLoad();
    // add(PlayerImageSpriteComponent());
    add(PlayerSpriteSheetComponent());
}
```

And we will have the following.

Figure 3-15. *Animation of a sprite sheet in Flame*

Practical Case: Animate the Sprite Sheet

Now that the process of changing between each of the states in the sprite sheet has been made clear by means of the function

```
spriteSheet. getSprite(1, 1);
```

once the sprite sheet–type image is loaded

```
final spriteSheet = SpriteSheet(image: spriteImages, srcSize:
Vector2(spriteSheetWidth, spriteSheetHeight));
```

we are going to create a walking sprite or animate the sprite. To create an animation based on sprites, we have the following function:

```
SpriteAnimation.spriteList
```

This function receives three parameters:

1. *A list of sprites*: (**List<Sprite>**) that corresponds to the sprites in the animation

2. Animation speed

3. Whether it is going to be executed in cycle

So that we can easily create a sprite list, we are going to create an auxiliary function that receives the range and builds the list and animates the list at once. Before presenting the solution, let's work with the image called **dino.png** shown in Figure 3-14.

With the function that we are going to create, we are going to be able to define the complete ranges to go through the entire image or fragments of it (since it is very common that in the same sprite sheet–type image, there are steps for many states, e.g., walk, run, jump, die, etc.).

Given the initial and final value of the range (among other parameters), the function that we are going to create must be capable of generating a list with each of the sprites; for example, if we want to generate a sprite list that goes from steps (0,0) to (3,0), the sprites to store correspond to ten steps and would be

$$(0,0) \cdot (0,1) \cdot (0,2) \cdot (1,0) \cdot (1,1) \cdot (1,2) \cdot (2,0) \cdot (2,1) \cdot (2,2) \cdot (3,0)$$

If we want the list of sprites to be from steps (1.1) to (2.1), this corresponds to four steps:

$$(1,1) \cdot (1,2) \cdot (2,0) \cdot (2,1)$$

If we want the list of sprites to be from steps (1.1) to (3.0), this corresponds to six steps:

$$(1,1) \cdot (1,2) \cdot (2,0) \cdot (2,1) \cdot (2,2) \cdot (3,0)$$

In short, the important thing is to note that we can generate lists of partial or complete animations, in the order in which the steps are defined.

Function for Animation

For this function, we will need the following parameters:

1. Initial step in X (e.g., (**3**,0))

2. Initial step in Y (e.g., (3,**0**))

3. Number of steps (e.g., the value of 6 corresponds to six sprites)

4. The width of the matrix (in the **dino.png** image, the sprite matrix would be 3 × 3, so the width would be 3)

5. Animation speed

6. If it is to be executed in a loop

With this in mind, we'll create the following extension function that extends the **SpriteSheet** class:

lib/utils/create_animation_by_limit.dart

```
extension CreateAnimationByLimit on SpriteSheet {
  SpriteAnimation createAnimationByLimit({
    required int xInit,
    required int yInit,
    required int step,
    required int sizeX,
    required double stepTime,
    bool loop = true,
  }) {
    final List<Sprite> spriteList = [];

    int x = xInit;
    int y = yInit - 1;

    for (var i = 0; i < step; i++) {
      if (y >= sizeX) {
        y = 0;
        x++;
      } else {
        y++;
      }

      spriteList.add(getSprite(x, y));
      // print(x.toString() + ' ' + y.toString());
    }
```

```
    return SpriteAnimation.spriteList(spriteList,
        stepTime: stepTime, loop: loop);
  }
}
```

For loop blocks are where we loop through the sprite array just like in the examples explained previously; with this sprite list, we generate the animation using **SpriteAnimation.spriteList()**.

SpriteAnimationComponent

We are going to use the image loaded in the project called **dino.png**. Since we are now working with an animated sprite, we now need to change from a **SpriteComponent** to a **SpriteAnimationComponent**. We are going to implement the following content:

```
class PlayerSpriteSheetComponent extends SpriteAnimationComponent with
HasGameReference {

  late double screenWidth;
  late double screenHeight;
  late double centerX;
  late double centerY;

  final double spriteWidth = 512.0;
  final double spriteHeight = 512.0;
  final double spriteSheetWidth = 680;
  final double spriteSheetHeight = 472;

  late SpriteAnimation dinoAnimation;

  @override
  void onLoad() async {
    super.onLoad();
    screenWidth = game.size.x;
    screenHeight = game.size.y;

    centerX = (screenWidth / 2) - (spriteSheetWidth / 2);
    centerY = (screenHeight / 2) - (spriteSheetHeight / 2);
```

```
    var spriteImages = await Flame.images.load('dino.png');

    final spriteSheet = SpriteSheet(
        image: spriteImages,
        srcSize: Vector2(spriteSheetWidth, spriteSheetHeight));

    //sprite = spriteSheet.getSprite(1, 1);
    position = Vector2(centerX, centerY);
    size = Vector2(spriteSheetWidth, spriteSheetHeight);
    //sprite = await Sprite.load('Sprite.png');

    dinoAnimation = spriteSheet.createAnimationByLimit(
        xInit: 0, yInit: 0, step: 10, sizeX: 2, stepTime: .08);

    animation = dinoAnimation;
  }
}
```

The code is almost the same as before, but now instead of loading a sprite

```
sprite = spriteSheet.getSprite(1, 1);
```

we create the animation of the sprites using the function created previously:

```
dinoAnimation = spriteSheet.createAnimationByLimit(
        xInit: 0, yInit: 0, step: 10, sizeX: 2, stepTime: .08,);
```

Now, instead of using the **sprite** property, we use the **animation** property, which is available in the **SpriteAnimationComponent** class using the sprite sheet:

```
// sprite = spriteSheet.getSprite(1, 1);
animation = dinoAnimation;
```

Practical Case: Multiple Animations

In this section, we are going to create several animations based on the sequence of corresponding images, using a single sprite sheet. Let's start by creating a new sprite sheet with all the animations available with the TexturePacker program indicating a size of 4096, which looks like the following.

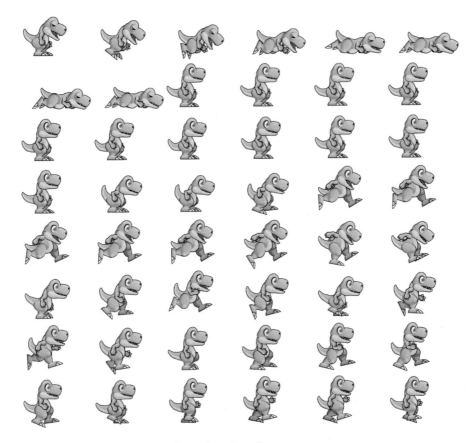

Figure 3-16. *Complete sprite sheet for the player*

We load and reference the preceding image in the project:

pubspec.yaml

```
assets:
  - assets/images/dino.png
  - assets/images/dinofull.png
```

The next step is to create separate animations for each state using the helper function we created earlier:

```
class PlayerSpriteSheetComponent extends SpriteAnimationComponent with
HasGameReference {

  final double spriteSheetWidth = 680;
  final double spriteSheetHeight = 472;
```

```
late double screenWidth;
late double screenHeight;
late double centerX;
late double centerY;

late SpriteAnimation deadAnimation;
late SpriteAnimation idleAnimation;
late SpriteAnimation jumpAnimation;
late SpriteAnimation runAnimation;
late SpriteAnimation walkAnimation;

@override
void onLoad() async {
  //sprite = await Sprite.load('tiger.png');

  final spriteImage = await Flame.images.load('dinofull.png');
  final spriteSheet = SpriteSheet(
      image: spriteImage,
      srcSize: Vector2(spriteSheetWidth, spriteSheetHeight));

  //sprite = spriteSheet.getSprite(2, 1);

  // init animation
    dinoDeadAnimation = spriteSheet.createAnimationByLimit(xInit: 0,
    yInit: 0, step: 8, sizeX: 5, stepTime: .08);
    dinoIdleAnimation = spriteSheet.createAnimationByLimit(xInit: 1,
    yInit: 2, step: 10, sizeX: 5, stepTime: .08);
    dinoJumpAnimation = spriteSheet.createAnimationByLimit(xInit: 3,
    yInit: 0, step: 12, sizeX: 5, stepTime: .08);
    dinoRunAnimation = spriteSheet.createAnimationByLimit(xInit: 5,
    yInit: 0, step: 8, sizeX: 5, stepTime: .08);
    dinoWalkAnimation = spriteSheet.createAnimationByLimit(xInit: 6,
    yInit: 2, step: 10, sizeX: 5, stepTime: .08);
  // end animation

  animation = dinoWalkAnimation;
```

39

```
//animation = spriteSheet.createAnimationByLimit(xInit: 0, yInit: 0,
 step: 7, sizeX: 2, stepTime: .08);

screenWidth = game.size.x;
screenHeight = game.size.y;

size = Vector2(spriteSheetWidth, spriteSheetHeight);

centerX = (screenWidth / 2) - (spriteSheetWidth / 2);
centerY = (screenHeight / 2) - (spriteSheetHeight / 2);

position = Vector2(centerX, centerY);
  }
}
```

To vary between the animations, you simply have to vary the **animation** property; with this, we have learned the most important aspects of using sprite animations in Flame.

Input: Keyboard

A user can interact with the game through

- Keyboard

- Drag-and-drop

- Gestures

- Tap (in most cases, equivalent to the click event)

- Virtual joystick

Among others, inputs are a fundamental functionality in any game today. In Flame, we can implement this type of functionality through events, which are listened to by a listener function.

In this section, we are going to work with keyboard input. Flame offers two different ways to take keyboard input:

1. At the level of the **Game** class

2. At the component level

In any of the scenarios, its use is very simple and is similar to other approaches, for example, JavaScript, in which we have a listener function called **onKeyEvent** that is executed every time a key is pressed. In said function, we receive the event with the key pressed to which we can apply any logic.

Game Class Level

In order for the application to recognize keyboard events, that is, when a key is pressed, and to be able to assign some function, we can use the **KeyboardEvents** class on the Game-type class.

This has been the most global way, since the events are executed at the level of the **Game** class, which we remember is global to the entire application, in contrast to the level of the components, which is where most of the time we are interested in interacting. That is, as we saw in the previous example, we draw a sprite for a component. If we want to move that sprite, which our player can simulate, we are interested in that said component receiving keyboard events (or input in general). Even so, it is important to know that at the level of the **Game** class, we can add this type of interactivity, since most of the time it is necessary that several components need to perform some functionality when, for example, a keyboard input occurs. Suppose we have two components:

- A player

- A stage

As we saw, they are two separate classes. Depending on the logic of your game, it may be that by pressing, for example, the movement key (up arrow or W key), this applies movement to the player and a change on the stage; in these cases, two components must be communicated and not just one.

At the **FlameGame** class level, we must add the **KeyboardEvents** mixin and, with this, override the **onKeyEvent** function; this method receives two parameters that return the keys pressed:

1. The RawKeyEvent

2. The LogicalKeyboardKeys

Practical Case

Continuing with our application, we are going to place the keyboard input listener at the **FlameGame** class level:

```
class MyGame extends FlameGame with KeyboardEvents {
  ***
  @override
  KeyEventResult onKeyEvent(
    RawKeyEvent event,
    Set<LogicalKeyboardKey> keysPressed,
  ) {
    super.onKeyEvent(event, keysPressed);

    //print(keysPressed);
    print(event);

    return KeyEventResult.handled;
  }
}
```

When pressing different keys, with any of the events, we will see an output like the following:

```
{LogicalKeyboardKey#00301(keyId: "0x100000301", keyLabel: "Arrow Down",
debugName: "Arrow Down")}
```

```
RawKeyUpEvent#881c1(logicalKey: LogicalKeyboardKey#00304(keyId:
"0x100000304", keyLabel: "Arrow Up", debugName: "Arrow Up"), physicalKey:
PhysicalKeyboardKey#70052(usbHidUsage: "0x00070052", debugName:
"Arrow Up"))
```

In the preceding case, the arrow up or arrow up key was pressed.

For this experiment, we will not make any further adaptations in the application, since the game logic will be implemented in the components and not at the game level.

You can create conditions like

```
keysPressed.contains(LogicalKeyboardKey.arrowUp)
```

to ask for the key pressed.

Component Level

In order to use the events locally in a component, we must use the HasKeyboardHandlerComponents mixin at the **FlameGame** class level:

lib/main.dart

```
class <LevelGame> extends FlameGame
    with
        HasKeyboardHandlerComponents {}
```

And now, at the component level, where we are going to place the keyboard event listener, we use the **KeyboardHandler** mixin:

```
class <Component> extends <TypeComponent> with KeyboardHandler {}
```

Practical Case

For the experiment that we are carrying out on the component class called "PlayerImageSpriteComponent," we are going to add the event to move the sprite:

lib/components/player_image_sprite_component.dart

```
import 'package:flame/components.dart';

class PlayerImageSpriteComponent extends SpriteComponent with
KeyboardHandler {
  ***
  @override
  bool onKeyEvent(
    RawKeyEvent event,
    Set<LogicalKeyboardKey> keysPressed,
  ) {
    if (keysPressed.contains(LogicalKeyboardKey.arrowUp)) {
      position = Vector2(centerX, centerY--);
    } else if (keysPressed.contains(LogicalKeyboardKey.arrowDown)) {
      position = Vector2(centerX, centerY++);
    } else if (keysPressed.contains(LogicalKeyboardKey.arrowRight)) {
      position = Vector2(centerX++, centerY);
```

43

```
  } else if (keysPressed.contains(LogicalKeyboardKey.arrowLeft)) {
    position = Vector2(centerX--, centerY);
  }

  return true;
  }
}
```

As you can see in the preceding code, we can easily move the sprite by using the arrow keys on the keyboard and modifying the position vector provided by the **Sprite Component/PositionComponent** class.

As you can see, it's a simple conditional logic to ask for the typical keys to move the player up, down, right, and left; with this, if you run the application and press the keys defined before, you will see that the sprite scrolls on the screen.

Challenge

As a challenge, adapt the previous code, and in addition to the arrows, you can use the W (up), D (right), S (down), and A (left) keys.

Resolution for the Challenge

To add the typical WASD keys in our script, we can do a simple conditional with an OR:

lib/components/player_image_sprite_component.dart

```
@override
bool onKeyEvent(
    RawKeyEvent event,
    Set<LogicalKeyboardKey> keysPressed,
  ) {
    if (keysPressed.contains(LogicalKeyboardKey.arrowUp) ||
        keysPressed.contains(LogicalKeyboardKey.keyW)) {
      position = Vector2(centerX, centerY--);
    } else if (keysPressed.contains(LogicalKeyboardKey.arrowDown) ||
        keysPressed.contains(LogicalKeyboardKey.keyS)) {
      position = Vector2(centerX, centerY++);
    } else if (keysPressed.contains(LogicalKeyboardKey.arrowRight) ||
```

```
    keysPressed.contains(LogicalKeyboardKey.keyD)) {
    position = Vector2(centerX++, centerY);
  } else if (keysPressed.contains(LogicalKeyboardKey.arrowLeft) ||
      keysPressed.contains(LogicalKeyboardKey.keyA)) {
    position = Vector2(centerX--, centerY);
  }
  return true;
}
```

And with this, we can use two keys for the same function.

Input: Tap

Another input that we can use in Flame is a tap on the screen, which is equivalent to the click event. Just like with keyboard input, we can use the tap event at the class level as well as at the component level.

Game Class level

In order to use the tap event at the Game class level, we have to use the **TapDetector** mixin:

```
class MyGame extends FlameGame with TapDetector {
  @override
  void onTapDown(TapDownInfo info) {
    print("Player tap down on ${info.eventPosition.game}");
    super.onTapDown(info);
  }

  @override
  void onTapUp(TapUpInfo info) {
    print("Player tap up on ${info.eventPosition.game}");
    super.onTapUp(info);
  }
}
```

With the preceding class, we can override several types of events.

onTapDown

Each touch/tap starts with a "tap down" event, which you receive via the function

```
void onTapDown(TapDownEvent)
```

Any tap event begins with the **onTapDown** event with whose parameter we can obtain information about where the touch was on the screen.

onLongTapDown

If the user holds their finger down for some time (as set by the **.longTapDelay** property on **HasTappableComponents**), the "long tap" will be generated, which is received by the function

```
void onLongTapDown(TapDownEvent)
```

In those components that previously received the **onTapDown** event.

onTapUp

This event indicates that the tap event completed successfully; this event will only be executed after the **onTapDown** event.

The **TapUpEvent object** passed to the event handler contains the information about the event, including where the user tapped on the screen.

onTapCancel

This event occurs when the tap does not materialize. Most of the time, this will happen if the user moves their finger, which turns the gesture from "tap" to "drag." Less frequently, this can happen when the component being touched moves away from the user's finger or when another widget appears on top of the game widget or when the device powers off or similar situations.

Practical Case

You can implement the preceding functions and evaluate the result on the screen:

```
class MyGame extends FlameGame with TapDetector {
}
```

Component Level

In order to use the tap event at the component level, we must first enable it at the Flame level:

lib/main.dart

```
class <LevelGame> extends FlameGame
    with
        HasTappablesBridge {}
```

And from the component, we implement the mixin **TapCallbacks**:

```
class <Component> extends <TypeComponent> with TapCallbacks {}
```

With this, we have access to the same functions as those used at the Game class level that we showed before.

For example, a possible implementation looks like the following:

lib\components\player_sprite_sheet_component.dart

```
class PlayerSpriteSheetComponent extends SpriteAnimationComponent with
TapCallbacks {
  ***
  @override
  void onTapDown(TapDownEvent event) {
    print("Player tap down on ${info.eventPosition.game}");
    super.onTapDown(event);
  }

  @override
  void onTapUp(TapUpEvent event) {
    print("Player tap up on ${info.eventPosition.game}");
    super.onTapUp(event);
  }
}
```

Challenge: Practical Case

As a small challenge, you must implement the following logic in the component of the animated sprite sheets, and you must implement a very simple logic to vary the animation each time a tap is given on the screen. To do this, you can use a numeric property, which will indicate the animation to be executed:

- ***animationIndex*** *with the value of zero*: The death animation is displayed.

- ***animationIndex*** *with the value of one*: The idle animation is displayed.

- ***animationIndex*** *with the value of two*: The jumping animation is displayed.

- ***animationIndex*** *with the value of three*: The walking animation is displayed.

- ***animationIndex*** *with the value of four*: The running animation is displayed.

Resolution for the Challenge

As a resolution, we can use a **switch** in which we change the animation according to the value of **animationIndex** that we will increase each time a "tap" on the screen occurs:

```
lib\components\player_sprite_sheet_component.dart
```

```
***
  int animationIndex = 0;
***

  @override
  void onTapDown(TapDownEvent event) {
    super.onTapDown(event);
    print(info);

    animationIndex++;

    if (animationIndex > 4) animationIndex = 0;
```

```
switch (animationIndex) {
  case 1:
    animation = dinoIdleAnimation;
    break;
  case 2:
    animation = dinoJumpAnimation;
    break;
  case 3:
    animation = dinoWalkAnimation;
    break;
  case 4:
    animation = dinoRunAnimation;
    break;
  case 0:
  default:
    animation = dinoDeadAnimation;
    break;
}

return true;
}
```

Challenge: Animations and Inputs (Keyboard) – Walk and Idle Animations

Varying the state of our sprite/player according to the user's interaction is very common. As we have seen, we have animations for different states; walking, running, dying, and simply the base state are some of them. Therefore, it is time to activate these animations according to the operation to perform; for example, if we press the A and D keys or the left and right arrows, the animation that should occur would be walking or running; if we don't press any key, the animation that should occur would be the idle state.

We've already seen how to use keyboard input in components and how to create the animations and run them programmatically based on a state. Now, the next thing to do is to act based on the criteria mentioned before:

No key is pressed, so the idle animation is executed.

If the key pressed is the

- Right arrow or D key, move to the right.

- Left arrow or A key, move to the left.

Resolution for the Challenge

For this challenge, we will clearly use the callback function for the pressed key, and depending on the pressed key (right arrow or D key, move to the right; left arrow or A key, move to the left), we activate the walking animation and move the sprite:

lib\components\player_sprite_sheet_component.dart

```
@override
bool onKeyEvent(
  RawKeyEvent event,
  Set<LogicalKeyboardKey> keysPressed,
) {
  if (keysPressed.isEmpty) {
    animation = dinoIdleAnimation;
  }

  if (keysPressed.contains(LogicalKeyboardKey.arrowRight) ||
      keysPressed.contains(LogicalKeyboardKey.keyD)) {
    animation = dinoWalkAnimation;
    position.x++;
  }

  if (keysPressed.contains(LogicalKeyboardKey.arrowLeft) ||
      keysPressed.contains(LogicalKeyboardKey.keyA)) {
    animation = dinoWalkAnimation;
    position.x--;
  }

  return true;
}
```

We also put in additional validation to return to the base state when a key is no longer being pressed; in this case the **keysPressed** parameter returns void:

```
if (keysPressed.isEmpty) {
  animation = dinoIdleAnimation;
}
```

With this, we complete the horizontal movement of the sprite on the screen by pressing the right arrow or D and left arrow or A keys.

Mirror or Flip the Sprite

One problem we currently have is that when moving the sprite from right to left, the sprite appears to be walking backward; we can fix this problem in two ways.

The first way is to generate all the states (walk, die, run, jump, etc.) also in reverse.

Figure 3-17. *Inverted sprite sheet*

This solution can be valid when we have an object with few movements.

The other solution is to flip the sprite from the component, that is, using code, which is generally the best solution. In Flame, we have the function

```
flipVertically();
```

to move the component vertically or

```
flipHorizontally();
```

to move the component horizontally. We can use this function in any component that implements or inherits the **PositionComponent** class.

In the case of the application that we are building, we want the mirror or flip effect to be done horizontally.

It is important to note that, when we are talking about the component and not directly about the sprite, the component has a larger size than the sprite and it is the one that is applying the flip; therefore, apart from making the flip effect, we must make another configuration so that, when we apply the flip effect, there are no sudden jumps in the positioning of the sprite when moving from right to left or left to right.

Practical Case

The logic that we are going to implement for the application is very simple. We need a Boolean to indicate if the sprite is aligned to the right or to the left, and depending on its value and the key pressed, we apply the flip using the **flipHorizontally()** function when necessary. We finally have the following:

```
lib\components\player_sprite_sheet_component.dart

bool right = true;

@override
bool onKeyEvent(
  RawKeyEvent event,
  Set<LogicalKeyboardKey> keysPressed,
) {
  if (keysPressed.isEmpty) {
    animation = dinoIdleAnimation;
  }
```

```
if (keysPressed.contains(LogicalKeyboardKey.arrowUp) ||
    keysPressed.contains(LogicalKeyboardKey.keyW)) {
  position.y--;
}

if (keysPressed.contains(LogicalKeyboardKey.arrowDown) ||
    keysPressed.contains(LogicalKeyboardKey.keyS)) {
  position.y++;
}

if (keysPressed.contains(LogicalKeyboardKey.arrowRight) ||
    keysPressed.contains(LogicalKeyboardKey.keyD)) {
  position.x++;
  if (!right) flipHorizontally();
  right = true;
  animation = dinoWalkAnimation;
}

if (keysPressed.contains(LogicalKeyboardKey.arrowLeft) ||
    keysPressed.contains(LogicalKeyboardKey.keyA)) {
  position.x--;
  if (right) flipHorizontally();
  right = false;
  animation = dinoWalkAnimation;
}

return true;
}
```

The problem we have is that, when flipping the sprite, an abrupt change in positioning occurs; this is because each of the states is poorly positioned in the sprite sheet. If you observe, the state has an empty space to the right and is not centered; for the sprite sheet we are using, each state is distributed as follows.

Figure 3-18. *Sprite with proportion problems*

And we need it to be as follows.

Figure 3-19. *Centered sprite*

To correct this, you can add/subtract the number of pixels when applying the flip effect on the scroll. For the sprite we are using, it would be something like this:

```
if (keysPressed.contains(LogicalKeyboardKey.arrowRight) ||
    keysPressed.contains(LogicalKeyboardKey.keyD)) {
  position.x += 80;
  ***
}
```

```
if (keysPressed.contains(LogicalKeyboardKey.arrowLeft) ||
    keysPressed.contains(LogicalKeyboardKey.keyA)) {
  position.x -= 80;
  ***
}
```

This would imply additional logic to our game to avoid adding a constant value in each interaction. Another option is to correct the image so that the affected states appear centered and not thrown to one side; in this case, the states to correct are all except the one of death.

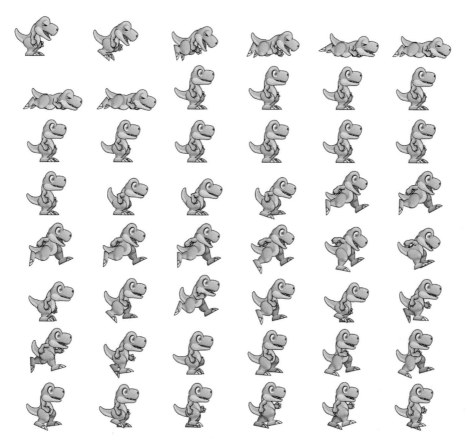

Figure 3-20. *Centered sprite sheet*

You can compare this image with the one generated previously, and you will see that all the states (except the death one) were centered. To correct this positioning, you can use programs like Photoshop or GIMP.

Even with the preceding correction, the problem of abrupt changes in the positioning continues to occur; this is because, when performing the flip effect, the entire component is flipped and not only the sprite and it is being performed at an incorrect angle. So we are going to correct the angle of incidence for this type of operations; to do this, we must use the width property defined in any component that inherits from **PositionComponent**.

---

anchor is the place defined in the component from which to set the position and rotation (the default is **anchor.topLeft**).

We place the component such that it is centered:

```
@override
@override
void onLoad() async {
  super.onLoad();
  ***
  anchor = Anchor.center;
}
```

With this change, no snap changes will occur when flipping.

Constant Velocity

As we mentioned in Chapter 2 when we introduced the use of the **update()** function, it is recommended that the value of **deltaTime (dt)** passed as a parameter be used in the calculations for positioning, rotation, scaling, etc. For the application that we are building, it would be for movement; therefore, we are going to create some more properties with which we can indicate a value to define the speed

```
int playerSpeed = 500;
```

and to indicate the positioning of the sprite:

```
double posX = 0;
double posY = 0;
```

With this, when pressing the keys, we will give them a non-zero value, and that is used in the **update()** function:

```
@override
void update(double dt) {
  position.x += playerSpeed * dt * posX;
  position.y += playerSpeed * dt * posY;
  posX = 0;
  posY = 0;
  super.update(dt);
}
```

Finally, here's the complete code:

```
class PlayerSpriteSheetComponent extends SpriteAnimationComponent
    with KeyboardHandler {
  ***

  int playerSpeed = 500;
  double posX = 0;
  double posY = 0;

  @override
  bool onKeyEvent(
    RawKeyEvent event,
    Set<LogicalKeyboardKey> keysPressed,
  ) {
    if (keysPressed.isEmpty) {
      animation = dinoIdleAnimation;
    }

    if (keysPressed.contains(LogicalKeyboardKey.arrowRight) ||
        keysPressed.contains(LogicalKeyboardKey.keyD)) {
      // position.x++;
      posX++;

      if (!right) flipHorizontally();
      right = true;
      animation = dinoWalkAnimation;
    }
```

```dart
  if (keysPressed.contains(LogicalKeyboardKey.arrowUp) ||
      keysPressed.contains(LogicalKeyboardKey.keyW)) {
    // position.y--;
    posY--;
  }

  if (keysPressed.contains(LogicalKeyboardKey.arrowDown) ||
      keysPressed.contains(LogicalKeyboardKey.keyS)) {
    // position.y++;
    posY++;
  }

  if (keysPressed.contains(LogicalKeyboardKey.arrowLeft) ||
      keysPressed.contains(LogicalKeyboardKey.keyA)) {
    // position.x -= 5;
    posX--;
    if (right) flipHorizontally();
    right = false;
    animation = dinoWalkAnimation;
  }

  return true;
}

@override
void update(double dt) {
  position.x += playerSpeed * dt * posX;
  position.y += playerSpeed * dt * posY;
  posX = 0;
  posY = 0;
  super.update(dt);
}
}
```

Key Combination

Another aspect to take into account in this type of applications when integrating keyboard input is that we can combine keys to perform other actions. For example, the famous combination of Shift+W so that the player (our sprite) starts running can be perfectly implemented in Flame with Flutter; of course, this combination is just an example, and you can create custom combinations at will.

For the app we're building, we can't use Shift+W but Shift+D/right arrow or Shift+A/left arrow instead to run; this implies that you have to increase the speed of the player and change the animation. To combine two keys, for example, Shift+D/right arrow, we have

```
(keysPressed.contains(LogicalKeyboardKey.arrowRight) ||
        keysPressed.contains(LogicalKeyboardKey.keyD)) &&
    keysPressed.contains(LogicalKeyboardKey.shiftLeft)
```

As you can see, the only thing we have to indicate is an additional condition to verify if the keys we want to listen to exist – in the preceding case, by pressing the D or right arrow key and the left Shift key. You have to do the same in the rest of the cases that you want to combine your keys.

One aspect that you must take into account when carrying out this kind of functionality is that, depending on the type of validation that we are carrying out, if the user presses only the D key or the combination of Shift+D, they will enter the following conditional:

```
if (keysPressed.contains(LogicalKeyboardKey.keyD){
  // TODO
}
```

The same applies to any combination that includes the D key. Therefore, to prevent the two conditionals from being executed (the one on the D key and the one on the Shift+D key), we put an **if else**.

Taking the aforementioned into consideration, we create an additional conditional for the combination of the D/A or right/left arrow key and the left Shift key, where the running animation will be used and the speed is increased:

```
class PlayerSpriteSheetComponent extends SpriteAnimationComponent
    with KeyboardHandler {
  ***

  @override
  bool onKeyEvent(RawKeyEvent event, Set<LogicalKeyboardKey> keysPressed) {
    if (keysPressed.isEmpty) {
      animation = dinoIdleAnimation;
    }

    print(keysPressed);

    //***X */
    // Running
    if ((keysPressed.contains(LogicalKeyboardKey.arrowRight) ||
            keysPressed.contains(LogicalKeyboardKey.keyD)) &&
        keysPressed.contains(LogicalKeyboardKey.shiftLeft)) {
      animation = dinoRunAnimation;

      playerSpeed = 1500;

      if (!right) flipHorizontally();
      right = true;
      // position.x += 5;
      posX++;
    } else if (keysPressed.contains(LogicalKeyboardKey.arrowRight) ||
        keysPressed.contains(LogicalKeyboardKey.keyD)) {
      animation = dinoWalkAnimation;
      playerSpeed = 500;
      if (!right) flipHorizontally();
      right = true;
      // position.x += 5;
      posX++;
    }

    if ((keysPressed.contains(LogicalKeyboardKey.arrowLeft) ||
            keysPressed.contains(LogicalKeyboardKey.keyA)) &&
        keysPressed.contains(LogicalKeyboardKey.shiftLeft)) {
      animation = dinoRunAnimation;
```

```
playerSpeed = 1500;

if (right) flipHorizontally();
right = false;

//position.x -= 5;
posX--;
} else if (keysPressed.contains(LogicalKeyboardKey.arrowLeft) ||
    keysPressed.contains(LogicalKeyboardKey.keyA)) {
animation = dinoWalkAnimation;

playerSpeed = 500;

if (right) flipHorizontally();
right = false;

//position.x -= 5;
posX--;
}
***

return true;
    }
}
```

With the preceding code, we complete the walking and running functionality for our player.

PositionComponent: Components to Render Objects

We are going to go a step back and let our dinosaur sprite rest a bit, and we are going to know the use of a more general component, **PositionComponent**, which we remember is an implementation of **SpriteComponent**. This class represents an object positioned on the screen, for example, a rectangle or other shapes, and thus its use is more general than **SpriteComponent**. Therefore, it is a component that we can use to present more features of Flame.

Let's remember that this class implements some properties just like the **SpriteComponent** class:

1. *position*: position is simply a Vector2 that represents the position of the component relative to its parent; if the parent is a **FlameGame**, it is relative to the viewport.

2. *size*: The size of the component when the camera zoom level is 1.0.

Remember that you can see the complete list at `https://docs.flame-engine.org/latest/flame/components.html#positioncomponent`.

Practical Case

Let's draw a circle on the screen that moves from the center to the right.

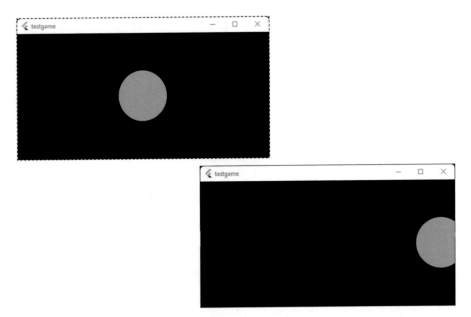

***Figure 3-21.** Moving a circle from one side to another in Flame*

To do this, we will create a new component with the following content:

`lib\components\circle_position_component.dart`

```
import 'package:flame/collisions.dart';
import 'package:flame/components.dart';
import 'package:flutter/material.dart';
```

```dart
import 'package:flame/palette.dart';

class CirclePositionComponent extends PositionComponent with
HasGameReference {
  static const int circleSpeed = 250;
  static const circleWidth = 100.0;
  static const circleHeight = 100.0;

  int circleDirection = 1;
  late double screenWidth;
  late double screenHeight;
  late double centerX;
  late double centerY;

  final ShapeHitbox hitbox = CircleHitbox();

  @override
  void onLoad() async {
    super.onLoad();

    screenWidth = game.size.x;
    screenHeight = game.size.y;

    centerX = (screenWidth / 2) - (circleWidth / 2);
    centerY = (screenHeight / 2) - (circleHeight / 2);

    position = Vector2(centerX, centerY);
    size = Vector2(circleWidth, circleHeight);

    hitbox.paint.color = BasicPalette.green.color;
    hitbox.renderShape = true;
    add(hitbox);
  }

  @override
  void update(double deltaTime) {
    super.update(deltaTime);
    // position.x += circleSpeed * circleDirection * deltaTime;
  }
```

```dart
@override
void render(Canvas canvas) {
  super.render(canvas);
}
}
```

And we register the component in the **main.dart**:

lib/main.dart

```dart
@override
void onLoad() async {
  super.onLoad();
  add(CirclePositionComponent());
}
```

Explanation of the preceding **code**

- With the **circleWidth** and **circleHeight** properties, we indicate the size of the circle to draw.

- The speed factor of the animation is **circleSpeed**.

- With the **circleDirection** property, we indicate if the circle goes from left to right (1) or right to left (–1).

- We calculate the screen size:

```dart
screenWidth = game.size.x;
screenHeight = game.size.y;
```

- And we calculate the center of the screen:

```dart
centerX = (screenWidth / 2) - (squareWidth / 2);
centerY = (screenHeight / 2) - (squareHeight / 2);
```

- We calculate the position and size and indicate the color of the circle:

```dart
position = Vector2(centerX, centerY);
size = Vector2(circleWidth, circleHeight);
hitbox.paint.color = BasicPalette.green.color;
```

- We are going to draw a circle; for this, we will use an existing Flame component, a hitbox, which is used to detect collisions between components. However, for now, we will only use a circle to represent the element visually on the screen and nothing else. To draw the hitbox circle, we use

```
final ShapeHitbox hitbox = CircleHitbox();
```

- We indicate a green color:

```
hitbox.paint.color = BasicPalette.green.color;
```

- Or you can indicate a random color:

```
hitbox.paint.color = ColorExtension.random();
```

- And we indicate that the hitbox component is visible:

```
hitbox.renderShape = true;
```

- Finally, we add the component to the **PositionComponent** class:

```
add(hitbox);
```

Of course, we can draw all kinds of graphic elements, be they images, squares, rectangles, or other kinds of figures, and animate them, place the collision detection, etc. Before working with the animations on an image, we are going to animate a geometric figure, a circle. With this, we will have a simpler example of how we can animate some element on the screen, which, in this case, would simply be moving a circle.

Through the **update()** function, we move the circle. This time, the **deltaTime** parameter is used as a part of the calculation to move the component, which in this case is a circle, but it could be anything else like a sprite like we saw before. Using the deltaTime function, as mentioned before, guarantees that the component will have the same speed regardless of the speed of the processor it is running on:

```
@override
void update(double deltaTime) {
  super.update(deltaTime);
  position.x += circleSpeed * circleDirection * deltaTime;
}
```

Debug Mode

We can activate debug mode to obtain more data at the component level with

```
@override
void onLoad() async {
    debugMode = true;
}
```

If we enable the preceding property, we will see more information on the screen such as the position and dimensions of the object.

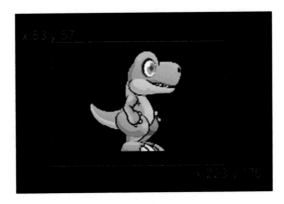

Figure 3-22. *Enable debug mode in Flame*

As you can see, you have the position of the sprite at its origin and end; with these data, you can calculate the dimensions of the object, which in this case is 170 × 118 or (223 – 53) × (175 – 57). In this case, remember that for the sprite, we calculate the size as

```
final double spriteSheetWidth = 680, spriteSheetHeight = 472;
size = Vector2(spriteSheetWidth / 4, spriteSheetHeight / 4);  // 680/4 = 170
472/4 = 118
```

The debug mode is ideal for getting our objects positioned exactly where we want and knowing exactly how Flame is positioning the object in its 2D space.

Detect Collisions

Collision detection is necessary in most games to do something when two components interact, that is, when they make contact, for example, when a stone hits an enemy, when a player picks up an item, etc.

In the different game engines, components called hitboxes that also exist in Flame are used. These can have different shapes, such as circles, rectangles, or polygons. For this reason, we can create delimiters for the sprites or other components and, with this, detect the contact between components.

Practical Case

In order to use collision detection in components, we must first enable it at the **FlameGame** class level:

```
class MyGame extends FlameGame with HasCollisionDetection {
    ***
}
```

And enable it from the component:

```
class <Component> extends <TypeComponent> with CollisionCallbacks {}
```

With this, we have access to the following function:

```
@override
void onCollision(Set<Vector2> points, PositionComponent other) {
    ***
}
```

Challenge: Change Direction

For the example we created earlier, the circle, we are going to avoid the scenario where when it reaches one end of the screen, it follows its course and disappears from the scene; to do this, we must detect the edges of the screen. An easy way to do this is by adding an existing Flame component that allows us to detect collisions between the circle and the edges of the screen (**ScreenHitbox**); from the Game class, we add

lib\main.dart

```
@override
void onLoad() async {
  super.onLoad();
  add(CirclePositionComponent());
  add(ScreenHitbox());
}
```

And from the hitbox component, we implement the **CollisionCallbacks** mixin to be able to overwrite the **onCollision()** function that receives the component with which it collided; this function is logically executed every time the component that said function overwrites collides with another component of hitbox type:

lib\components\circle_position_component.dart

```
@override
void onCollision(Set<Vector2> points, PositionComponent other) {
  ***
}
```

In the **points** parameter, we have the collision points, for example:

```
{[701.0,135.0099435710236], [701.0,112.9900564289764]}
```

And the **other** parameter corresponds to the component with which the circle collided, which in our example can be another circle or the edge of the screen (**ScreenHitbox**):

```
Instance of 'ScreenHitbox<FlameGame>'
```

With this of course, you can create the logic for your game. Above all, the parameter **other** is used to know with which component there was a collision; for example, if the collision was between a player and the enemy, then the player would lose a life.

In the preceding function, as you can see, we ask for the component with which the hitbox circle could collide, which would be the **ScreenHitbox** added in the **main.dart**; from that collision, we create a simple logic to change the direction of the circle:

lib\components\circle_position_component.dart

```
@override
void onCollisionStart(Set<Vector2> points, PositionComponent other) {
  if (other is ScreenHitbox) {
    if (circleDirection == 1) {
      circleDirection = -1;
    } else {
      circleDirection = 1;
    }
  }
}
```

We can simplify the preceding conditional as

lib\components\circle_position_component.dart

```
@override
void onCollision(Set<Vector2> points, PositionComponent other) {
  if (other is ScreenHitbox) {
    circleDirection *=-1;
  }
}
```

And add additional logic like changing the color of the circle:

lib\components\circle_position_component.dart

```
@override
void onCollision(Set<Vector2> points, PositionComponent other) {
  if (other is ScreenHitbox) {
    circleDirection *=-1;
    hitbox.paint.color = ColorExtension.random();
  }
}
```

The **onCollision()** method keeps on executing while the collision is still occurring, making the process very inefficient; for the preceding experiment, we can use the **onCollisionStart()** function that is only executed once, when entering a collision, leaving the preceding code as

```
@override
void onCollisionStart(Set<Vector2> points, PositionComponent other) {
  if (other is ScreenHitbox) {
    circleDirection *=-1;
    hitbox.paint.color = ColorExtension.random();
  }
}
```

Challenge: Colliding Circles

As a challenge, you must create two hitbox components that, when colliding with each other, take opposite directions. To make the exercise more interesting, also add movement on the Y axis. To do this, you can create a couple of properties like

```
int circleDirectionX = 1;
int circleDirectionY = 1;
```

instead of just

```
int circleDirection = 1;
```

With this, we have more movement between the spheres.

You can also use the **nextBool()** method instead of **nextInt()**:

```
circleDirectionX = random.nextBool();
circleDirectionY = random.nextBool();
```

Tips

As additional considerations, as an aid in the challenge, you must register from the **FlameGame** class at least two instances of the previous component, but you can place more:

lib/main.dart

```
@override
void onLoad() async {
  super.onLoad();
  add(CirclePositionComponent());
  add(CirclePositionComponent());
  add(ScreenHitbox());
}
```

Now, to generate a random move, you can generate a random starting position by

```
import 'dart:math';
***
Random random = Random();
random.nextDouble() // 0 - 1
```

The function generates values between 0 and 1 of type **double**; to increase the range, we can use it for a fixed value like

```
random.nextDouble() * 500
```

However, remember that the screen must be at least 500 pixels wide and high; otherwise, the circle may appear in a position off the emulator screen.

To avoid linear moves like we currently have, you must create additional logic in the **onCollision()** function; for this, you can take as additional values those provided by the **points** parameter. Remember that if the sphere collides with the top of the emulator, in position Y it will have a value of zero:

```
{[401.0,135.0099435710236], [0]}
```

And if it enters from the left, that of X would be zero in the same way:

```
{[0],[401.0,112.9900564289764]}
```

With this, you can create conditionals to, for example, reverse direction:

```
if (points.first[1] == 0.0) {
  // top
  circleDirectionY = 1;
  circleDirectionX *= -1; // inverts the direction of x
}
```

Resolution for the Challenge

To solve the challenge, once at least duplicate the component in the **main.dart**, as shown previously. We must create a couple of properties for the X and Y directions, respectively:

```
int circleDirectionX = 1;
int circleDirectionY = 1;
```

We compute a random starting position for the circles and generate random directions:

lib\components\circle_position_component.dart

```
@override
void onLoad() async {
  super.onLoad();

  circleDirectionX = random.nextBool() ? 1 : -1;
  circleDirectionY = random.nextBool() ? 1 : -1;

  screenWidth = game.size.x;
  screenHeight = game.size.y;

  centerX = (screenWidth / 2) - (circleWidth / 2);
  centerY = (screenHeight / 2) - (circleHeight / 2);

  position = Vector2(random.nextDouble() * 500, random.nextDouble() * 500);
  size = Vector2(circleWidth, circleHeight);
  hitbox.paint.color = ColorExtension.random();

  hitbox.renderShape = true;
  add(hitbox);
}
```

The **random** property is defined at the class level:

```
class CirclePositionComponent extends PositionComponent
    with CollisionCallbacks {
  ***
  Random random = Random();
}
```

And in the collision function, we add the movement on the X and Y axes, and we invert them at key points when detecting collisions. To make it more interesting, some values are random:

lib\components\circle_position_component.dart

```
@override
void onCollision(Set<Vector2> points, PositionComponent other) {
  if (other is ScreenHitbox) {
    if (points.first[1] <= 0.0) {
      // top
      circleDirectionX = random.nextInt(2) == 1 ? 1 : -1;
      circleDirectionY *= -1;
    } else if (points.first[1] >=
        game.size.y) {
      // bottom
      circleDirectionX = random.nextInt(2) == 1 ? 1 : -1;
      circleDirectionY *= -1;
    } else
    if (points.first[0] <= 0.0) {
      // left
      circleDirectionX *= -1;
      circleDirectionY = random.nextInt(2) == 1 ? 1 : -1;
    }  // o else -- caso base
     else if (points.first[0] >=
        game.size.x) {
      // right
      circleDirectionX *= -1;
      circleDirectionY = random.nextInt(2) == 1 ? 1 : -1;
    }
    hitbox.paint.color = ColorExtension.random();
  }
```

```
  if( other is CirclePositionComponent){
    circleDirectionX *=-1;
    circleDirectionY *=-1;
  }

  super.onCollision(points, other);
}
```

The preceding script is far from perfect, since many times the circle is left in a loop bouncing between the corners or colliding with the other circle; but, if we carry out several tests, you will see that, when interacting with the circle from the X axis, the directions are reversed, giving the sensation of a rebound effect.

This script can be improved by limiting the update time between circles, but more on that later:

lib\components\circle_position_component.dart

```
import 'dart:math';

import 'package:flame/collisions.dart';
import 'package:flame/palette.dart';
import 'package:flutter/material.dart';

import 'package:flame/components.dart';

class CirclePositionComponent extends PositionComponent
    with CollisionCallbacks, HasGameReference {
  static const int circleSpeed = 500;
  static const double circleWidth = 100.0;
  static const double circleHeight = 100.0;

  int circleDirectionX = 1;
  int circleDirectionY = 1;

  Random random = Random();

  late double screenWidth;
  late double screenHeight;

  final ShapeHitbox hitbox = CircleHitbox();
```

```dart
@override
void update(double dt) {
  position.x += circleDirectionX * circleSpeed * dt;
  position.y += circleDirectionY * circleSpeed * dt;
  super.update(dt);
}

@override
void onLoad() {
  screenWidth = game.size.x;
  screenHeight = game.size.y;

  circleDirectionX = random.nextInt(2) == 1 ? 1 : -1;
  circleDirectionY = random.nextInt(2) == 1 ? 1 : -1;

  position = Vector2(random.nextDouble() * 500, random.
  nextDouble() * 500);
  size = Vector2(circleWidth, circleHeight);

  hitbox.paint.color = BasicPalette.green.color;
  hitbox.renderShape = true;

  add(hitbox);
}

@override
void onCollision(Set<Vector2> points, PositionComponent other) {
  if (other is ScreenHitbox) {
    if (points.first[1] <= 0.0) {
      // top
      circleDirectionX = random.nextInt(2) == 1 ? 1 : -1;
      circleDirectionY *= -1;
    } else if (points.first[1] >=
        game.size.y) {
      // bottom
      circleDirectionX = random.nextInt(2) == 1 ? 1 : -1;
      circleDirectionY *= -1;
    } else
```

```
  if (points.first[0] <= 0.0) {
    // left
    circleDirectionX *= -1;
    circleDirectionY = random.nextInt(2) == 1 ? 1 : -1;
  } else if (points.first[0] >=
      game.size.x) {
    // right
    circleDirectionX *= -1;
    circleDirectionY = random.nextInt(2) == 1 ? 1 : -1;
  }

  // hitbox.paint.color = BasicPalette.red.color;
  hitbox.paint.color = ColorExtension.random();
}

if( other is CirclePositionComponent){
  circleDirectionX *=-1;
  circleDirectionY *=-1;
}

super.onCollision(points, other);
}
}
```

Counter for Collisions

Based on the preceding code, it's easy to implement a counter to keep track of how many collisions have occurred; we simply use one more property on the class and increment by one for each detected collision:

```
lib/components/circle_position_component.dart
```

```
class CirclePositionComponent extends PositionComponent
    with CollisionCallbacks {

  int count = 0;

  @override
  void onCollision(Set<Vector2> points, PositionComponent other) {
    ***
```

```
    count++;
    print(count);
  }
}
```

`lib/main.dart`

```
@override
void onLoad() {
  add(CirclePositionComponent(countActive: true));
  add(CirclePositionComponent());
  add(ScreenHitbox());
}
```

As you can see if you run the code, counting is done for both circles (since we added the component to **lib\components\circle_position_component.dart** twice); we could implement an additional logic in which, through a conditional, we can indicate in which instance of the component we want to carry the count:

`lib/components/circle_position_component.dart`

```
class CirclePositionComponent extends PositionComponent
    with CollisionCallbacks {

  CirclePositionComponent({this.countActive = false});

  bool countActive;
  int count = 0;

  @override
  void onCollision(Set<Vector2> points, PositionComponent other) {
    ***

    if (this.countActive) {
      count++;
      print(count);
    }
  }
}
```

And we register it in the component that we want to use the count:

lib/main.dart

```
@override
void onLoad() {
  add(CirclePositionComponent(countActive: true));
  add(CirclePositionComponent());
  add(ScreenHitbox());
}
```

This is useful if we have components of the same type and we want to keep a count, for example, for a global score of the application.

Sprite Collisions

Returning to our animated dinosaur sprite, we are going to implement the screen collision so that it does not go off the screen, as we saw before. To do this, we add ScreenHitbox from the **FlameGame** class:

lib/main.dart

```
class MyGame extends FlameGame
    with
        KeyboardEvents,
        HasKeyboardHandlerComponents,
        HasCollisionDetection {
  @override
  void onLoad() {
    add(PlayerSpriteSheetComponent());
    add(ScreenHitbox());
  }
}
```

And from the sprite animation component, we define the callback:

lib/components/player_sprite_sheet_component.dart

```
class PlayerSpriteSheetComponent extends SpriteAnimationComponent
    with TapCallbacks, KeyboardHandler, CollisionCallbacks {
```

```
@override
void onCollision(Set<Vector2> points, PositionComponent other) {
  print(other);

  super.onCollision(points, other);
  }
}
```

Just placing a sprite is not enough to activate a hitbox; we must indicate its use explicitly. You can test this by moving the sprite to the edge of the screen, and you will see that the **onCollision()** function is not activated. We must add the hitbox specifically to our sprite, as follows:

lib/components/player_sprite_sheet_component.dart

```
class PlayerSpriteSheetComponent extends SpriteAnimationComponent
    with TapCallbacks, KeyboardHandler, CollisionCallbacks {
  @override
  void onLoad() async {
    add(RectangleHitbox());
  }
}
```

We have hitboxes of other types, for example, circular, but rectangular-type ones are usually used. For adjusting their size relative to the object in question, see https://docs.flame-engine.org/latest/flame/collision_detection.html.

The problem is our sprite has a lot of space left over that is taken into account to generate the hitbox container. If you activate the debug mode, you will see exactly what the size of the container is and that the collision with the edge of the screen is triggered long before the sprite hits the edge.

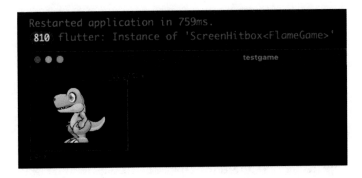

Figure 3-23. *Very large player hitbox*

For this, remember to activate the debug mode of the component:

lib/components/player_sprite_sheet_component.dart

```
@override
void onLoad() async {
    debugMode = true;
    ***
}
```

Like any other object, we can manipulate the size, position, and rotation of the hitbox. To know exactly which are the properties that we can customize, Ctrl/Command-click, and you will see

```
RectangleHitbox({
    super.position,
    super.size,
    super.angle,
    super.anchor,
    super.priority,
    bool isSolid = false,
}) : shouldFillParent = size == null && position == null {
    this.isSolid = isSolid;
}
```

To fit the hitbox more to the screen, we can reduce the width of the hitbox and adjust its position:

lib/components/player_sprite_sheet_component.dart

```
add(RectangleHitbox(
    size: Vector2(spriteSheetWidth / 4 - 70, spriteSheetHeight / 4),
    position: Vector2(25, 0),),),);
```

And we will have the following.

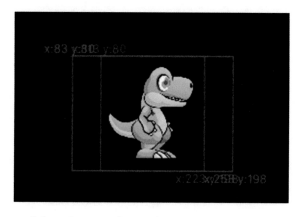

Figure 3-24. *Hitbox of the player adapted*

With this, we have the bases of our player with which we can go from walking to jumping from one side of the screen to the other, along with the possibility of using it in collision detection. With this, we can implement some very simple games as we will see in the next chapters. Remember to test the generated hitbox component for the sprite with the screen borders and detect when collisions are triggered.

Chapter source code:

https://github.com/libredesarrollo/flame-curso-libro-bases-01

CHAPTER 4

Game 1: Meteor Shower

Let's start by creating a new project called **dinometeor02** by the process shown in Chapter 1.

    With everything we have learned, we can implement a very simple game, in which we will have our sprite and several randomly generated figures will fall on our dinosaur.

    Let's start by defining the player, which will be a copy of the file

```
lib/components/player_sprite_sheet_component.dart
```

generated in the project of the previous chapter:

```
lib/components/player_component.dart
```

```dart
import 'package:flame/collisions.dart';
import 'package:flame/input.dart';
import 'package:flame/sprite.dart';
import 'package:flutter/material.dart';

import 'package:flame/flame.dart';
import 'package:flame/components.dart';

import 'package:flutter/services.dart';

class PlayerComponent extends SpriteAnimationComponent
    with  KeyboardHandler, CollisionCallbacks {
  late double screenWidth, screenHeight, centerX, centerY;
  final double spriteSheetWidth = 680, spriteSheetHeight = 472;
  int posX = 0, posY = 0;
  double playerSpeed = 500;

  int animationIndex = 0;

  bool right = true;
```

© Andrés Cruz Yoris 2024
A. Cruz Yoris, *Flame Game Development*, https://doi.org/10.1007/979-8-8688-0063-4_4

```
late SpriteAnimation dinoDeadAnimation,
    dinoIdleAnimation,
    dinoJumpAnimation,
    dinoRunAnimation,
    dinoWalkAnimation;

@override
void onLoad() async {
  //sprite = await Sprite.load('tiger.png');

  anchor = Anchor.center;
  debugMode = true;

  final spriteImage = await Flame.images.load('dinofull.png');
  final spriteSheet = SpriteSheet(
      image: spriteImage,
      srcSize: Vector2(spriteSheetWidth, spriteSheetHeight));

  //sprite = spriteSheet.getSprite(2, 1);

  // init animation
  dinoDeadAnimation = spriteSheet.createAnimationByLimit(
      xInit: 0, yInit: 0, step: 8, sizeX: 5, stepTime: .08);
  dinoIdleAnimation = spriteSheet.createAnimationByLimit(
      xInit: 1, yInit: 2, step: 10, sizeX: 5, stepTime: .08);
  dinoJumpAnimation = spriteSheet.createAnimationByLimit(
      xInit: 3, yInit: 0, step: 12, sizeX: 5, stepTime: .08);
  dinoRunAnimation = spriteSheet.createAnimationByLimit(
      xInit: 5, yInit: 0, step: 8, sizeX: 5, stepTime: .08);
  dinoWalkAnimation = spriteSheet.createAnimationByLimit(
      xInit: 6, yInit: 2, step: 10, sizeX: 5, stepTime: .08);
  // end animation

  animation = dinoIdleAnimation;

  screenWidth = game.size.x;
  screenHeight = game.size.y;

  size = Vector2(spriteSheetWidth / 4, spriteSheetHeight / 4);
```

```
  centerX = (screenWidth / 2) - (spriteSheetWidth / 2);
  centerY = (screenHeight / 2) - (spriteSheetHeight / 2);

  position = Vector2(centerX, centerY);

  add(RectangleHitbox(
      size: Vector2(spriteSheetWidth / 4 - 70, spriteSheetHeight / 4),
      position: Vector2(25, 0)));
}

@override
bool onKeyEvent(RawKeyEvent event, Set<LogicalKeyboardKey> keysPressed) {
  if (keysPressed.isEmpty) {
    animation = dinoIdleAnimation;
  }

  // print(keysPressed);

  //***X */
  // run
  if ((keysPressed.contains(LogicalKeyboardKey.arrowRight) ||
          keysPressed.contains(LogicalKeyboardKey.keyD)) &&
      keysPressed.contains(LogicalKeyboardKey.shiftLeft)) {
    animation = dinoRunAnimation;

    playerSpeed = 1500;

    if (!right) flipHorizontally();
    right = true;
    // position.x += 5;
    posX++;
  } else if (keysPressed.contains(LogicalKeyboardKey.arrowRight) ||
      keysPressed.contains(LogicalKeyboardKey.keyD)) {
    animation = dinoWalkAnimation;
    playerSpeed = 500;
    if (!right) flipHorizontally();
    right = true;
```

```
  // position.x += 5;
  posX++;
}

if ((keysPressed.contains(LogicalKeyboardKey.arrowLeft) ||
        keysPressed.contains(LogicalKeyboardKey.keyA)) &&
    keysPressed.contains(LogicalKeyboardKey.shiftLeft)) {
  animation = dinoRunAnimation;

  playerSpeed = 1500;

  if (right) flipHorizontally();
  right = false;

  //position.x -= 5;
  posX--;
} else if (keysPressed.contains(LogicalKeyboardKey.arrowLeft) ||
    keysPressed.contains(LogicalKeyboardKey.keyA)) {
  animation = dinoWalkAnimation;

  playerSpeed = 500;

  if (right) flipHorizontally();
  right = false;

  //position.x -= 5;
  posX--;
}

//***Y */
if (keysPressed.contains(LogicalKeyboardKey.arrowUp) ||
    keysPressed.contains(LogicalKeyboardKey.keyW)) {
  animation = dinoWalkAnimation;

  //position.y -= 5;
  posY--;
}
if (keysPressed.contains(LogicalKeyboardKey.arrowDown) ||
    keysPressed.contains(LogicalKeyboardKey.keyS)) {
  animation = dinoWalkAnimation;
```

```dart
      //position.y ++= 5;
      posY++;
    }

    return true;
  }

  @override
  void update(double dt) {
    position.x += playerSpeed * dt * posX;
    position.y += playerSpeed * dt * posY;
    posX = 0;
    posY = 0;

    super.update(dt);
  }

  @override
  void onCollision(Set<Vector2> points, PositionComponent other) {
    print('collision');
    super.onCollision(points, other);
  }
}

extension CreateAnimationByLimit on SpriteSheet {
  SpriteAnimation createAnimationByLimit({
    required int xInit,
    required int yInit,
    required int step,
    required int sizeX,
    required double stepTime,
    bool loop = true,
  }) {
    final List<Sprite> spriteList = [];

    int x = xInit;
    int y = yInit - 1;
```

```
    for (var i = 0; i < step; i++) {
      if (y >= sizeX) {
        y = 0;
        x++;
      } else {
        y++;
      }

      spriteList.add(getSprite(x, y));
      // print(x.toString() + ' ' + y.toString());
    }

    return SpriteAnimation.spriteList(spriteList,
        stepTime: stepTime, loop: loop);
  }
}
```

For the impact component, it will also be a copy of the one generated in the previous chapter:

lib/components/circle_position_component.dart

And it will have the following content:

lib/components/meteor_component.dart

```
import 'dart:math';

import 'package:flame/collisions.dart';
import 'package:flame/palette.dart';
import 'package:flutter/material.dart';

import 'package:flame/components.dart';

class MeteorComponent extends PositionComponent
    with CollisionCallbacks, HasGameReference {
  MeteorComponent({this.countActive = false});

  static const int circleSpeed = 500;
  static const double circleWidth = 100.0;
  static const double circleHeight = 100.0;
```

```
int circleDirectionX = 1;
int circleDirectionY = 1;

Random random = Random();

int count = 0;
bool countActive;

late double screenWidth;
late double screenHeight;

final ShapeHitbox hitbox = CircleHitbox();

@override
void update(double dt) {
  position.x += circleDirectionX * circleSpeed * dt;
  position.y += circleDirectionY * circleSpeed * dt;
  super.update(dt);
}

@override
void onLoad() {
  screenWidth = game.size.x;
  screenHeight = game.size.y;

  circleDirectionX = random.nextInt(2) == 1 ? 1 : -1;
  circleDirectionY = random.nextInt(2) == 1 ? 1 : -1;

  position = Vector2(random.nextDouble() * 500, random.
  nextDouble() * 500);
  size = Vector2(circleWidth, circleHeight);

  hitbox.paint.color = BasicPalette.green.color;
  hitbox.renderShape = true;

  add(hitbox);

}
```

```
@override
void onCollision(Set<Vector2> points, PositionComponent other) {
  if (other is ScreenHitbox) {
    if (points.first[1] <= 0.0) {
      // top
      circleDirectionX = random.nextInt(2) == 1 ? 1 : -1;
      circleDirectionY *= -1;
    } else if (points.first[1] >= game.size.y) {
      // bottom
      circleDirectionX = random.nextInt(2) == 1 ? 1 : -1;
      circleDirectionY *= -1;
    } else if (points.first[0] <= 0.0) {
      // left
      circleDirectionX *= -1;
      circleDirectionY = random.nextInt(2) == 1 ? 1 : -1;
    } else if (points.first[0] >=
        game.size.x) {
      // right
      circleDirectionX *= -1;
      circleDirectionY = random.nextInt(2) == 1 ? 1 : -1;
    }

    // hitbox.paint.color = BasicPalette.red.color;
    hitbox.paint.color = ColorExtension.random();
  }

  if (other is MeteorComponent) {
    circleDirectionX *= -1;
    circleDirectionY *= -1;
  }

  if (countActive) {
    count++;
    print(count);
  }
```

```
      super.onCollision(points, other);
   }
}
```

The **MeteorComponent** will be one of the key elements in our initial game, which
consists of the dinosaur/player escaping from the circles by walking/running in the
horizontal plane.

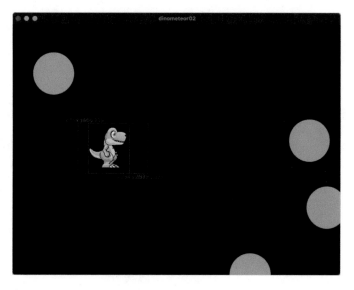

Figure 4-1. *Collision circles falling from above*

We will call the meteors "collision circles," but of course, they can be anything else
like a meteorite sprite, but we'll see that later.

Finally, the main.dart is as follows:

lib/main.dart

```
import 'package:dinometeor02/components/meteor_component.dart';
import 'package:dinometeor02/components/player_component.dart';
import 'package:flutter/material.dart';

import 'package:flame/game.dart';
import 'package:flame/input.dart';

class MyGame extends FlameGame with HasKeyboardHandlerComponents,
HasCollisionDetection {
```

```
  @override
  void onLoad() {
    // add(MeteorComponent());
    add(PlayerComponent());
  }
}

void main() {
  runApp(GameWidget(game: MyGame()));
}
```

Offset Collision Circles on the Vertical Axis

We are going to want to adapt the movement of the circles so that it is only on the Y axis, that is, vertically. In addition, the collision circles are generated randomly along the X axis, that is, from 0 to the width of the screen defined by **screenWidth**. Thinking about this, the implementation looks like the following:

lib/components/meteor_component.dart

```
import 'dart:math';

import 'package:flame/collisions.dart';
import 'package:flame/palette.dart';
import 'package:flutter/material.dart';

import 'package:flame/components.dart';

class MeteorComponent extends PositionComponent with CollisionCallbacks,
HasGameReference {

  static const int circleSpeed = 500;
  static const double circleWidth = 100.0;
  static const double circleHeight = 100.0;

  Random random = Random();
  late double screenWidth;
  late double screenHeight;
  final ShapeHitbox hitbox = CircleHitbox();
```

```
@override
void onLoad() {
  screenWidth = game.size.x;
  screenHeight = game.size.y;

  position = Vector2(random.nextDouble() * screenWidth, -circleHeight);
  size = Vector2(circleWidth, circleHeight);

  hitbox.paint.color = BasicPalette.green.color;
  hitbox.renderShape = true;

  add(hitbox);
}

@override
void update(double dt) {
  position.y += circleSpeed * dt;
  super.update(dt);
}

@override
void onCollision(Set<Vector2> points, PositionComponent other) {
  if (other is ScreenHitbox) {
  }

  super.onCollision(points, other);
}
}
```

It is important to note the calculation made for the positioning on the Y axis:

```
position = Vector2(random.nextDouble() * screenWidth, -circleHeight) ;
```

In the calculation, the size of the collision circle must be taken into account to prevent it from being generated within the visible space.

Add Collision Circles by Time

Just one circle component isn't enough to make a challenging game. Although we managed to generate a circle randomly that seeks to collide with our defenseless dinosaur, one circle is not enough; we need to create more from time to time. Consider a function like the following:

```
class MyGame extends FlameGame
    with
        KeyboardEvents,
        HasKeyboardHandlerComponents,
        HasCollisionDetection {

  @override
  void update(double dt) {
    add(CirclePositionComponent());
    super.update(dt);
  }
}

void main(List<String> args) {
  runApp(GameWidget(game: MyGame()));
}
```

This will generate too many circles in a short amount of time resulting in an unplayable game as the collisions would be constant and impossible to escape.

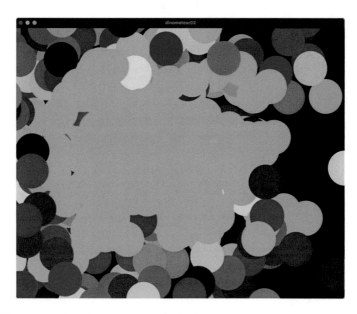

Figure 4-2. *Many randomly generated circles*

We are going to generate circles of collisions every certain time, defining a time in a personalized way, for example, generate a circle every half second, one second, three seconds, etc. This can also be a factor to modify the difficulty; that is, if we generate more collision circles in the same period of time, the game will have a greater difficulty.

In the same **update()** function, we can register a timer like the following:

lib/main.dart

```
import 'package:dinometeor02/components/meteor_component.dart';
import 'package:dinometeor02/components/player_component.dart';
import 'package:flame/collisions.dart';
import 'package:flutter/material.dart';

import 'package:flame/game.dart';
import 'package:flame/input.dart';

class MyGame extends FlameGame with HasKeyboardHandlerComponents,
HasCollisionDetection{

  double elapsedTime = 0.0;
```

```
***
@override
void update(double dt) {

  if(elapsedTime > 1.0){
    add(MeteorComponent());
    elapsedTime = 0.0;
  }

  elapsedTime += dt;
  super.update(dt);
 }
}
```

With this, we are adding a circle about every second.

Remove Invisible Components (Collision Circles)

Once the collision circles are no longer visible on the screen, there is no point in keeping the same renderings; this is a very important factor in games, and it is to optimize resources. Even though the collision circles are not visible on the screen, they continue to consume computer resources, and by generating these from time to time, it can cause performance problems in the application. There are several solutions for this problem; one of them could be to reuse the circles, restoring their position. But, to keep it simple, we are going to simply remove them from the game and, with this, free up the resources, as follows:

lib/components/meteor_component.dart

```
@override
void update(double dt) {
  position.y += circleSpeed * dt;
  super.update(dt);
  print('update');
  if (position.y > screenHeight) {
    removeFromParent();
  }
}
```

How can you evaluate, in the preceding code, when the circle is no longer visible? We simply remove it from the application using the **removeFromParent()** function.

Prevent the Player from Crossing the Screen

One big bug we have in the game that makes it impossible to lose is that the player can escape indefinitely from collision circles if it is placed in an invisible region of the screen, something like the following.

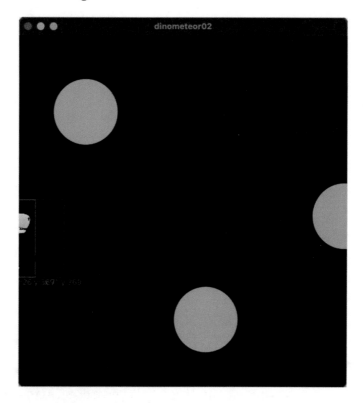

Figure 4-3. *Player hidden at the edge of the screen*

For this, we have to add the collisions on the edges of the screen and prevent the player from escaping. To do this, we will implement the following logic:

```
import 'package:flame/collisions.dart';
import 'package:flame/input.dart';
import 'package:flame/sprite.dart';
import 'package:flutter/material.dart';
```

```dart
import 'package:flame/flame.dart';
import 'package:flame/components.dart';

import 'package:flutter/services.dart';

class PlayerComponent extends SpriteAnimationComponent
    with KeyboardHandler, CollisionCallbacks {

  bool collisionXRight = false, collisionXLeft = false;
  ***

  @override
  bool onKeyEvent(RawKeyEvent event, Set<LogicalKeyboardKey> keysPressed) {
    if (keysPressed.isEmpty) {
      animation = dinoIdleAnimation;
    }

    // print(keysPressed);

    //***X */
    // run
    if ((keysPressed.contains(LogicalKeyboardKey.arrowRight) ||
            keysPressed.contains(LogicalKeyboardKey.keyD)) &&
        keysPressed.contains(LogicalKeyboardKey.shiftLeft)) {
      animation = dinoRunAnimation;
      playerSpeed = 1500;
      if (!right) flipHorizontally();
      right = true;

      if (!collisionXRight) posX++;
    } else if (keysPressed.contains(LogicalKeyboardKey.arrowRight) ||
        keysPressed.contains(LogicalKeyboardKey.keyD)) {
      animation = dinoWalkAnimation;
      playerSpeed = 500;
      if (!right) flipHorizontally();
      right = true;

      if (!collisionXRight) posX++;
    }
```

```
if ((keysPressed.contains(LogicalKeyboardKey.arrowLeft) ||
        keysPressed.contains(LogicalKeyboardKey.keyA)) &&
    keysPressed.contains(LogicalKeyboardKey.shiftLeft)) {
  animation = dinoRunAnimation;
  playerSpeed = 1500;
  if (right) flipHorizontally();
  right = false;

  if (!collisionXLeft) posX--;
} else if (keysPressed.contains(LogicalKeyboardKey.arrowLeft) ||
    keysPressed.contains(LogicalKeyboardKey.keyA)) {
  animation = dinoWalkAnimation;
  playerSpeed = 500;
  if (right) flipHorizontally();
  right = false;

  if (!collisionXLeft) posX--;
}

//***Y */
if (keysPressed.contains(LogicalKeyboardKey.arrowUp) ||
    keysPressed.contains(LogicalKeyboardKey.keyW)) {
  animation = dinoWalkAnimation;

  posY--;
}

if (keysPressed.contains(LogicalKeyboardKey.arrowDown) ||
    keysPressed.contains(LogicalKeyboardKey.keyS)) {
  animation = dinoWalkAnimation;

  posY++;
}

return true;
}
```

```
  @override
  void onCollision(Set<Vector2> points, PositionComponent other) {
    if (other is ScreenHitbox) {
      if (points.first[0] <= 0.0) {
        // left
        collisionXLeft = true;
      } else if (points.first[0] >=
          game.size.x) {
        // left
        collisionXRight = true;
      }
    }

    super.onCollision(points, other);
  }

  @override
  void onCollisionEnd(PositionComponent other) {
    collisionXLeft = collisionXRight = false;
    super.onCollisionEnd(other);
  }
}
```
***

As you can see, we have a couple of properties to check if the player is making contact (collision) with the right side

```
bool collisionXRight = false;
```

or left:

```
bool collisionXLeft = false;
```

At the moment of the collision, we detect the edges of the screen as we showed before with the implementation of the randomly generated circles in Chapter 3:

```
if (points.first[0] <= 0.0) {
  // left
  collisionXLeft = true;
```

```
} else if (points.first[0] >=
    game.size.x) {
  // left
  collisionXRight = true;
}
```

As long as the corner collision is maintained, the corresponding properties will be set to **true**. When the player is no longer colliding with the borders of the screen, the following method executes:

```
@override
void onCollisionEnd(PositionComponent other) {
  if (other is ScreenHitbox) {
    print('end');
    collisionXLeft = collisionXRight = false;
  }
}
```

The **onCollisionEnd()** method is executed when the collision ends. For the player component implementation, we can use the preceding method to reset the properties:

```
bool collisionXLeft = false, collisionXRight = false;
```

In a nutshell, the preceding properties indicate when a collision occurs and at which corner; in this state, we can prevent the player from scrolling off the screen, by setting the motion to zero (or, in practice, preventing the **posX** property from being incremented by the keyboard event), for example:

```
@override
bool onKeyEvent(RawKeyEvent event, Set<LogicalKeyboardKey> keysPressed) {
  if (!collisionXRight) {
    posX++;
  }
}
```

With this, we solved the small bug.

Player: Vary Animation When Detecting Screen Edge

A common detail that these types of games have when hitting a wall or, in this case, the limit of the screen established before is to vary the animation when the scroll key is held down, that is, if the player is already in contact with the limit of the screen, we can interrupt the walking/running animation and leave it in the idle one or define another type of animation. For this change, we are going to use the walking animation, but playing the animation more slowly:

lib/components/player_component.dart

```
class PlayerComponent extends SpriteAnimationComponent
    with KeyboardHandler, CollisionCallbacks {
  ***

  late SpriteAnimation dinoDeadAnimation,
      dinoIdleAnimation,
      dinoJumpAnimation,
      dinoRunAnimation,
      dinoWalkAnimation,
      dinoWalkSlowAnimation;

  @override
  void onLoad() async {
    ***
    dinoWalkSlowAnimation = spriteSheet.createAnimationByLimit(
        xInit: 6, yInit: 2, step: 10, sizeX: 5, stepTime: .32,);
  }

  @override
  bool onKeyEvent(RawKeyEvent event, Set<LogicalKeyboardKey> keysPressed) {
    if (keysPressed.isEmpty) {
      animation = dinoIdleAnimation;
    }

    //***X */
    // run
    if ((keysPressed.contains(LogicalKeyboardKey.arrowRight) ||
            keysPressed.contains(LogicalKeyboardKey.keyD)) &&
```

```
      keysPressed.contains(LogicalKeyboardKey.shiftLeft)) {
    playerSpeed = 1500;

    if (!right) flipHorizontally();
    right = true;

  if (!collisionXRight) {
      animation = dinoRunAnimation;
      posX++;
    } else {
      animation = dinoWalkSlowAnimation;
    }
} else if (keysPressed.contains(LogicalKeyboardKey.arrowRight) ||
      keysPressed.contains(LogicalKeyboardKey.keyD)) {
    playerSpeed = 500;
    if (!right) flipHorizontally();
    right = true;

    if (!collisionXRight) {
      animation = dinoWalkAnimation;
      posX++;
    } else {
      animation = dinoWalkSlowAnimation;
    }
}

if ((keysPressed.contains(LogicalKeyboardKey.arrowLeft) ||
        keysPressed.contains(LogicalKeyboardKey.keyA)) &&
      keysPressed.contains(LogicalKeyboardKey.shiftLeft)) {
    playerSpeed = 1500;

    if (right) flipHorizontally();
    right = false;

    if (!collisionXLeft) {
      animation = dinoRunAnimation;
      posX--;
    } else {
```

```
      animation = dinoWalkSlowAnimation;
    }
  } else if (keysPressed.contains(LogicalKeyboardKey.arrowLeft) ||
      keysPressed.contains(LogicalKeyboardKey.keyA)) {
    playerSpeed = 500;

    if (right) flipHorizontally();
    right = false;

    if (!collisionXLeft) {
      animation = dinoWalkAnimation;
      posX--;
    } else {
      animation = dinoWalkSlowAnimation;
    }
  }

  return true;
  }
}
```

As you can see, the animation is set when the collision exists; to do this, we use the **else** of the conditional set before to determine whether or not the player moves based on the same collision with the screen edge.

It is important where you define this type of animation, since, if you define it elsewhere in the class, for example, in the collision function

```
@override
void onCollision(Set<Vector2> points, PositionComponent other) {
  if (other is ScreenHitbox) {
    if (points.first[0] <= 0.0) {
      // left
      collisionXLeft = true;
    } else if (points.first[0] >=
        game.size.x) {
      // left
      collisionXRight = true;
    }
```

```
    animation = dinoWalkSlowAnimation;
  }

  super.onCollision(points, other);
}
```

the result will be that the player will always continue with the slow walking animation while the collision with the border of the screen is maintained, which is not what we want; instead, the animation is set as long as the arrow key is held down and the player is colliding with the edge of the screen.

Gravity for the Player

Another feature that we will use later when we implement character jumping is gravity. To understand the importance of this, it is important to note that gravity influences all bodies and attracts bodies downward (its center). To take a more practical approach to this, **the world will always push the player down only if the player is not on the ground**. Currently, we don't have a floor in the game, but we can create a limit (for now, an imaginary limit) for this. For example, we indicate that the floor is about 900 pixels on the screen on the Y axis, below this limit the player cannot go down, but they can go up by means of a jump that we will implement later.

Let's create a couple of properties to simulate gravity. The first indicates a constant value over the object:

```
double gravity = 1.8;
```

The other property is to calculate the velocity, which will be incremental and is assigned to the body, in this case to the player to simulate a body being attracted by gravity:

```
Vector2 velocity = Vector2(0, 0);
```

To make the experiment more interesting, we are going to position the player in the upper part of the window:

```
@override
void onLoad() async {
  ***
  position = Vector2(centerX, 0);
}
```

The code to implement it is very easy to understand; it is simply an incremental value that is applied to the body/player until it comes into contact with the ground. This is the same behavior that happens in the real world where when an object is thrown into the void, it gains speed until it touches the ground:

```
if (position.y < 900 - size[1]) {
  velocity.y += gravity;
  position.y += velocity.y * dt;
}
```

Such code is placed in the **update()** function.

Finally, here's the complete code:

lib\components\player_component.dart

```
class PlayerComponent extends SpriteAnimationComponent
    with TapCallbacks, KeyboardHandler, CollisionCallbacks {

  double gravity = 1.8;
  Vector2 velocity = Vector2(0, 0);
  ***

  @override
  void onLoad() async {
    ***

    position = Vector2(centerX, 0);
  }

  @override
  void update(double dt) {
    position.x += playerSpeed * dt * posX;
    position.y += playerSpeed * dt * posY;
    posX = 0;
    posY = 0;

    if (position.y < 900 - size[1]) {
      velocity.y += gravity;
      position.y += velocity.y * dt;
    }
```

```
    super.update(dt);
  }
}
```

Try executing the preceding code and evaluate the result. You should see the player falling at the beginning until reaching the limit or floor at about 900 pixels.

Player: Implement Jump

The next functionality that we are going to implement in the game is the jumping ability for the player. This ability is not necessary for the game we are playing since being able to walk/run horizontally is more than enough to escape from the meteorites. Still, it's an interesting ability and one that we'll use in other games.

We will create a property that we will use to detect whether or not the player is on the floor:

```
bool inGround = false;
```

To detect the state, we'll use the conditional we defined earlier to handle gravity:

```
@override
void update(double dt) {
  ***

  if (position.y < 900 - size[1]) {
    velocity.y += gravity;
    inGround = false;
  } else {
    inGround = true;
  }
  ***
}
```

The use of this property is to avoid performing multiple jumps in the air in a row without touching the ground.

The jump is very easy to implement; for it, we need to implement a property that indicates the applied force:

```
final double jumpForce = 130;
```

We also need the variation of the position on the Y axis of the player in some factor:

```
position.y -= 15;
```

And we also need the calculation made to handle gravity that we saw before (since the player is going to jump, when moving on the Y axis, the logic implemented to handle gravity is applied again):

```
@override
void update(double dt) {
  position.x += playerSpeed * dt * posX;
  position.y += playerSpeed * dt * posY;
  posX = 0;
  posY = 0;

  if (position.y < 900 - size[1]) {
    velocity.y += gravity;
    position.y += velocity.y * dt;
    inGround = false;
  } else {
    inGround = true;
  }

  super.update(dt);
}
```

It is also possible to convert this

```
position.y += velocity.y * dt;
```

to use the entire vector

```
position += velocity * dt;
```

since the position of X is not being affected.

At the time of the jump, we vary the position on the Y axis of the player and apply a force on the velocity vector, which is also used in the logic of gravity:

```
if ((keysPressed.contains(LogicalKeyboardKey.arrowUp) ||
        keysPressed.contains(LogicalKeyboardKey.keyW)) &&
    !inGround) {
  animation = dinoJumpAnimation;
  velocity.y = -jumpForce;
  position.y -= 15;
}
```

Remember that negative values are applied to "up" or move upward; negative values must be applied to the Y axis.

You can try other values of **jumpForce** and the movement of the player on the Y axis (in this implementation, –15px) and see the changes.

Finally, the implementation looks like the following:

lib\components\player_component.dart

```
class PlayerComponent extends SpriteAnimationComponent
    with KeyboardHandler, CollisionCallbacks {
  int animationIndex = 0;
  ***

  double playerSpeed = 500;
  final double jumpForce = 130;

  bool inGround = true,
      right = true,
      collisionXRight = false,
      collisionXLeft = false;
  ***

  @override
  bool onKeyEvent(RawKeyEvent event, Set<LogicalKeyboardKey> keysPressed) {
    if (keysPressed.isEmpty) {
      animation = dinoIdleAnimation;
    }
```

```
//***X */
***
//***Y */
if ((keysPressed.contains(LogicalKeyboardKey.arrowUp) ||
    keysPressed.contains(LogicalKeyboardKey.keyW)) && inGround) {
  animation = dinoWalkAnimation;
  velocity.y = -jumpForce;
  position.y -= 15;

  animation = dinoJumpAnimation;
}
// if (keysPressed.contains(LogicalKeyboardKey.arrowDown) ||
//     keysPressed.contains(LogicalKeyboardKey.keyS)) {
//   animation = dinoWalkAnimation;

//   posY++;
// }

  return true;
}

@override
void update(double dt) {
  position.x += playerSpeed * dt * posX;
  position.y += playerSpeed * dt * posY;
  posX = 0;
  posY = 0;

  if (position.y < 900 - size[1]) {
    velocity.y += gravity;
    position.y += velocity.y * dt;
    inGround = false;
  } else {
    inGround = true;
  }
```

```
    super.update(dt);
  }
  ***
}

***
```

And we will have the following.

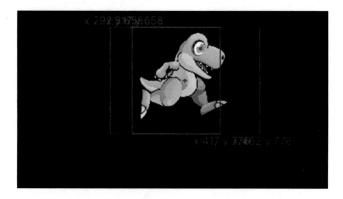

Figure 4-4. *Player jumping*

The figure shows the player's jumping ability.

Modularize the Player Class

Let's simplify the player class

lib/components/player_component.dart

so that we can reuse part of the implementation in other components, since the functionalities that we implement for the player, such as walking, running, rest state, and gravity, among others, can be implemented more easily in other components, for example, enemies and other players, among others. For this, let's start by creating a file for the creation of the animated list:

lib/utils/create_animation_by_limit.dart

```
extension CreateAnimationByLimit on SpriteSheet {
  SpriteAnimation createAnimationByLimit({
    required int xInit,
```

```dart
    required int yInit,
    required int step,
    required int sizeX,
    required double stepTime,
    bool loop = true,
  }) {
    final List<Sprite> spriteList = [];
    int x = xInit;
    int y = yInit - 1;

    for (var i = 0; i < step; i++) {
      if (y >= sizeX) {
        y = 0;
        x++;
      } else {
        y++;
      }

      spriteList.add(getSprite(x, y));
      // print(x.toString() + ' ' + y.toString());
    }

    return SpriteAnimation.spriteList(spriteList,
        stepTime: stepTime, loop: loop);
  }
}
```

The generic class, let's call it as **Character**, will only have inheritance, mixins, and properties:

`lib/components/character.dart`

```dart
import 'package:flame/collisions.dart';
import 'package:flame/input.dart';
import 'package:flame/sprite.dart';
import 'package:flutter/material.dart';

import 'package:flame/flame.dart';
import 'package:flame/components.dart';
```

```
import 'package:flutter/services.dart';

class Character extends SpriteAnimationComponent
    with KeyboardHandler, CollisionCallbacks {

  int animationIndex = 0;

  double gravity = 1.8;
  Vector2 velocity = Vector2(0, 0);
  late double screenWidth, screenHeight, centerX, centerY;
  final double spriteSheetWidth = 680, spriteSheetHeight = 472;

  int posX = 0, posY = 0;
  double playerSpeed = 500;
  final double jumpForce = 130;

  bool inGround = true,
      right = true,
      collisionXRight = false,
      collisionXLeft = false;

  late SpriteAnimation deadAnimation,
      idleAnimation,
      jumpAnimation,
      runAnimation,
      walkAnimation,
      walkSlowAnimation;
}
```

We'll leave the rest of the content in the player class:

lib/components/player_component.dart

```
import 'package:dinometeor02/components/meteor_component.dart';
import 'package:flutter/material.dart';
import 'package:flutter/services.dart';

import 'package:flame/collisions.dart';
import 'package:flame/sprite.dart';
import 'package:flame/flame.dart';
import 'package:flame/components.dart';
```

```dart
import 'package:dinometeor02/components/character.dart';
import 'package:dinometeor02/utils/create_animation_by_limit.dart';

class PlayerComponent extends Character  {

  @override
  void onLoad() async {
    anchor = Anchor.center;
    debugMode = true;

    final spriteImage = await Flame.images.load('dinofull.png');
    final spriteSheet = SpriteSheet(
        image: spriteImage,
        srcSize: Vector2(spriteSheetWidth, spriteSheetHeight));

    // init animation
    deadAnimation = spriteSheet.createAnimationByLimit(
        xInit: 0, yInit: 0, step: 8, sizeX: 5, stepTime: .08);
    idleAnimation = spriteSheet.createAnimationByLimit(
        xInit: 1, yInit: 2, step: 10, sizeX: 5, stepTime: .08);
    jumpAnimation = spriteSheet.createAnimationByLimit(
        xInit: 3, yInit: 0, step: 12, sizeX: 5, stepTime: .08);
    runAnimation = spriteSheet.createAnimationByLimit(
        xInit: 5, yInit: 0, step: 8, sizeX: 5, stepTime: .08);
    walkAnimation = spriteSheet.createAnimationByLimit(
        xInit: 6, yInit: 2, step: 10, sizeX: 5, stepTime: .08);
    walkSlowAnimation = spriteSheet.createAnimationByLimit(
        xInit: 6, yInit: 2, step: 10, sizeX: 5, stepTime: .32);
    // end animation

    animation = idleAnimation;

    screenWidth = game.size.x;
    screenHeight = game.size.y;

    size = Vector2(spriteSheetWidth / 4, spriteSheetHeight / 4);

    centerX = (screenWidth / 2) - (spriteSheetWidth / 2);
    centerY = (screenHeight / 2) - (spriteSheetHeight / 2);
```

```
    position = Vector2(centerX, centerY);

    add(RectangleHitbox(
        size: Vector2(spriteSheetWidth / 4 - 70, spriteSheetHeight / 4),
        position: Vector2(25, 0)));
}

@override
bool onKeyEvent(RawKeyEvent event, Set<LogicalKeyboardKey> keysPressed) {
    if (keysPressed.isEmpty) {
        animation = idleAnimation;
    }

    //***X */
    // Running
    if ((keysPressed.contains(LogicalKeyboardKey.arrowRight) ||
            keysPressed.contains(LogicalKeyboardKey.keyD)) &&
        keysPressed.contains(LogicalKeyboardKey.shiftLeft)) {
        playerSpeed = 1500;

        if (!right) flipHorizontally();
        right = true;

        if (!collisionXRight) {
            animation = runAnimation;
            posX++;
        } else {
            animation = walkSlowAnimation;
        }
    } else if (keysPressed.contains(LogicalKeyboardKey.arrowRight) ||
        keysPressed.contains(LogicalKeyboardKey.keyD)) {
        playerSpeed = 500;

        if (!right) flipHorizontally();
        right = true;
        if (!collisionXRight) {
            animation = walkAnimation;
            posX++;
        } else {
```

```
      animation = walkSlowAnimation;
    }
  }

  if ((keysPressed.contains(LogicalKeyboardKey.arrowLeft) ||
          keysPressed.contains(LogicalKeyboardKey.keyA)) &&
      keysPressed.contains(LogicalKeyboardKey.shiftLeft)) {
    playerSpeed = 1500;

    if (right) flipHorizontally();
    right = false;
    if (!collisionXLeft) {
      animation = runAnimation;
      posX--;
    } else {
      animation = walkSlowAnimation;
    }
  } else if (keysPressed.contains(LogicalKeyboardKey.arrowLeft) ||
      keysPressed.contains(LogicalKeyboardKey.keyA)) {
    playerSpeed = 500;

    if (right) flipHorizontally();
    right = false;

    if (!collisionXLeft) {
      animation = walkAnimation;
      posX--;
    } else {
      animation = walkSlowAnimation;
    }
  }

  //***Y */
  if ((keysPressed.contains(LogicalKeyboardKey.arrowUp) ||
          keysPressed.contains(LogicalKeyboardKey.keyW)) &&
      inGround) {
    animation = walkAnimation;
    velocity.y = -jumpForce;
```

```
    position.y -= 15;

    animation = jumpAnimation;
  }
  // if (keysPressed.contains(LogicalKeyboardKey.arrowDown) ||
  //     keysPressed.contains(LogicalKeyboardKey.keyS)) {
  //   animation = walkAnimation;

  //   posY++;
  // }

  return true;
}

@override
void update(double dt) {
  position.x += playerSpeed * dt * posX;
  position.y += playerSpeed * dt * posY;
  posX = 0;
  posY = 0;

  if (position.y < 900 - size[1]) {
    velocity.y += gravity;
    position.y += velocity.y * dt;
    inGround = false;
  } else {
    inGround = true;
  }

  super.update(dt);
}

@override
void onCollisionStart(Set<Vector2> points, PositionComponent other) {
  if (other is ScreenHitbox) {
    if (points.first[0] <= 0.0) {
      // left
      collisionXLeft = true;
    } else if (points.first[0] >=
```

```
        game.size.x) {
      // left
      collisionXRight = true;
    }
  }

  super.onCollisionStart(points, other);
}

@override
void onCollisionEnd(PositionComponent other) {
  collisionXLeft = collisionXRight = false;
  super.onCollisionEnd(other);
}
}
```

If you run the game, everything should still work.

Meteor Animated Sprite

Finally, we're going to want to change the look of our meteor, so that it's not a circle but some animated sprite instead; in this book, we will use the following image.

Figure 4-5. *Meteorite sprite sheet*

This image was taken from

`www.freepik.es/vector-gratis/conjunto-animacion-llama-fuego-brillante_9586183.htm`

and edited to remove the frames that are not going to be used and change the format to PNG.

We import the image into the project:

`pubspec.yaml`

```
assets:
  **

  - assets/images/meteor.png
```

The implementation that we must do to use a sprite sheet instead of a hitbox consists of changing a **PositionComponent** to a **SpriteAnimationComponent**, similar to how we did before with the player, and using the **animate property** to use the preceding sprite sheet. In the rest of the implementation, there are no additional major changes to mention from the original implementation:

`lib/components/meteor_component.dart`

```
import 'dart:math';

import 'package:flutter/material.dart';

import 'package:flame/collisions.dart';
import 'package:flame/flame.dart';
import 'package:flame/palette.dart';
import 'package:flame/sprite.dart';
import 'package:flame/components.dart';

import 'package:dinometeor02/utils/create_animation_by_limit.dart';

class MeteorComponent extends SpriteAnimationComponent with
CollisionCallbacks {

  static const int circleSpeed = 500;
  static const double circleWidth = 100.0;
  static const double circleHeight = 100.0;
```

```
Random random = Random();

late double screenWidth;
late double screenHeight;

final ShapeHitbox hitbox = CircleHitbox();

final double spriteSheetWidth = 79;
final double spriteSheetHeight = 100;

@override
void onLoad() async {
  screenWidth = game.size.x;
  screenHeight = game.size.y;

  position = Vector2(random.nextDouble() * screenWidth, -circleHeight);
  size = Vector2(circleWidth, circleHeight);

  hitbox.paint.color = BasicPalette.green.color;
  hitbox.renderShape = false;
  hitbox.position = Vector2(0, 50);
  hitbox.collisionType = CollisionType.passive;

  final spriteImage = await Flame.images.load('meteor.png');
  final spriteSheet = SpriteSheet(
      image: spriteImage,
      srcSize: Vector2(spriteSheetWidth, spriteSheetHeight));

  // init animation
  animation = spriteSheet.createAnimationByLimit(
      xInit: 0, yInit: 0, step: 3, sizeX: 3, stepTime: .08);

  add(hitbox);
}
***
}
```

And we will have the following.

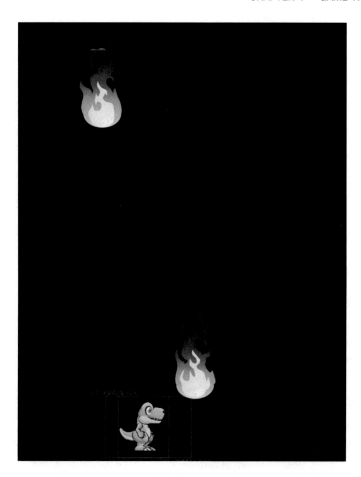

Figure 4-6. *Generate meteorites in the Flame game*

Impact Counter

Now with the meteorites implemented, the next thing we want to do is count the collisions; to do this, for each collision of a meteorite on the player, we will want to increase a counter by one unit.

Remember that the use of collisions is through the **onCollisionStart()** function, and it will be executed in both collided components; in the case of our implementation, it would be in **PlayerComponent** and **MeteorComponent**. However, we only want to implement the counter in the player, which there's only one instance of in the application. We could try something like this:

lib/components/player_component.dart

```
class PlayerComponent extends Character {
  int count = 0;
  ***

  @override
  void onCollisionStart(Set<Vector2> points, PositionComponent other) {
    if (other is ScreenHitbox) {
      ***
    }

    if (other is MeteorComponent) {
      print('meteor');
    }

    super.onCollisionStart(points, other);
  }
}
```

The problem we are going to have is that, when the meteorite (collision circle) comes into contact with the player, this contact is consecutive and is maintained while the meteorite crosses the hitbox defined in the player; this causes the counter to increase by more than one unit, which is not what we want. To correct this, we have several ways; one of them is to place a timer, so that the operation is only performed once. However, a better option is to disable the hitbox component defined in the **MeteorComponent** by a property:

lib/components/player_component.dart

```
class PlayerComponent extends Character {
  int count = 0;
  ***

  @override
  void onCollision(Set<Vector2> points, PositionComponent other) {
    if (other is ScreenHitbox) {
      ***
    }
```

```
    if (other is MeteorComponent) {
      print('meteor');

      other.hitbox.removeFromParent();
    }

    super.onCollision(points, other);
  }
}
```

With this implementation, when the components come into contact, we remove the **hitbox**, and with this, there are no more collisions except the first one in which we increment the counter. Another implementation could be to remove the meteorite:

lib/components/player_component.dart

```
class PlayerComponent extends Character {
  int count = 0;
  ***

  @override
  void onCollision(Set<Vector2> points, PositionComponent other) {
    if (other is ScreenHitbox) {
      ***
    }

    if (other is MeteorComponent) {
      print('meteorito');

      // other.hitbox.removeFromParent();
      other.removeFromParent();
    }

    super.onCollision(points, other);
  }
}
```

With these implementations, we can be completely sure that, for each meteor component colliding on the player, it will only be counted once.

One of the aspects that we must work is the background of the game we are building, but we will do that in the next chapter.

Chapter source code:

```
https://github.com/libredesarrollo/flame-curso-libro-dinometeor-02/
releases/tag/v0.1
```

CHAPTER 5

Background Color and Image

One of the missing elements in the dinosaur game that we started to create in the previous chapter is a good background for our game. For this, we have some ways, and they are a solid color or an image. In this chapter, we will present both options, and remember that we will continue using the **dinometeor02** project created in the previous chapter.

Background Color

We can easily change the background color of the game by

lib\main.dart

```
class MyGame extends FlameGame {
  ***
  @override
  Color backgroundColor() {
    return Colors.purple;
  }
}
```

You can specify the color of your preference, in the preceding case purple.

© Andrés Cruz Yoris 2024
A. Cruz Yoris, *Flame Game Development*, https://doi.org/10.1007/979-8-8688-0063-4_5

Figure 5-1. *Change the background color*

We can also create a component to define the color of our application, which consists of using the **render()** function to draw a rectangle that will serve as the background:

lib/components/background_color_component.dart

```
import 'package:flame/components.dart';
import 'package:flame/palette.dart';
import 'package:flutter/material.dart';

class Background extends PositionComponent {
  static final backgroundPaint = BasicPalette.white.paint();
  late double screenWidth;
  late double screenHeight;

  @override
  void onLoad() async {
    super.onLoad();
    screenWidth = game.size.x;
    screenHeight = game.size.y;
```

```
    position = Vector2(0, 0);
    size = Vector2(screenWidth, screenHeight);
  }

  @override
  void render(Canvas canvas) {
    super.render(canvas);
    canvas.drawRect(
        Rect.fromPoints(position.toOffset(), size.toOffset()),
        backgroundPaint);
  }
}
```

Of course, if you only want to change the background color, you can use the first implementation. Apart from that, the implementation based on the component has the problem that it is built based on the size of the screen and, if the user rescales it, it does not update.

From the main:

lib/main.dart

```
import 'package:dinometeor02/components/background_color_component.dart';
***
@override
void onLoad() {
  add(BackgroundImageComponent());
  add(PlayerComponent());
  add(ScreenHitbox());
}
```

it is important to place the background first before the rest of the components, which in this case would be the player and the meteorites, since if you place it after

```
add(PlayerComponent());
add(ScreenHitbox());
add(BackgroundImageComponent());
```

the background will overlap the player component.

Background Image

We can also specify a background image for our game; to do this, first, we load an image that serves as a background in our project. You can select any, but for the tests we are going to perform, it is recommended that you use an image that is higher than the resolution of your monitor.

Figure 5-2. *Background image*

You can get the image from

```
www.freepik.com/free-vector/space-game-background-neon-night-alien-
landscape_7671274.htm#query=game%20background&position=6&from_view=keyword
```

We copy the image to the project.

```
pubspec.yaml
```

```
  assets:
      - assets/images/dinofull.png
      - assets/images/meteor.png
      - assets/images/background.jpg
```

And we use the image in a new component:

```
lib/components/background_image_component.dart
```

```
import 'package:flame/components.dart';
import 'package:flutter/widgets.dart';
```

```
class BackgroundImageComponent extends SpriteComponent with
HasGameReference {

  late double screenWidth;
  late double screenHeight;

  @override
  void onLoad() async{
    screenWidth = game.size.x;
    screenHeight = game.size.y;

    position = Vector2(0, 0);

    sprite = await Sprite.load('background.jpg');

    size = Vector2(screenWidth, screenHeight);
    //size = sprite!.originalSize;
  }
}
```

With

```
sprite!.originalSize
```

we can specify the original size of the image; that is, if we have a 6500 × 2889 image (like the one used in this section), this will be the size specified for the component.

However, we can adjust the size of the background to that of the window:

```
size = Vector2(screenWidth, screenHeight);
```

And from the main, we add the component:

```
lib/main.dart
```

```
import 'package:dinometeor02/components/background_image_component.dart';
***
@override
void onLoad() {
  add(BackgroundImageComponent());
  add(PlayerComponent());
  add(ScreenHitbox());
}
```

And we have the following.

Figure 5-3. *Background image in the Flame application*

It is important to place the background component before the player component so that the background component does not overlap the player component; the order in which the components are added is the order in which they will be added in the window overlaying them.

Get Component Information from the Game Class

Suppose we have a dynamic size for the background component, where the size of the components corresponds to the size of the image:

lib/components/background_image_component.dart

```
import 'package:flame/components.dart';
import 'package:flutter/widgets.dart';

class BackgroundImageComponent extends SpriteComponent {
  late double screenWidth;
  late double screenHeight;
```

```
@override
void onLoad() async{
  screenWidth = game.size.x;
  screenHeight = game.size.y;

  position = Vector2(0, 0);

  sprite = await Sprite.load('background.jpg');

  //size = Vector2(screenWidth, screenHeight);
  size = sprite!.originalSize;
  }
}
```

In this example, we are using an image with size

6500x2889

Depending on the image that we use, we will have one size or another. The important thing to note from the preceding code is that in no part of the code are we indicating fixed values to define the size; therefore, the size of the background can influence other components of the game, for example, the player. By having a background with a height of 2889 pixels and by positioning the player in

lib\components\player_component.dart

```
if (position.y < 900 - size[1]) {
  velocity.y += gravity;
  inGround = true;
}
```

or placing it somewhere that works from the height of the window

```
if (position.y < screenHeight - size[1]) {
  velocity.y += gravity;
  inGround = true;
}
```

if we have a window of 1080 pixels and the character of 118 pixels, the player would be positioned in the air at a height of 962 pixels.

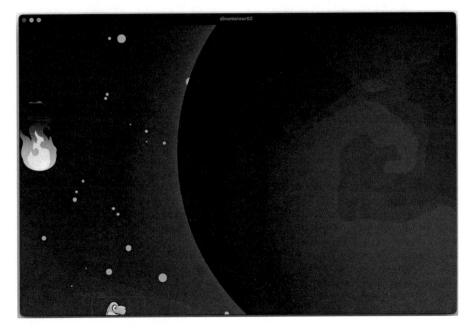

Figure 5-4. *Position of the player in the world*

And of course, the meteorite component has a similar problem, both to indicate its movement:

lib/components/meteor_component.dart

```
@override
void onLoad() async {
  position = Vector2(random.nextDouble() * screenWidth, -circleHeight);
}
```

Here's how to remove them:

lib/components/meteor_component.dart

```
@override
void update(double dt) {
  position.y += circleSpeed * dt;
  super.update(dt);
  if (position.y > screenHeight) {
    removeFromParent();
  }
}
```

It does not correspond to the size of the background or that of the window, resulting in a poor experience and game execution. Apart from that, you need to know the size of the background to determine how far the character will walk:

lib\components\player_component.dart

```
@override
void onCollision(Set<Vector2> points, PositionComponent other) {
  if (other is ScreenHitbox) {
    if (points.first[0] <= 0.0) {
      // left
      collisionXLeft = true;
    } else if (points.first[0] >=
        game.size.x) {
      // left
      collisionXRight = true;
    }
  }
}
```

In short, many times it is necessary to pass information between components so that they behave as expected, especially when it is the size of the background component that is used to perform the rest of the calculations by other components, without the need to define fixed values, such as the background size in the components.

To know the solution to the preceding problem, we are going to carry out some tests. We can convert the implementation we currently have into something like this:

lib\main.dart

```
@override
void onLoad() {
  var player = PlayerComponent();
  var background = Background();

  add(ScreenHitbox());
  add(background);
  add(player);
}
```

As you can see, it's the same implementation, but this time, the instance of the class (components) was registered in a variable. With this, we can access the component's properties, for example, the size:

lib\main.dart

```
@override
void onLoad() {
  var player = PlayerComponent();
  var background = Background();

  print(background.size.x.toString());

  add(ScreenHitbox());
  add(background);
  add(player);
}
```

But, if we run the preceding code, we'll see that the console returns a zero and not the width of the component (which we remember is the original width of the image – **sprite!.originalSize** – which would be 6500 pixels); the reason for this is that, although the instance of the class/component has been created, it has not yet been loaded. If you write

background.load

you will see some interesting matches.

Figure 5-5. *isLoaded property of the PositionComponent*

The

```
background.isLoaded
```

specifies via a Boolean whether the component has been loaded or not. But, to make an interesting test, you can put the preceding impression in the **update()** function:

```
lib\main.dart
```

```
@override
void onLoad() {
   print(background.size.x.toString());
   ***
}
```

You will see that the console returns the size of the window, which in this case is 6500 pixels, since, at this point, the background component has been loaded.

We have another interesting property

```
background.loaded
```

that we can use, which is a **Future** and is executed when the component has been loaded. So if we put print in said **Future**

```
lib\main.dart
```

```
@override
void onLoad() {
  var player = PlayerComponent();
  var background = Background();

  add(ScreenHitbox());
  add(background);
  add(player);

  background.loaded.then((value) {
    print(background.size.x.toString());
  });
}
```

we will see the size of the background component, which in this example is 6500 pixels. Therefore, we can create the rest of the components that need to know the dimensions of the background component when the background component has been loaded.

Update the Player Component with Map Dimensions

Continuing with the modifications to be able to use a background of any size, whether the size of the screen or less, we are going to modify the player component to obtain the size of the map and, with this, define the limits of the player:

lib\components\player_component.dart

```
class PlayerComponent extends Character {
  Vector2 mapSize;
  PlayerComponent({required this.mapSize}) : super() {
    anchor = Anchor.center;
    debugMode = true;
  }

  ***
  @override
  void update(double dt) {
    position.x += playerSpeed * dt * posX;
    position.y += playerSpeed * dt * posY;
    posX = 0;
    posY = 0;

    if (position.y < mapSize.y - size[1]) {
      velocity.y += gravity;
      inGround = true;
    } else {
      velocity = Vector2.all(0);
      inGround = false;
    }

    position += velocity * dt;

    super.update(dt);
  }

  @override
  void onCollision(Set<Vector2> points, PositionComponent other) {
    if (other is ScreenHitbox) {
```

```
    if (points.first[0] <= 0.0) {
      // left
      collisionXLeft = true;
    } else if (points.first[0] >= mapSize.x) {
      //game.size.x
      // left
      collisionXRight = true;
      //
    }
  }
  ***
  super.onCollision(points, other);
  }
}
```

Its changes are very subtle. Now, the lateral limit is done by the width of the map as well as the calculation of the floor with the calculation of gravity, in which the height of the map is taken and not the size of the screen.

And from the main class, we load the background:

```
lib\main.dart
```

```
@override
void onLoad() {
  var background = Background();
  add(background);
  add(ScreenHitbox());

  background.loaded.then((value) {
    final player = PlayerComponent(
        mapSize: Vector2(background.size.x, background.size.y));
    add(player);
  });
}
```

As you can see, when the background is loaded, it has the size of the map, and it is passed as a reference to the player instance.

Set the Camera to Follow the Component

We currently have a background that is larger than what can be displayed in the window, resulting in a large part of it that cannot be visible; in order to take advantage of this non-visible background and have it show up as the player scrolls, we need to place a camera following the player.

The camera concept has been worked on in any game engine like Unity or Unreal or 3D/2D content creation software like Blender and should be familiar to you; but in essence, the camera is nothing more than a mechanism through which we can observe a part of the world, where the world is nothing more than all the components that are within the game. Using coordinates, we can move this observer.

In these types of games, usually the camera follows the player, and with this, we can visualize parts of the background that are not visible as the player moves through the world.

You can get more information about it at

`https://docs.flame-engine.org/latest/flame/camera_component.html`

In Flame we have a component called **CameraComponent** with which we can indicate the display area.

World

The world component, as its name indicates, is a component that can be used to house all the other components that make up the game world. In the case of the game that we are implementing, these components would be

- The background
- The tiles
- The player
- The meteorites

All these components must be added in an instance of the world component so that they are in the same layer and, with this, to be able to interact with the player.

Using a world component is as simple as creating the instance:

```
final world = World();
```

Add it in Flame:

```
add(world);
```

And at this point, all the components that are part of the game must be added to the world instance:

```
world.add(<COMPONENT>);
```

The **world** component and **CameraComponent** are designed to work together; an instance of the **CameraComponent** class "looks" at the world, and this is why we introduced the world component along with the camera component.

It is usually not mandatory to use a world component for our Flame games, since we can add our game components directly into the Flame instance

```
add(player);
```

or in the same components, but, in this type of game that we have a bigger world than can fit on the screen, it is necessary to use a camera that follows or watches over our player.

CameraComponent

CameraComponent, as we mentioned before, is the component used to observe the world. We have several properties to set on this component so that it "looks" at exactly where we want and follows a component.

The viewport is a window through which the world is seen. That window has a certain size, shape, and position on the screen.

The viewfinder is responsible for knowing the location in the game world we are currently looking at. The viewfinder also controls the zoom level and rotation angle of the view; this property is key in these games since it is the one that is updated to "look" at the player.

Like any other game, the camera must observe the player who is moving through the world, although luckily this update is done automatically using the **follow()** function, which receives as a parameter a component to observe and updates the position of the camera as it moves across the screen:

```
cameraComponent.follow(player);
```

The viewfinder allows you to customize aspects of the display such as the anchor, with which we can specify the center of the camera; that is, our world looks like the following.

Figure 5-6. *World*

The camera must be centered in the lower-left corner, that is, in the **bottomLeft**.

Figure 5-7. *Camera observing the world*

And for this we have:

```
cameraComponent.viewfinder.anchor = Anchor.bottomLeft
```

Deploy the Camera Component

Having clarified how the world and camera components work, let's implement the logic in our application:

```
class MyGame extends FlameGame *** {
  ***

  late PlayerComponent player;

  final world = World();
  late final CameraComponent cameraComponent;

  @override
  void onLoad() {
    var background = Background();

    add(world);

    world.add(background);

    background.loaded.then(
      (value) {
        player = PlayerComponent();

        cameraComponent = CameraComponent(world: world);
        cameraComponent.follow(player);
        cameraComponent.setBounds(Rectangle.fromLTRB(0, 0, background.
        size.x, background.size.y)));

        // cameraComponent.viewfinder.anchor = Anchor.bottomLeft;
        cameraComponent.viewfinder.anchor = const Anchor(0.1, 0.9);
        add(cameraComponent);

        cameraComponent.world.add(player);
      },
    );

    add(ScreenHitbox());
  }
}
```

Key Points

We define and add to Flame the **world** object:

```
final world = World();
***
add(world);
```

When using the camera component, it is necessary to use a **world** object:

```
cameraComponent = CameraComponent(world: world);
```

With an instance of the preceding component, we can customize various aspects of the display, such as the camera following a component through the **follow()** function, which receives the component to follow as a parameter:

```
cameraComponent.follow(player);
```

The center of the camera is defined in the lower-left corner, but if we leave it in this form

```
cameraComponent.viewfinder.anchor = Anchor.bottomLeft; // Anchor(0, 1);
```

by positioning the camera that is following the player, we will see that the player is partly visible.

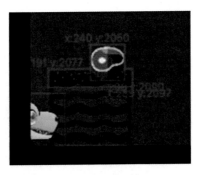

Figure 5-8. *Testing using the camera in the application*

This is because the camera "follows" the player's anchor, which is aligned in the center:

```
PlayerComponent({required this.mapSize}) : super() {
    anchor = Anchor.center;
    debugMode = true;
}
```

To avoid this behavior, we can specify numeric values for the camera's **anchor** that are not as constrained as the previous value:

```
cameraComponent.viewfinder.anchor = const Anchor(0.1, 0.9);
```

And with this we have a complete visualization of the player.

Figure 5-9. *Positioning the camera correctly in the application*

Added to this, we can also place restrictions on the camera display (the area visible by the camera, which in this case is precisely the size of the image or map). It is important to mention that the display area corresponds to a rectangle with the size of the background, therefore:

```
cameraComponent.setBounds(Rectangle.fromLTRB(0, 0, background.size.x,
background.size.y)));
```

And from the main, we pass the position of the camera:

`lib\main.dart`

```
@override
void update(double dt) {
  if (elapsedTime > 1.0) {
    Vector2 cp = cameraComponent.viewfinder.position;

    cp.y = cameraComponent.viewfinder.position.y -
        cameraComponent.viewport.size.y;
    world.add(MeteorComponent(cameraPosition: cp));
    elapsedTime = 0.0;
  }
  elapsedTime += dt;
  super.update(dt);
}
```

As you can see, we do not have the position of the camera directly; therefore, we must make a calculation, as we mentioned before, through the viewfinder:

`cameraComponent.viewfinder`

We have the position of the camera, which is updated through the player as it moves across the screen, and we can obtain it with

`cameraComponent.viewfinder.position`

But this gives us the position of the camera in the lower corner, that is, the bottom, and we need to generate the meteorites in the upper part. For this reason, we subtract the height of the camera that we can obtain with

`cameraComponent.viewport.size.y`

Update the Meteor Component with Map Dimensions

Now with the player component adapted to the size of the background and not the screen, we must do the same with the meteorite in which we have to take a different approach; for this component, it is necessary to avoid generating meteorites along the entire width of the map (the 6500 pixels wide) and generate the meteorites only in the space visible by the camera (where the camera is observing). We are going to carry out the following implementation:

lib\components\meteor_component.dart

```dart
import 'dart:math';

import 'package:flame/collisions.dart';
import 'package:flame/flame.dart';
import 'package:flame/palette.dart';
import 'package:flame/sprite.dart';
import 'package:flutter/material.dart';

import 'package:flame/components.dart';
import 'package:testgame/utils/create_animation_by_limit.dart';

class MeteorComponent extends SpriteAnimationComponent with
CollisionCallbacks, HasGameReference {
  Vector2 cameraPosition;
  MeteorComponent({required this.cameraPosition}) : super() {
    debugMode = true;
  }
  ***
  @override
  void onLoad() async {
    screenWidth = game.size.x;
    screenHeight = game.size.y;
    position = Vector2(random.nextDouble() * screenWidth + cameraPosition.x,
    cameraPosition.y - circleHeight);
    ***
  }

  @override
  void update(double dt) {
    ***
```

```
    if (position.y > cameraPosition.y + screenHeight) {
      removeFromParent();
    }
  }
  ***
}
```

As you can see, the camera is a component that also stores a position on the world and is moved according to the position of the player. We can use the position of the camera to determine the initial position, and together with the size of the screen, we can perform the calculation to determine in which portion of the screen the meteorites will be generated.

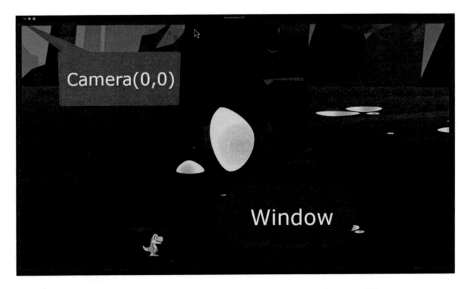

Figure 5-10. *Determine the position of the camera in the world*

And from the main, we pass the position of the camera:

```
lib\main.dart
```

```
@override
void update(double dt) {
  elapsedTime += dt;
  if (elapsedTime > 1.0) {
    add(MeteorComponent(cameraPosition: camera.position));
```

```
    elapsedTime = 0.0;
  }

  super.update(dt);
}
```

With the preceding changes, we have a more adaptive application, since the main elements of the game, such as the player and the meteorites, are not calculated based on the size of the screen, but instead on a more configurable element such as the image used as background.

Chapter source code:

https://github.com/libredesarrollo/flame-curso-libro-dinometeor-02/releases/tag/v0.2

CHAPTER 6

Tiled Background

In this chapter we are going to learn how to generate and use maps for our application using tiles; with these maps, we can design them so that they not only look the way we want but also establish different references in them where we can create sections for handling collisions, rendering consumables, etc. Therefore, in this chapter we will learn to

1. Generate tiled maps or backgrounds with Tiled Map Editor (or simply Tiled).

2. Use in-app tiled maps in Flutter with Flame.

The program that we are going to use to generate the maps is
`www.mapeditor.org/`

This is a very complete, free, and easy-to-use software (at least in a basic way) to create any 2D map, indicating through layers and many options how you want to compose the map based on tiles, which are nothing more than a set of textures included in the same image and with which the scene of a video game is composed; with these textures we can form a map using software like Tiled Map Editor (or simply Tiled). In this book, we will take the first steps with Tiled, although, in the code repositories attached to this book, you can find ready-to-use maps.

Surely what you have noticed if you have played 2D games is that, on the map, there are always a multitude of elements that are repeated, and it is precisely because they use the tiles to compose their maps since, with them, we can create a map large enough and generated in a very efficient way since the map does not consist of a huge image in PNG (as we used in the previous chapter for the game "Meteor Shower" or similar formats that we load in the game) but through a format generated by programs like Tiled using tilesets that are nothing more than a set of tiles with which to compose the map. For example, the following image is a tileset that we are going to use to generate a map.

© Andrés Cruz Yoris 2024
A. Cruz Yoris, *Flame Game Development*, https://doi.org/10.1007/979-8-8688-0063-4_6

Figure 6-1. *Tileset to place as floors and tiles in the game (`https://limezu.itch. io/basic-platformer-tileset-dirt-grass`)*

On the other hand, a tile is only a portion of a tileset that we can use independently like the following.

Figure 6-2. *Example tile for the game*

Creating Our First Map with Tiled Map Editor

Once Tiled Map Editor (or simply Tiled) is installed, when we open it, we will have an interface like the following.

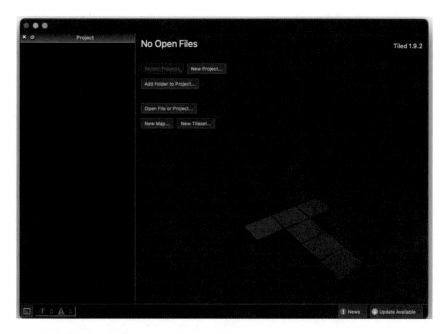

Figure 6-3. *Tiled Map Editor, main interface*

We must click "New Map…", and we must indicate some very basic configurations.

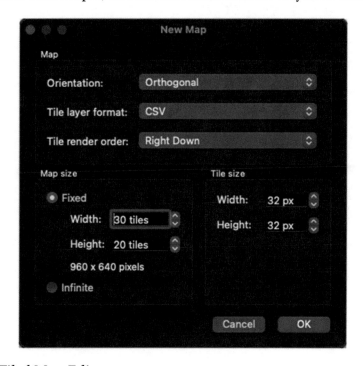

Figure 6-4. *Tiled Map Editor, new map*

We will see the size of the map, which is established based on patterns that are the tiles, like the one we saw before.

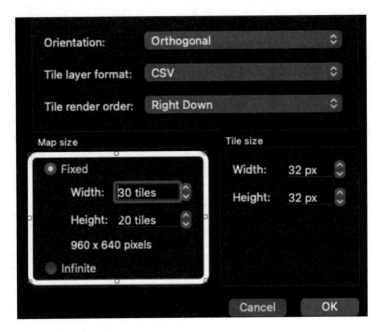

Figure 6-5. *Tiled Map Editor, map size*

And for the size of the pattern, here we must establish the sizes of the tiles that we are going to use to compose the map, in our case, 32 × 32 pixels.

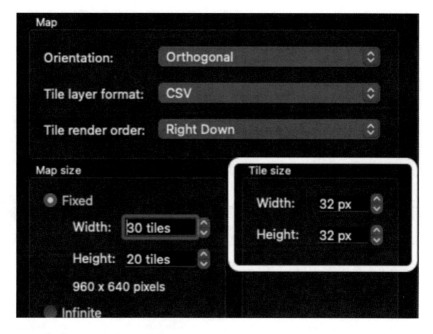

Figure 6-6. *Tiled Map Editor, tile size*

Another important aspect is the size of the map, which is calculated from the size of the pattern, and in the same configuration window, the total size of the map will appear based on the number of patterns established.

In the following figure, you can see the size of the tiles (remember that a tile is the pattern and the tiles are the ones that make up a tileset) in the previously shown tileset, the one in the previous figure, is also 32 × 32 pixels.

Figure 6-7. *Information about the tileset used*

If you wanted to use another pattern with a different size, you simply would have to establish it in the option presented before. Remember that the tileset image can be obtained from

https://limezu.itch.io/basic-platformer-tileset-dirt-grass

Once the preceding configurations have been established, we click the "OK" button. We will have a window like the following.

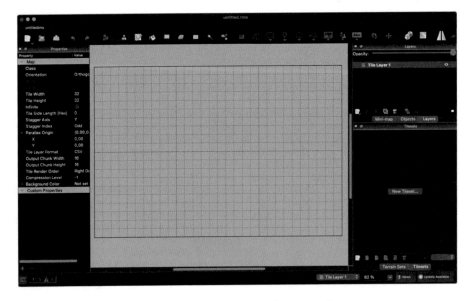

Figure 6-8. *Window to design the map in Tiled Map Editor*

Now, we need to register the tileset we downloaded earlier. On the desktop or in the place of your choice, create a folder called **jump** and save the project generated by Tiled in that folder, which we will call **map**; you can really put any name, but these are the ones we will use as reference. In that folder, copy the tileset you downloaded earlier and rename it simply as **tile.png**. You can see a summary of what was explained in the following figure.

Figure 6-9. *Files generated by Tiled Map Editor*

Clicking the "New Tileset..." button

Figure 6-10. *New Tileset... option in Tiled Map Editor*

we load the tileset; from the popup window, select the tileset.

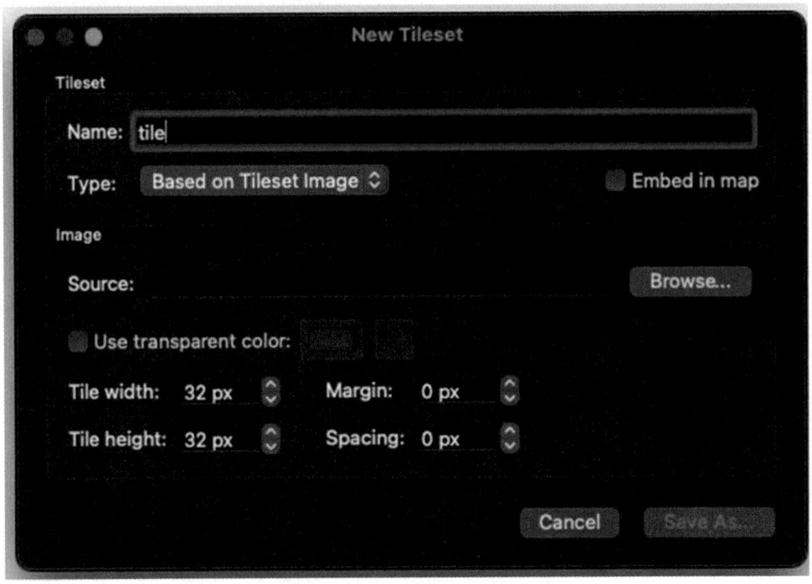

Figure 6-11. *Set a name for the tileset in Tiled Map Editor*

And click "Save As…"; you call the file as **tile**.

Figure 6-12. *Save the file in Tiled Map Editor*

In the Tiled editor, we will have loaded both the map and the pattern.

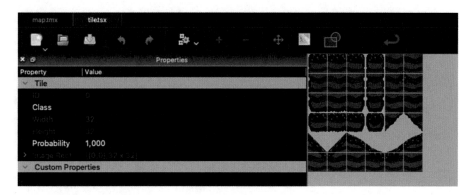

Figure 6-13. *Tileset loaded in Tiled Map Editor*

Click the map tag.

Figure 6-14. *Tag map in Tiled Map Editor*

And we will have the following.

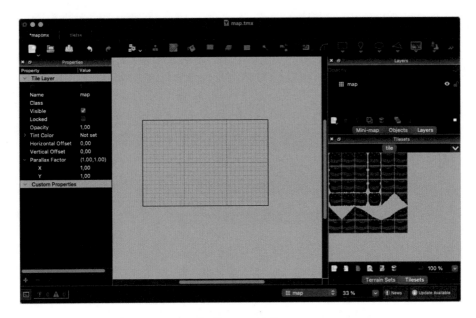

Figure 6-15. *Editing the map in Tiled Map Editor*

From here, we are ready to create a map; for this, we must keep several things in mind before starting. From the "Layers" section

Figure 6-16. *Tile layer in Tiled Map Editor*

we will have the layers of the map; there are different types of layers for maps.

Figure 6-17. *Types of layers in Tiled Map Editor*

However, in this book we will use a few. We rename the current layer to "map."

Figure 6-18. *Rename the layer to map*

Then, we are going to draw on the canvas; its use is very similar to what we have in other programs like Paint or GIMP in terms of tools to fill the entire canvas with a single color or use a brush. In this case, at the top we have the tools to fill or to draw on one tile at a time, respectively.

Figure 6-19. *Draw and fill options in Tiled Map Editor*

Once the "draw" option (the blue rectangle) is selected, we select the following pattern (although you can select any other).

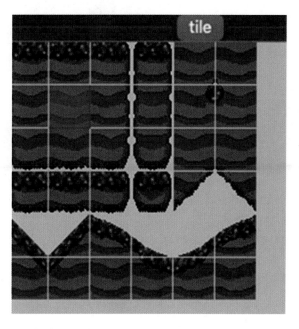

Figure 6-20. *Select a tile from the tileset in Tiled Map Editor*

Then we draw on the canvas; for this, we click the area where we want to draw.

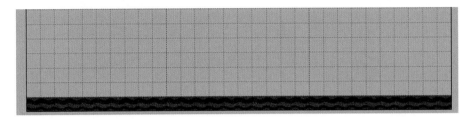

Figure 6-21. *Draw a floor in Tiled Map Editor*

And that's how it works, very, very easy to use. Finally, we will create the following map.

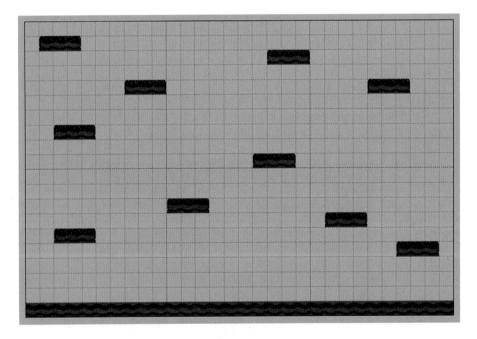

Figure 6-22. *Draw tiles in Tiled Map Editor*

If you make a mistake, you can use the delete option.

Figure 6-23. *Erase tool in Tiled Map Editor*

160

You can also select more than one pattern.

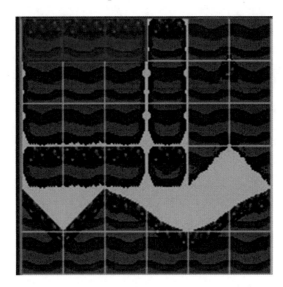

Figure 6-24. *Selecting multiple tiles in the tileset in Tiled Map Editor*

Now, we have to define the regions with which it will be possible to interact, in this case, all the tiles that we placed previously. For this, we have to do it from another layer; we create an "object layer."

Figure 6-25. *Create an object layer in Tiled Map Editor*

And we call it as **ground**.

Figure 6-26. *Rename the layer to ground in Tiled Map Editor*

Selecting the preceding layer (the **ground** layer), we will select the option "Insert Rectangle."

Figure 6-27. *Insert Rectangle tool in Tiled Map Editor*

This tool works like the selection option in image editing programs; you must select all the tiles established before, like the following.

Figure 6-28. *Selecting the tiles with the Insert Rectangle tool in Tiled Map Editor*

With all the tiles selected, we have the following.

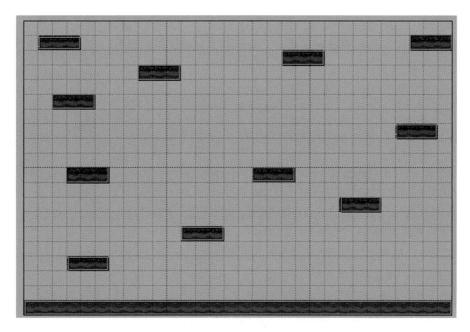

Figure 6-29. *Load the map designed in Tiled Map Editor in Flame*

And with this, we have our first map to use in our game. You can customize the map to your liking, that is, it does not have to be exactly the same as the one shown here, but remember to create tiles where our player can jump. Also remember to save your work before closing Tiled Map Editor.

Use the Tiled Map

We are going to create a new project in Flutter with Flame as we showed in Chapter 1 called **dinojump03** in which we will duplicate the following files from the previous project:

```
lib/components/player_component.dart
lib/components/character.dart
lib/utils/create_animation_by_limit.dart
lib/main.dart
assets/images/dinofull.png
```

Of course, we correct the local routes for those of the new project.

In this project, we are going to add an additional dependency apart from Flame, with which we can use the maps generated by Tiled:

```
https://pub.dev/packages/flame_tiled/
```

In our project, we add the following dependency:

```
$ flutter pub add flame_tiled
```

And with this, we can now use the previously defined map in our project; we copy the files to the following locations:

```
pubspec.yaml
```

```
    assets:
        - assets/images/dinofull.png
        - assets/images/tile.png
        - assets/tiles/map.tmx
        - assets/tiles/tile.tsx
```

As you can see, you must place the files to generate the map in a folder called **tiles**.

With the files copied into the project, some internal references need to be modified, specifically the location of the image. Tile-based maps refer to the tileset specified for their creation; we must update this location with the location within the project in Flutter:

```
assets\tiles\tile.tsx
```

```xml
<?xml version="1.0" encoding="UTF-8"?>
<tileset version="1.9" tiledversion="1.9.2" name="tile" tilewidth="32"
tileheight="32" tilecount="36" columns="6">
 <image source="tile.png" width="192" height="192"/>
</tileset>
```

to

```xml
assets\tiles\tile.tsx
<?xml version="1.0" encoding="UTF-8"?>
<tileset version="1.9" tiledversion="1.9.2" name="tile" tilewidth="32"
tileheight="32" tilecount="36" columns="6">
 <image source="../images/tile.png" width="192" height="192"/>
</tileset>
```

As a recommendation, you can observe the composition of both files:

```
assets/tiles/map.tmx
assets/tiles/tile.tsx
```

And you will see that they are nothing more than XMLs with attributes that reference the different positions of the tileset used in the map's creation, as well as its layers.

Create TiledComponent

We are going to create a new component in which we will use the previously generated map; to do this, you can consult the official documentation, which discusses using a component called **TiledComponent** in which we specify two arguments through the **load()** function:

1. The map

2. The size of the patterns, which, in the case of the map, is
   32 × 32 pixels

In the implementation that we are going to carry out, we use a component of type **PositionComponent** in which we use **TiledComponent** provided by the Flame Tiled package:

```
lib\components\tile_map_component.dart

import 'package:flame/collisions.dart';
import 'package:flame/components.dart';

import 'package:flame_tiled/flame_tiled.dart';
import 'package:testgame/map/ground.dart';

import 'package:tiled/tiled.dart';

class TileMapComponent extends PositionComponent {
  late TiledComponent tiledMap;

  @override
  void onLoad() async {
    tiledMap = await TiledComponent.load('map.tmx', Vector2.all(32));
```

```
   add(tiledMap);
  }
}
```

We load the component from the FlameGame class:

`lib\main.dart`

```
@override
void onLoad() {
  var background = TileMapComponent();
  world.add(background);
  add(ScreenHitbox());
}
```

And we will have the following.

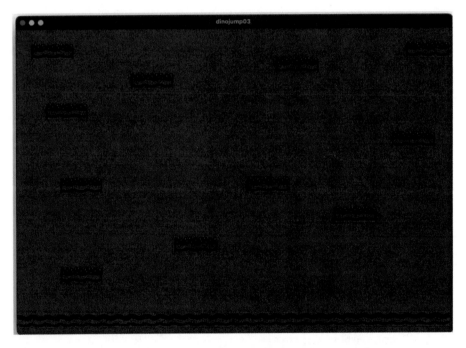

Figure 6-30. *Load the map designed in Tiled Map Editor in Flame*

The map is loaded in our game.

Iterate the Object Layer and Define a PositionComponent

As explained before, the reason we add a layer of objects to the map is so that from the **TiledComponent**, we can reference the layer and be able to do some process; this process can be anything like registering a zone to execute some event, placing some game item, or, in this case, placing a **PositionComponent**, which we will use later to detect collisions with the player. For this, we must indicate the name of the layer, which we remember was called as **ground** as you can see in Figure 6-26.

Therefore, to reference this layer, we have

```
final objGroup = tiledMap.tileMap.getLayer<ObjectGroup>("ground");
```

where **tiledMap** is the instance of **TiledComponent**. The **getLayer()** function is generic, and we can obtain different types of layers; in this case it is of the object type, that is, **ObjectGroup**.

In this layer, we have a list of objects, which consist of the positions that we established in said layer. Therefore, we can iterate through them to create any component with pixel precision. You can consult this list as follows:

assets\tiles\map.tmx

```
<objectgroup id="3" name="ground">
    <object id="1" x="3.89163" y="610.986" width="954.746" height="27.2414"/>
    <object id="2" x="99.8851" y="514.992" width="88.2103" height="27.2414"/>
    <object id="3" x="354.138" y="450.132" width="92.1019" height="27.2414"/>
    <object id="4" x="512.398" y="320.411" width="92.1019" height="28.5386"/>
    <object id="5" x="709.574" y="385.271" width="88.2103" height="29.8358"/>
    <object id="6" x="835.403" y="227.012" width="89.5075" height="28.5386"/>
    <object id="7" x="866.536" y="31.133" width="92.1019" height="31.133"/>
    <object id="8" x="35.0247" y="36.3219" width="90.8047" height="24.647"/>
    <object id="9" x="64.8605" y="160.854" width="93.3991" height="29.8358"/>
    <object id="10" x="95.9935" y="319.114" width="93.3991" height="32.4302"/>
    <object id="11" x="256.848" y="97.2907" width="92.1019" height="31.133"/>
    <object id="12" x="578.556" y="66.1577" width="90.8047" height="29.8358"/>
</objectgroup>
```

This is the list of objects that is being iterated, and you can see both the size and position. With this clear, the code is as follows:

lib\components\tile_map_component.dart

```
import 'package:flame/collisions.dart';
import 'package:flame/components.dart';

import 'package:flame_tiled/flame_tiled.dart';
import 'package:testgame/map/ground.dart';
import 'package:tiled/tiled.dart';

class TileMapComponent extends PositionComponent {

  late TiledComponent tiledMap;
  @override
  void onLoad() async {
    tiledMap = await TiledComponent.load('map.tmx', Vector2.all(32));
    add(tiledMap);

    final objGroup = tiledMap.tileMap.getLayer<ObjectGroup>("ground");

    for (final obj in objGroup!.objects) {
      add(Ground(
          size: Vector2(obj.width, obj.height),
          position: Vector2(obj.x, obj.y),),),);
    }
  }
}
```

The **ground** component is a **PositionComponent** that receives the size and position; it is very important to note the hitbox that will be used from the player to detect collisions with said component:

lib/components/ground.dart

```
import 'package:flame/collisions.dart';
import 'package:flame/components.dart';
```

```
class Ground extends PositionComponent {
  Ground({required size, required position}) : super(size: size, position:
  position) {
    debugMode = true;
    add(RectangleHitbox());
  }
}
```

As it happened with the image used as a background that we saw in the previous chapter, we must use the **loaded** property to detect when the background has been loaded. This time, when using a **TiledComponent**, we must reference the property that we created in the **TileMapComponent** component to obtain the size. It is recommended to place a breakpoint when adding the player and evaluate the **background** property:

lib\main.dart

```
@override
void onLoad() {
  var background = TileMapComponent();
  world.add(background);

  background.loaded.then(

    (value) {
      var player = PlayerComponent(mapSize:  background.tiledMap.size);
      world.add(player);

      ***

      // cameraComponent.setBounds(Rectangle.fromLTRB(
             0, 0, background.tiledMap.size.x, background.tiledMap.size.y));
    },
  );
  add(ScreenHitbox());
}
```

This time, since we are using a very small map, less than the size of the window, the camera component was removed.

Update the Gravity Component

Before testing the implementation, we need to adapt the player's gravity code. Since there exists on the map a region bounded as **ground**, whose purpose is to function as a ground for the game, we no longer have to use the size of the map as a factor to indicate the ground. We can use the **inGround** property to determine when the player is on the ground or not, and when it is on the ground (in collision with the **ground** component added via the tiled map), then, we suspend gravity. The following implementation is based on what was mentioned.

Since the player is thrown from the top, by default, the player is not on the ground:

lib\components\character.dart

```
class Character extends SpriteAnimationComponent
    with KeyboardHandler, CollisionCallbacks {
  int animationIndex = 0;
  ***
  bool inGround = false;
}
```

We make small changes in the player component taking into account what was commented before. For example, when the jump key is pressed, the player is no longer on the floor (since the position vector is updated), and therefore, the property **inGround** is updated; also, the **inGround** property is updated when it collides. Finally, gravity is applied based on the value of **inGround**:

lib\components\player_component.dart

```
class PlayerComponent extends Character {
  ***
  @override
  bool onKeyEvent(RawKeyEvent event, Set<LogicalKeyboardKey> keysPressed) {
    ***
    if ((keysPressed.contains(LogicalKeyboardKey.arrowUp) ||
            keysPressed.contains(LogicalKeyboardKey.keyW)) &&
        inGround) {
      animation = walkAnimation;
      velocity.y = -jumpForce;
```

```
    position.y -= 15;
    inGround = false;
    animation = jumpAnimation;
  }
  return true;
}

@override
void update(double dt) {
  position.x += playerSpeed * dt * posX;
  position.y += playerSpeed * dt * posY;
  posX = 0;
  posY = 0;

  if (!inGround) {
    velocity.y += gravity;
    position.y += velocity.y * dt;
  }

  super.update(dt);
}

@override
void onCollision(Set<Vector2> points, PositionComponent other) {
  ***

  if (other is Ground) {
    inGround = true;
  }

  super.onCollision(points, other);
}

@override
void onCollisionEnd(PositionComponent other) {
  collisionXLeft = collisionXRight = false;

  if (other is Ground) {
    inGround = false;
  }
```

```
    super.onCollisionEnd(other);
  }
}
```

With this, we have that, when the player comes into contact with one of the tiles, specifically with one of the **grounds** of type **PositionComponent** used for the floor, gravity is no longer applied to the player.

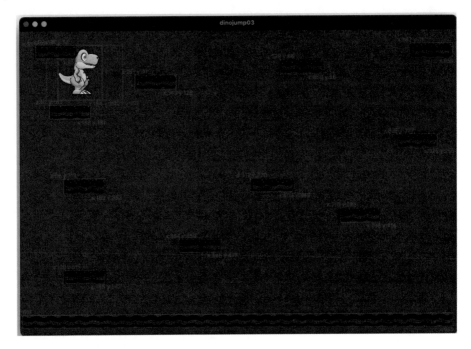

Figure 6-31. *Position the player is in on the map*

With this, we use our first tile-type map in a Flutter project with Flame. Through the object layer that the map has, we interact with the application, in this case, detecting collisions and stopping gravity. Therefore, we have exactly the same behavior that we apply in the player with the background image, but with a more precise (at the pixel level) and custom (at the object layer level) approach.

It is important to note

```
@override
void onCollisionEnd(PositionComponent other) {
  collisionXLeft = collisionXRight = false;

  if (other is Ground) {
    inGround = false;
  }

  super.onCollisionEnd(other);
}
```

since, when the player is no longer in collision with the ground, it means that it is no longer in contact; therefore, we update the **inGround** property.

Chapter source code:

https://github.com/libredesarrollo/flame-curso-libro-dinojump03/releases/tag/v0.1

CHAPTER 7

Game 2: Jump Between Tiles

In this chapter, we are going to continue with the **dinojump03** project created in the previous chapter with which we are going to implement the interaction of the player with the tiles and implement a simple logic for the game where, as the player goes up for the tiles, meteorites are falling.

Detect When the Player Is Jumping

An important problem that we have with the player is when it comes into contact with the floor or the tiles, the player is suspended.

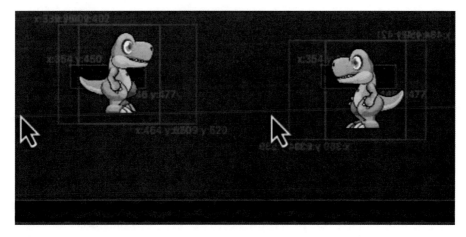

Figure 7-1. *Problem with the player hitbox*

© Andrés Cruz Yoris 2024
A. Cruz Yoris, *Flame Game Development*, https://doi.org/10.1007/979-8-8688-0063-4_7

To avoid this problem, we need to know when the player is jumping (when it scrolls up) to suspend collision detection; this way, when you are jumping, you can go through the tiles and avoid getting stuck on the tiles. For this, we create another property that handles this logic, which will be **true** when the player is jumping, which implies that the player moves up:

lib\components\character.dart

```
class Character extends SpriteAnimationComponent
    with KeyboardHandler, CollisionCallbacks {
  ***
  bool jumpUp = false;
}
```

Since the moment of pressing the up arrow/W is when the position vector of the player is updated

```
position.y -= 15;
```

it is precisely this moment in which the player is jumping, and therefore, we update the property:

```
if (inGround) {
  ***
  if ((keysPressed.contains(LogicalKeyboardKey.arrowUp) ||
      keysPressed.contains(LogicalKeyboardKey.keyW))) {
    ***
    jumpUp = true;
  }
}
```

Now, you need to determine when the **jumpUp** property is updated again. As we indicated before, we are interested in knowing when the player is jumping (preceding code) and when the player is falling, which is the next step after the jump. Just when it is falling, we must update the **jumpUp** property to activate the collisions with the floor.

Figure 7-2. *Property to know the status of the player's jump*

We can easily obtain this value based on the calculation we are making. When this value is negative

```
velocity.y * dt
```

the player is going up; when it is zero, the player is suspended; and when it is positive, the player is going down. Therefore, we can create a conditional for when the player's position is positive and the player is in the jump. Then we update the property **jumpUp** to indicate that the player is no longer jumping:

```
@override
void update(double dt) {
  ***
    if (jumpUp && velocity.y > 0) {
      jumpUp = false;
    }
}
```

Finally, with the logic implemented, we suspend the detection of collisions with the floor when the player is jumping:

```
@override
void onCollision(Set<Vector2> points, PositionComponent other) {
  ***

  if (other is Ground && !jumpUp) {
    inGround = true;
  }

  super.onCollision(points, other);
}
```

Here's the full code:

lib\components\player_component.dart

```
***
class PlayerComponent extends Character {
  Vector2 mapSize;

  ***

  @override
  bool onKeyEvent(RawKeyEvent event, Set<LogicalKeyboardKey> keysPressed) {
    ***

    if (inGround) {
      ***
      if ((keysPressed.contains(LogicalKeyboardKey.arrowUp) ||
          keysPressed.contains(LogicalKeyboardKey.keyW))) {
        ***
        jumpUp = true;
      }
    }

    return true;
  }

  @override
  void update(double dt) {
```

```
  ***
    if (jumpUp && velocity.y > 0) {
      jumpUp = false;
    }
  }


  super.update(dt);
}


@override
void onCollision(Set<Vector2> points, PositionComponent other) {
  ***
  if (other is Ground && !jumpUp) {
    inGround = true;
  }

  super.onCollision(points, other);
  }
}
```

Changes to the Jump and Move Component

We have implemented several functionalities that affect the gameplay, such as defining tiles in the application, detecting collisions between the floor and the player, adapting the jump, among others; in this section, we are going to create variations in the vertical and horizontal movement of the player.

Lock the Jump

One of the problems we have is that currently if the player jumps, they can move in the air to the sides. To correct this, it is important to note that, if the player is in the air, they cannot jump again (this implementation was already done by checking the state of **inGround** before making the jump) and they cannot move either; that is to say, **the player cannot carry out any type of movement** (walk, run, or jump) if they are in the air. So we put a global conditional to block movement in the air:

```
class PlayerComponent extends Character {
  @override
  bool onKeyEvent(RawKeyEvent event, Set<LogicalKeyboardKey> keysPressed) {
    ***
    if (inGround) {
      //*** walk, run or jump
    }
    return true;
  }
}
```

Arched Jump and Movement Modifications

Also, we're going to create additional properties so that at the moment of the jump, the player can move a bit at jump time, that is, not only to be able to jump vertically but also in an arc.

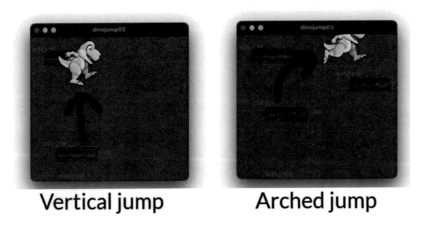

Figure 7-3. *Vertical and arche jumps of the player*

The properties to create will be as follows:

- Rename the **jumpForce** property to **jumpForceUp**, and it indicates the impulse on the Y axis at the moment of the jump.

- With **jumpForceSide** we indicate the impulse on the X axis (right and left) at the moment of the jump.

- With **jumpForceXY** we indicate the movement to the position vector of the player.

In the implementation that we are going to show, we already have established values that are going to be used in the game, but you can modify them at will to customize the experience.

With the preceding properties, we are going to enable the jump:

- In the form of an arc as long as the user presses the arrow key right (D) or left (A) and the arrow up (W)

- Vertically if the user only presses the up arrow key (W)

The following implementation allows us to do the aforementioned:

lib\components\character.dart

```
class Character extends SpriteAnimationComponent
    with KeyboardHandler, CollisionCallbacks {
  ***

  double gravity = 9.8;
  final double jumpForceUp = 300, jumpForceXY = 20, jumpForceSide = 100;
  ***

}
```

lib\components\player_component.dart

```
***
class PlayerComponent extends Character {
  ***
  @override
  bool onKeyEvent(RawKeyEvent event, Set<LogicalKeyboardKey> keysPressed) {

    //***Y */
    if ((keysPressed.contains(LogicalKeyboardKey.arrowUp) ||
        keysPressed.contains(LogicalKeyboardKey.keyW))) {
      animation = walkAnimation;
      velocity.y = -jumpForceUp;
      position.y -= jumpForceXY;
      inGround = false;
      animation = jumpAnimation;
      jumpUp = true;
```

```
        if ((keysPressed.contains(LogicalKeyboardKey.arrowLeft) ||
            keysPressed.contains(LogicalKeyboardKey.keyA))) {
          if (right) flipHorizontally();
          right = false;

          if (!collisionXLeft) {
            velocity.x = -jumpForceSide;
            position.x -= jumpForceXY;
          }
        } else if ((keysPressed.contains(LogicalKeyboardKey.arrowRight) ||
            keysPressed.contains(LogicalKeyboardKey.keyD))) {
          if (!right) flipHorizontally();
          right = true;

          if (!collisionXRight) {
            velocity.x = jumpForceSide;
            position.x += jumpForceXY;
          }
        }
      }
    }
  }

  return true;
}

@override
void update(double dt) {
  position.x += playerSpeed * dt * posX;
  position.y += playerSpeed * dt * posY;
  posX = 0;
  posY = 0;

  if (!inGround) {
    // in the air

    if (velocity.y * dt > 0 && jumpUp) {
      jumpUp = false;
    }
```

```
      velocity.y += gravity;
      position += velocity * dt;
    }

    super.update(dt);
  }

  @override
  void onCollisionStart(Set<Vector2> points, PositionComponent other) {
    ***

    if (other is Ground && !jumpUp) {
      inGround = true;
      velocity = Vector2.all(0);
    }

    super.onCollisionStart(points, other);
  }

  ***
}
```

It is important to note that we are updating the entire position vector of the player when interacting with gravity:

```
position += velocity * dt;
```

This is essential to get the arched jump.

Also, the velocity vector is reinitialized at the end of the jump:

```
velocity = Vector2.all(0);
```

When making the jump, the animation is done in a loop; therefore, if the jump is long (or depending on the values established in the preceding properties), the animation is repeated multiple times giving a somewhat strange effect. We are going to indicate that the jump animation only executes once:

```
jumpAnimation = spriteSheet.createAnimationByLimit(xInit: 3, yInit: 0,
step: 12, sizeX: 5, stepTime: .08, loop: false);
```

Movement of the Player in the Tiles

We still need to solve several problems that we have with the interaction between the player and the tiles/floor; one of these problems is of detecting collisions with the floor and tiles in the entire hitbox component of the player, which currently occupies the entire sprite.

Figure 7-4. *Very large player hitbox*

This does similar behavior to the one presented previously; when the player is falling (**jumpUp** is false), the player does not have enough force in the jump and gets stuck, and it is precisely because the collision is being detected in the entire sprite as shown in Figure 7-1.

To correct this behavior, we need to create a hitbox that only occupies the feet.

Figure 7-5. *Hitbox for the player's feet*

For this, we adjust the current hitbox:

lib\components\player_component.dart

```
@override
void onLoad() async {
  ***

  // add(RectangleHitbox(
  //     size: Vector2(spriteSheetWidth / 4 - 70, spriteSheetHeight / 4 - 20),
  //     position: Vector2(25, 10)));
```

```
add(RectangleHitbox(
      size: Vector2(50, 10),
      position: Vector2(55, spriteSheetHeight / 4 - 20),),),);
}
```

Also, we need to do some reduction in tile size. If we look at the current implementation, it is not necessary for the contact or collision to occur on the entire tile.

Figure 7-6. *Tile size*

Only the part that the player is going to touch with the feet is necessary.

Figure 7-7. *Shrink the tile hitbox*

Therefore, we can reduce the width of the tiles and the floor:

lib\components\tile_map_component.dart

```
@override
void onLoad() async {
  tiledMap = await TiledComponent.load('map.tmx', Vector2.all(32));
  add(tiledMap);

  final objGroup = tiledMap.tileMap.getLayer<ObjectGroup>("ground");

  for (final obj in objGroup!.objects) {
    add(Ground(size: Vector2(obj.width, , /*obj.height*/ 5), position:
    Vector2(obj.x, obj.y)));
  }
}
```

You can try multiple values since, if the hitboxes of the player and the tiles were minimal (5 in this example), it might be the case that, when making the updates, the collision does not occur and the player crosses the tile; therefore, very small values should not be used. Finally, it looks like the following.

Figure 7-8. *Player and tile*

Horizontal Movement with the Velocity Vector

As we saw in the previous section, it was possible to implement an arched jump using the movement on the X axis. Nothing prevents us from implementing horizontal scrolling using the velocity vector instead of the **posX** and related properties; with this, the application will be more modular and simpler in general, since it will not use two different mechanisms to handle the movement (velocity vector and properties of **posX** and **posY**) but only one mechanism.

We are going to remove all the properties that we used for horizontal movement of the player:

lib\components\character.dart

```
class Character extends SpriteAnimationComponent
    with KeyboardHandler, CollisionCallbacks {
  int animationIndex = 0;

  // int posX = 0, posY = 0;
  // double playerSpeed = 500;
  ***

}
```

And we use the current approach of the velocity vector and the applied force:

lib\components\player_component.dart

```
@override
bool onKeyEvent(RawKeyEvent event, Set<LogicalKeyboardKey> keysPressed) {
  if (keysPressed.isEmpty) {
    animation = idleAnimation;
  }

  if (inGround) {
//***X */
    // run
    if ((keysPressed.contains(LogicalKeyboardKey.arrowRight) ||
            keysPressed.contains(LogicalKeyboardKey.keyD)) &&
        keysPressed.contains(LogicalKeyboardKey.shiftLeft)) {
      ***
      if (!collisionXRight) {
        animation = runAnimation;
        // posX++;
        velocity.x = jumpForceSide;
        position.x += jumpForceXY * 2;
      } else {
        animation = walkSlowAnimation;
      }
    } else if ((keysPressed.contains(LogicalKeyboardKey.arrowRight) ||
        keysPressed.contains(LogicalKeyboardKey.keyD))) {
      ***
      if (!collisionXRight) {
        ***
        // posX++;
        velocity.x = jumpForceSide;
        position.x += jumpForceXY;
      } else {
        animation = walkSlowAnimation;
      }
    }
```

```
if ((keysPressed.contains(LogicalKeyboardKey.arrowLeft) ||
        keysPressed.contains(LogicalKeyboardKey.keyA)) &&
    keysPressed.contains(LogicalKeyboardKey.shiftLeft)) {
  ***

  if (!collisionXLeft) {
    ***
    // posX--;
    velocity.x = -jumpForceSide;
    position.x -= jumpForceXY * 2;
  } else {
    animation = walkSlowAnimation;
  }
} else if ((keysPressed.contains(LogicalKeyboardKey.arrowLeft) ||
    keysPressed.contains(LogicalKeyboardKey.keyA))) {
  playerSpeed = 500;

  if (right) flipHorizontally();
  right = false;

  if (!collisionXLeft) {
    ***
    // posX--;
    velocity.x = -jumpForceSide;
    position.x -= jumpForceXY;
  } else {
    animation = walkSlowAnimation;
  }
}

//***Y */
if ((keysPressed.contains(LogicalKeyboardKey.arrowUp) ||
    keysPressed.contains(LogicalKeyboardKey.keyW))) {
  ***

  if ((keysPressed.contains(LogicalKeyboardKey.arrowLeft) ||
      keysPressed.contains(LogicalKeyboardKey.keyA))) {
    ***

    if (!collisionXLeft) {
```

```
            velocity.x = -jumpForceSide;
            position.x -= jumpForceXY;
        }
    } else if ((keysPressed.contains(LogicalKeyboardKey.arrowRight) ||
        ***
      if (!collisionXRight) {
            velocity.x = jumpForceSide;
            position.x += jumpForceXY;
        }
      }
    }
  }

  return true;
}
```

With this, we have the same movement, but now unified.

Create Multiple Hitbox Components for the Player

At the moment, we only have one hitbox defined for the player, at the feet, which works quite well for us to handle collisions with tiles and the ground. The problem occurs **when we want to develop other real features of the game, such as, in this case, detecting collisions with meteorites, that is, functionalities that have to do with the actual gameplay of the game**. Obviously we cannot count the collisions of the meteors with only the player's feet, but with the entire body of the sprite; therefore, we are going to handle two hitboxes for the player, one for the feet and the other for the whole body:

lib\components\character.dart

```
class Character extends SpriteAnimationComponent
    with KeyboardHandler, CollisionCallbacks {
  int animationIndex = 0;
  ***
  late RectangleHitbox foot, body;
}
***
}
```

And we use them from the component. The arguments we use are the same ones that we have used in the previous sections:

lib\components\player_component.dart

```
@override
void onLoad() async {
  ***

  body = RectangleHitbox(
      size: Vector2(spriteSheetWidth / 4 - 70, spriteSheetHeight / 4 - 20),
      position: Vector2(25, 10));

  foot = RectangleHitbox(
      size: Vector2(50, 10),
      position: Vector2(55, spriteSheetHeight / 4 - 20));

  add(foot);
  add(body);
}
```

From the collision function, we can use the **foot.isColliding** property to handle the collision of the **ground** component for the foot hitbox only:

lib\components\player_component.dart

```
@override
void onCollisionStart(Set<Vector2> points, PositionComponent other) {
  if (other is Ground && !jumpUp) {
    if (foot.isColliding) {
      inGround = true;
    }
  }
  super.onCollisionStart(points, other);
}
```

Modify Movement

An important development that needs to be implemented is to know at all times what the player is doing, if it is walking, running, jumping, in a rest state, or, in general, in any other state that you want to implement. For this, we will create an **enum**:

lib\components\character.dart

```
enum MovementType {
  walkingright,
  walkingleft,
  runright,
  runleft,
  idle,
  jump,
  jumpright,
  jumpleft
}

class Character extends SpriteAnimationComponent {***}
```

And now, the implementation that we currently have in which we verify the key pressed and apply the corresponding functionalities is divided into two parts, leaving the implementation as follows:

lib\components\player_component.dart

```
@override
bool onKeyEvent(RawKeyEvent event, Set<LogicalKeyboardKey> keysPressed) {
  if (keysPressed.isEmpty) {
    movementType = MovementType.idle;
    animation = idleAnimation;
  }

  if (inGround) {
    //*** RIGHT
    if (keysPressed.contains(LogicalKeyboardKey.arrowRight) ||
        keysPressed.contains(LogicalKeyboardKey.keyD)) {
      if (keysPressed.contains(LogicalKeyboardKey.shiftLeft)) {
```

```
    //RUN
    movementType = MovementType.runright;
  } else {
    movementType = MovementType.walkingright;
  }
}
//*** LEFT
if ((keysPressed.contains(LogicalKeyboardKey.arrowLeft) ||
    keysPressed.contains(LogicalKeyboardKey.keyA))) {
  if (keysPressed.contains(LogicalKeyboardKey.shiftLeft)) {
    //RUN
    movementType = MovementType.runleft;
  } else {
    movementType = MovementType.walkingleft;
  }
}
//*** JUMP
if ((keysPressed.contains(LogicalKeyboardKey.arrowUp) ||
    keysPressed.contains(LogicalKeyboardKey.keyW))) {
  movementType = MovementType.jump;

  if ((keysPressed.contains(LogicalKeyboardKey.arrowRight) ||
      keysPressed.contains(LogicalKeyboardKey.keyD))) {
    movementType = MovementType.jumpright;
  } else if ((keysPressed.contains(LogicalKeyboardKey.arrowLeft) ||
      keysPressed.contains(LogicalKeyboardKey.keyA))) {
    movementType = MovementType.jumpleft;
  }
}

switch (movementType) {
  case MovementType.walkingright:
  case MovementType.runright:
    if (!right) flipHorizontally();
    right = true;
```

```
    if (!collisionXRight) {
      animation = (movementType == MovementType.walkingright
          ? walkAnimation
          : runAnimation);

      velocity.x = jumpForceSide;
      position.x += jumpForceXY *
          (movementType == MovementType.walkingright ? 1 : 2);
    } else {
      animation = walkSlowAnimation;
    }
    break;

  case MovementType.walkingleft:
  case MovementType.runleft:
    if (right) flipHorizontally();
    right = false;

    if (!collisionXLeft) {
      animation = (movementType == MovementType.walkingleft
          ? walkAnimation
          : runAnimation);
      velocity.x = -jumpForceSide;
      position.x -= jumpForceXY *
          (movementType == MovementType.walkingleft ? 1 : 2);
    } else {
      animation = walkSlowAnimation;
    }
    break;

  default:
  }
}
```

Player Position

Another of the modifications that we are going to make is to simplify the player position process, starting by removing the properties that would not be necessary:

lib\components\character.dart

```
late double screenWidth, screenHeight, centerX, centerY;
```

And we use simpler logic; the only thing that is necessary is to place the player in a corner. For this, the size of the sprite can be occupied to prevent it from appearing hidden on the edge of the screen:

lib\components\player_component.dart

```
position = Vector2(spriteSheetWidth / 4, 0);
```

Add the Meteorite Component

Just like we did in the previous game's implementation, we'll be using the meteor component in this game; for this, remember that you have to copy the following component:

lib/components/meteor_component.dart

Change the references and update the **pubspec.yaml** to add the image from **assets/images/meteor.png**. And in the main, put

lib/main.dart

```
@override
void update(double dt) {
  if (elapsedTime > 1.0) {
    Vector2 cp = cameraComponent.viewfinder.position;

    cp.y = cameraComponent.viewfinder.position.y -
        cameraComponent.viewport.size.y;
    world.add(MeteorComponent(cameraPosition: cp));
    elapsedTime = 0.0;
  }
```

```
    elapsedTime += dt;
    super.update(dt);
}
```

New Map

Before continuing in the following sections, we are going to create a larger map following the same guidelines that we followed to build the map in the previous chapter (we add a floor, tiles, and the object layer called ground).

This time, the map will be larger than the size of the device's screen; being a large map, we will activate the camera so that it follows the player as we showed in previous chapters. The map looks like the following.

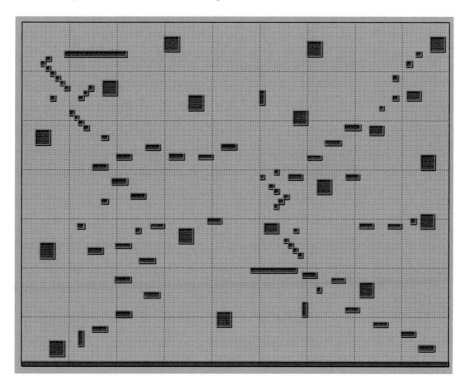

Figure 7-9. *Design of a larger map*

The map has a size as shown in the following figure.

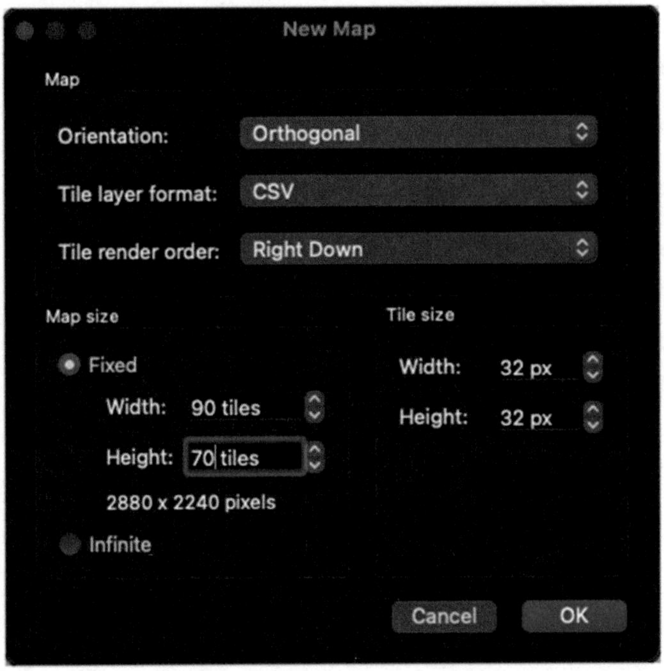

Figure 7-10. *Defined size for the new map in Tiled Map Editor*

The map does not have to be exactly the same as the preceding one; it does not even have to be similar. It is enough that the player can jump from one tile to another and that the size used to define the map is larger than the window. Finally, the map is added to the project:

pubspec.yaml

```
assets:
   - assets/tiles/map2.tmx
```

And it is used at the component level:

lib/components/tile_map_component.dart

```
class TileMapComponent extends PositionComponent {
  late TiledComponent tiledMap;

  @override
  void onLoad() async{
```

```
    tiledMap = await TiledComponent.load('map2.tmx', Vector2.all(32));
    add(tiledMap);
    ***
  }
}
```

With this, it is demonstrated that it is very easy to use different maps in the application, since it only consists of loading the tmx file in a component.

Overlay

Flame incorporates a property called **overlayBuilderMap** with which we can indicate a widget that we want to overlay the application; this is extremely useful to indicate any control data such as the amount of life, impact, or any other average. With this property we can even indicate more than one widget that we want to superimpose (e.g., one for the statistics and another for the end of the game) among other options that we will see throughout the chapter.

In this section, we will learn how to use the overlays to show data about the game, as well as implement many options such as the end of the game. Also, we will see how the components communicate with the overlays.

Overlay: Show the Number of Collisions

We will create a property to indicate the number of hits:

lib/main.dart

```
class MyGame extends FlameGame
    with HasKeyboardHandlerComponents, HasCollisionDetection {
  int collisionMeteors = 0;
  ***
}
```

And it is registered in the **GameWidget** instance:

`lib/main.dart`

```dart
void main() {
  runApp(GameWidget(
    game: MyGame(),
    overlayBuilderMap: {
      'Statistics': (context, MyGame game) {
        return Statistics(
          game: game,
        );
      },
    },
    initialActiveOverlays: const ['Statistics'],
  ));
}
```

As you can see, since it is a map, we can indicate as many overlays as the application needs, and using the **initialActiveOverlays**, since it is an array, it is possible to have more than one overlay active at the same time.

Regarding the implementation of the widget to show the number of hits at the top, as you can see, it is simply a basic Flutter widget to display text. We pass the **game** property to this widget, with which we can access the preceding property to display it on the screen:

`lib/overlays/statistics.dart`

```dart
import 'package:dinojump03/main.dart';
import 'package:flutter/material.dart';

class Statistics extends StatefulWidget {
  final MyGame game;
  Statistics({Key? key, required this.game}) : super(key: key);

  @override
  State<Statistics> createState() => _StatisticsState();
}
class _StatisticsState extends State<Statistics> {
```

```
  @override
  Widget build(BuildContext context) {
    return Padding(
      padding: const EdgeInsets.all(8.0),
      child: Text(
        'Count collision ${widget.game.collisionMeteors}',
        style: const TextStyle(color: Colors.white, fontSize: 30),
      ),
    );
  }
}
```

And we will have the following.

Count collision 0

Figure 7-11. *Overlay for the collision counter*

As you can see, this is very useful to be able to indicate game statistics, in this case, the number of hits.

Overlay: Game Over

We are going to create another very important overlay that is used to restart the game, that is, the end of the game or game over:

lib/overlays/game_over.dart

```
import 'package:dinojump03/main.dart';
import 'package:flutter/material.dart';

class GameOver extends StatefulWidget {
  final MyGame game;
  GameOver({Key? key, required this.game}) : super(key: key);

  @override
  State<GameOver> createState() => _GameOverState();
}
```

```
class _GameOverState extends State<GameOver> {
  @override
  Widget build(BuildContext context) {
    return Center(
      child: Container(
        padding: const EdgeInsets.all(10.0),
        height: 200,
        width: 300,
        decoration: const BoxDecoration(
            color: Colors.black,
            borderRadius: BorderRadius.all(Radius.circular(20))),
        child: Column(children: [
          const Text(
            'Game Over',
            style: TextStyle(color: Colors.white, fontSize: 24),
          ),
          const SizedBox(
            height: 40,
          ),
          SizedBox(
            width: 200,
            height: 75,
            child: ElevatedButton(
              onPressed: () {
                print('hello');
              },
              style: ElevatedButton.styleFrom(backgroundColor:
              Colors.white),
              child: const Text(
                'Play Again',
                style: TextStyle(fontSize: 28, color: Colors.black),
              ),
            ),
          )
        ]),
```

```
      ),
    );
  }
}
```

From here, the most important thing is to notice the **Center** widget with which we can center the widget in the middle of the parent component, which, in this case, would be the game rendered by **MyGame**; therefore, you can use the same structure that you would use in basic Flutter to align widgets.

And from the main, we register the overlay:

`lib/main.dart`

```
void main() {
  runApp(GameWidget(
    game: MyGame(),
    overlayBuilderMap: {
      'Statistics': (context, MyGame game) {
        return Statistics(
          game: game,
        );
      },
      'GameOver': (context, MyGame game) {
        return GameOver(
          game: game,
        );
      }
    },
    initialActiveOverlays: const ['Statistics', 'GameOver'],
  ));
}
```

And we will have both overlays active at the same time.

Figure 7-12. *Overlay to play again*

Overlay Functions

We currently have two well-defined layers that make up the application:

1. The one for the game, for components like the player, tiles, and
    the meteorite

2. The one for the overlays that we created previously

Both layers must be able to communicate in order to perform all kinds of operations:

1. *It is necessary for the layer of the components to communicate
    with that of the overlays*: For example, it is necessary to show the
    number of collisions each time a collision occurs; therefore, when
    executing any of the onCollision-type functions from the player
    component, the stats overlay needs to be updated.

2. *It is necessary for the layer of the overlays to communicate with that
    of the components*: For example, when we click the "Play Again"
    button of the overlay, it is necessary to restore statistics and the
    initial position of the player.

We are going to see in the following sections how to carry out each of these steps, but before that, it is important to know that, through the instance of the Game-type class, we can access and manipulate the overlays that we have defined in **overlayBuilderMap**; we have methods to manipulate them individually or together as if it were a list:

To add an overlay:

```
game.overlays.add('Statistics');
```

To add multiple overlays:

```
game.overlays.addAll(['Statistics','GameOver']);
```

```
To remove an overlay:
game.overlays.remove('Statistics');
```

To remove multiple overlays:

```
game.overlays.removeAll(['Statistics','GameOver']);
```

To remove all overlays:

```
game.overlays.clear();
```

In these **game** is an instance of the **FlameGame** class. We will see a practical implementation of these methods throughout the book.

Game Instance in Components and Communication with Overlays

In order to communicate from any component to any defined overlay, first, we must pass an instance of the game to the component or components. In this example, we use the **Player** class:

lib/main.dart

```
player = PlayerComponent(mapSize: background.tiledMap.size, game: this);
```

Remember that **this** refers to the instance where it is defined, which in this case is **MyGame**.

From the preceding component, we make the changes in the constructor, and from any part of the component, we have access to the overlays using the methods presented in the previous section. In the case of the component, we are interested in updating the statistics overlay when there are collisions; for this reason, we add and remove the statistics overlay when having the collision with the meteorite:

lib/components/player_component.dart

```
class PlayerComponent extends Character {
  MyGame game;

  PlayerComponent({required this.mapSize, required this.game}) :
super() {***}

  @override
  void onCollisionEnd(PositionComponent other) {
    collisionXLeft = collisionXRight = false;

    if (other is Ground) {
      inGround = false;
    }

    if(other is MeteorComponent && body.isColliding){
      game.collisionMeteors++;
      print('collision ${game.collisionMeteors}');

      game.overlays.remove('Statistics');
      game.overlays.add('Statistics');

      // game.overlays.removeAll(['Statistics','GameOver']);
      // game.overlays.addAll(['Statistics','GameOver']);
      // game.overlays.clear();
      // print(game.overlays.isActive('Statistics'));
    }
    super.onCollisionEnd(other);
  }
}
```

With this, when collisions occur on the screen, we should see the update of the collisions by the statistics overlay.

Game Instance in Overlays and Communication with Components

As we saw before, we were able to access the overlays using the Game class instance; therefore, from the overlay classes, we need to access the components through the Game instance. So, for the components that we want to update through the overlays, we must define them at the component level, as we do with the player:

lib/main.dart

```
class MyGame extends FlameGame
    with HasKeyboardHandlerComponents, HasCollisionDetection {
  late PlayerComponent player;
  ***
  @override
  void onLoad() {
    var background = TileMapComponent();
    add(background);
    background.loaded.then(
      (value) {
        player = PlayerComponent(mapSize: background.tiledMap.size,
        game: this);
        cameraComponent.world.add(player);
    );
    }
    ***
  }
}
```

Once the player component has been converted to a property, from the game instance passed from the component definition

lib/main.dart

```
'GameOver': (context, MyGame game) {
  return GameOver(
    game: game,
  );
}
```

we can update any of the properties defined within the player or the **PositionComponent**, as in this case it is the position, since when clicking the "Play Again" button, we are going to want to reset the collision counter and the position of the player. For it, we have the following:

lib/overlays/game_over.dart

```
class GameOver extends StatefulWidget {
  final MyGame game;
  GameOver({Key? key, required this.game}) : super(key: key);

  @override
  State<GameOver> createState() => _GameOverState();
}

class _GameOverState extends State<GameOver> {
  @override
  Widget build(BuildContext context) {
    return Center(
      child: Container(
        padding: const EdgeInsets.all(10.0),
        height: 200,
        width: 300,
        decoration: const BoxDecoration(
            color: Colors.black,
            borderRadius: BorderRadius.all(Radius.circular(20))),
        child: Column(children: [
          const Text(
            'Game Over',
            style: TextStyle(color: Colors.white, fontSize: 24),
          ),
          const SizedBox(
            height: 40,
          ),
          SizedBox(
            width: 200,
            height: 75,
```

```
        child: ElevatedButton(
          onPressed: () {
            widget.game.collisionMeteors = 0;
            widget.game.player.position = Vector2.all(0);
          },
          style: ElevatedButton.styleFrom(backgroundColor:
          Colors.white),
          child: const Text(
            'Play Again',
            style: TextStyle(fontSize: 28, color: Colors.black),
          ),
        ),
      ),
    )
  ]),
    ),
  );
  }
}
```

Reset

Let's create a function to reset the stats overlay, position, and velocity vector and show the death animation once:

```
void reset(){}
```

We will call this function every time a meteorite collides with the dinosaur according to the number of lives specified (we will see this implementation later); for this function, we're going to display the death animation based on the value of the dead parameter:

```
void reset({bool dead = false}) {
   velocity = Vector2.all(0);
   game.overlays.remove('Statistics');
   game.overlays.add('Statistics');

  movementType = MovementType.idle;
  velocity = Vector2.all(0);
```

```
  if (dead) {
    animation = deadAnimation;
  } else {
    animation = idleAnimation;
    game.collisionMeteors = 0;
    position = Vector2(spriteSheetWidth / 4, mapSize.y -
    spriteSheetHeight);
  }
}
```

And we can use this same function as part of the player initialization:

```
@override
void onLoad() async {
  ***
  reset();
}
```

Remember that you can customize the position of the player as you consider best; this function will be used in other parts of the game we are creating, for example, when the player loses their life (game over).

Introduction to SpriteAnimationTickers

An **AnimationTicker** is a technique used in various animation libraries and allows to control an animation. In the case of Flame, it also allows you to listen to the states of the animation, for example, when the animation is complete

```
animationTicker.onComplete = () {
    ***
  }
};
```

or when a frame of the animation is executed:

```
animationTicker.onFrame = (index) {
  ***
  }
};
```

This is all done by Flame's **SpriteAnimationTicker** class. For the game we are implementing, it is necessary to know when the "dying" animation ends to restart the game; for this, we can use any of the listeners shown previously.

First, we need to initialize the ticker:

lib/components/player_component.dart

```
class PlayerComponent extends Character {
  ***
  late SpriteAnimationTicker deadAnimationTicker;

  @override
  void onLoad() async {
    ***
    deadAnimationTicker = deadAnimation.createTicker();
  }

  @override
  void update(double dt) {
    ***
    deadAnimationTicker.update(dt);
    super.update(dt);
  }
}
```

With the **createTicker()** function, we create a ticker (**SpriteAnimationTicker**) on the animation that we are going to control; in the case of the game that we are implementing, we are interested in detecting when the dying animation ends, which will be executed only when the player runs out of lives, and when the animation ends, the level restarts. The reason that the **deadAnimationTicker** property is initialized in the **onLoad()** and not when the **deadAnimation** animation is used (when the player runs out of lives) is that it is necessary to update the ticker in the **upload()** function according to the ticker life cycle:

deadAnimationTicker.update(dt)

With the ticker, a listener is created to detect when the animation has finished running. To do this, we can execute the **onComplete()** listener

```
deadAnimationTicker.onComplete = () {
  // TODO
};
```

or the **onFrame()** one, which is executed for each frame, but asking if the current frame is the last one:

```
deadAnimationTicker.onFrame = (index) {
  if (deadAnimationTicker.isLastFrame) {
    // TODO
  }
};
```

Finally, the complete code looks like the following:

lib/components/player_component.dart

```
class PlayerComponent extends Character {
  void reset({bool dead = false}) async {
    game.overlays.remove('Statistics');
    game.overlays.add('Statistics');
    velocity = Vector2.all(0);
    game.paused = false;
    blockPlayer = true;
    invinciblePlayer = true;
    movementType = MovementType.idle;
    if (dead) {
      animation = deadAnimation;

      deadAnimationTicker = deadAnimation.createTicker();
      deadAnimationTicker.onFrame = (index) {
        // print("-----" + index.toString());
        if (deadAnimationTicker.isLastFrame) {
          animation = idleAnimation;
          position =
              Vector2(spriteSheetWidth / 4, mapSize.y - spriteSheetHeight);
        }
      };
```

```
    deadAnimationTicker.onComplete = () {
      if (animation == deadAnimation) {
        animation = idleAnimation;
        position =
            Vector2(spriteSheetWidth / 4, mapSize.y - spriteSheetHeight);
      }
    };
  } else {
    animation = idleAnimation;
    position = Vector2(spriteSheetWidth / 4, mapSize.y - spriteSheetHeight);
    size = Vector2(spriteSheetWidth / 4, spriteSheetHeight / 4);
  }
  game.collisionMeteors = 0;
  game.addConsumables();

  //position = Vector2(spriteSheetWidth / 4, 0);
  }
}
```

Finally, as you can see, when the death animation is completed, the player's position and animation are reset, as well as the meteor collision counter.

Lives

In the statistics overlay, we are going to place another widget to define the number of lives, which is usually three for this type of game:

lib\overlay\statistics.dart

```
import 'package:flutter/material.dart';
import 'package:testgame/main.dart';

class Statistics extends StatefulWidget {
  final MyGame game;
  Statistics({Key? key, required this.game}) : super(key: key);

  @override
  State<Statistics> createState() => _StatisticsState();
}
```

```dart
class _StatisticsState extends State<Statistics> {
  @override
  Widget build(BuildContext context) {
    return Padding(
      padding: const EdgeInsets.all(8.0),
      child: Column(
        crossAxisAlignment: CrossAxisAlignment.start,
        children: [
          Text(
            'Count collision ${widget.game.collisionMeteors}',
            style: const TextStyle(color: Colors.white, fontSize: 30),
          ),
          const SizedBox(
            height: 10,
          ),
          Row(
            children: [
              const SizedBox(
                width: 10,
              ),
              Icon(
                widget.game.collisionMeteors >= 3
                    ? Icons.favorite_border
                    : Icons.favorite,
                color: Colors.red,
              ),
              Icon(
                widget.game.collisionMeteors >= 2
                    ? Icons.favorite_border
                    : Icons.favorite,
                color: Colors.red,
              ),
              Icon(
                widget.game.collisionMeteors >= 1
                    ? Icons.favorite_border
```

```
                    : Icons.favorite,
                color: Colors.red,
              )
           ],
         )
       ],
     ),
   );
  }
}
```

As you can see, we put three heart icons in a row. For this implementation, we are going to handle fixed values for lives, but you can define the amount of life dynamically by using some property that determines the number of lives and representing its value in heart icons.

In the preceding implementation, we are replacing the filled hearts with bordered hearts as the player takes hits, and we will have the following.

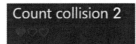

Figure 7-13. *Overlay for player lives*

Restart the Level at End of Lives

Already with the life counter, the following implementation consists of restarting the game when the player runs out of lives:

```
@override
void onCollisionStart(Set<Vector2> points, PositionComponent other) {
  ***

  if (game.collisionMeteors >= 3) {
    reset(dead: true);
  }
  super.onCollisionStart(points, other);
}
```

Pause

In the Flame Game class, we have a **bool** property called **paused** with which we can pause the game; to use it, we will create the corresponding option from the statistics overlay:

lib\overlay\statistics.dart

```
import 'package:flutter/material.dart';
import 'package:testgame/main.dart';

class Statistics extends StatefulWidget {
  final MyGame game;
  Statistics({Key? key, required this.game}) : super(key: key);

  @override
  State<Statistics> createState() => _StatisticsState();
}

class _StatisticsState extends State<Statistics> {
  @override
  Widget build(BuildContext context) {
    return Padding(
      padding: const EdgeInsets.all(8.0),
      child: Column(
        children: [
          Row(
            crossAxisAlignment: CrossAxisAlignment.end,
            children: [
              Text(
                'Count collision ${widget.game.collisionMeteors}',
                style: const TextStyle(color: Colors.white, fontSize: 30),
              ),
              const Expanded(
                child: SizedBox(
                  height: 10,
                ),
              ),
```

```
    GestureDetector(
        onTap: () {
          widget.game.paused = !widget.game.paused;
          setState(() {});
        },
        child: Icon(
            widget.game.paused == true
                ? Icons.play_arrow
                : Icons.pause,
            color: Colors.white,
            size: 40)),
  ],
),
Row(
  children: [
    const SizedBox(
      width: 10,
    ),
    Icon(
      widget.game.collisionMeteors >= 3
          ? Icons.favorite_border
          : Icons.favorite,
      color: Colors.red,
    ),
    Icon(
      widget.game.collisionMeteors >= 2
          ? Icons.favorite_border
          : Icons.favorite,
      color: Colors.red,
    ),
    Icon(
      widget.game.collisionMeteors >= 1
          ? Icons.favorite_border
          : Icons.favorite,
      color: Colors.red,
```

```
            )
          ],
        )
      ],
    ),
  );
}
}
```

We will have the following.

Figure 7-14. *Pause/play overlay*

Restart Level Button

In this implementation, we show how to restart the level, which consists of calling the **reset()** function of the player:

```
GestureDetector(/* pause */)

GestureDetector(
    onTap: () {
      widget.game.player.reset();
    },
    child:
        const Icon(Icons.replay, color: Colors.white, size: 40)),
```

We will have the following.

Figure 7-15. *Overlay to restart the level*

Types of Collisions

Hitboxes have a field called collision type that defines when one hitbox should collide with another. Usually, you set as many hitboxes as possible in **CollisionType.passive** to make collision detection more efficient. By default, **CollisionType** is set to **active**.

CollisionType contains the following values:

- **CollisionType.active** collides with other collidables of type active or passive.

- **CollisionType.passive** collides with other collidables of type active.

- **CollisionType.inactive** will not collide with any other collidable objects.

So if you have hitboxes where you don't need to check for collisions with each other (or with other passives), you can mark them as passive. This is useful, for example, in ground components; in the case of our game, it would be the floor component together with the tiles. Another example is that of enemies, which usually do not need to check for collisions with each other.

For the player, we are interested in being active since we are interested in colliding with passives such as the floor or the enemies. These are not rules that must be complied with 100%, since everything depends on the needs of each application, as we will see in the game.

Use Case: Correct the Counter of Collisions with Meteorites

Currently, there is a problem in the counting of collisions with meteorites, since according to the logic we have implemented

lib/components/player_component.dart

```
class PlayerComponent extends Character {
  MyGame game;

  PlayerComponent({required this.mapSize, required this.game}) :
  super() {***}
```

```
@override
void onCollisionEnd(PositionComponent other) {
  collisionXLeft = collisionXRight = false;

  if (other is Ground) {
    inGround = false;
  }
  if(other is MeteorComponent && body.isColliding){
    game.collisionMeteors++;
    ***
  }
  super.onCollisionEnd(other);
 }
}
```

the counter will be incremented by two on collision with one meteor when it collides with the **body** hitbox and **foot** hitbox. The preceding function will be called twice, once for each collision that occurs. Since the **foot** hitbox is inside the **body** hitbox, if the meteor collided with the **body** hitbox, it would also collide with the **foot** hitbox.

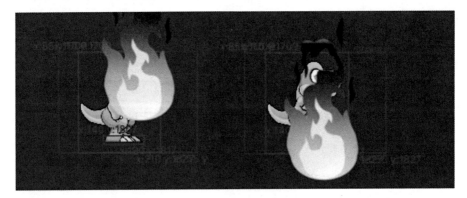

Figure 7-16. *Meteorite collision with the player*

To correct this, we can change the types of collisions. Initially, we could define it as follows:

- The meteor being an enemy could have a passive-type collision.

- The floor and tiles, by not colliding with anyone else, could have a passive-type collision.

- The player, for both hitboxes, could have a type collision active.

But the preceding configuration does not solve the problem we currently have of a double collision with the same meteorite, since the foot hitbox being active and the meteorite passive will collide with each other, which we do not want. To avoid this, we can implement the following structure:

- The meteor being an enemy could have a passive-type collision.

- The floor and tiles will have an active type, to be able to come into contact with the player's feet.

- The player for the body hitbox will be active and for the feet will be passive.

And, at the code level, we are left with the following:

lib\components\player_component.dart

```
body = RectangleHitbox(
    size: Vector2(spriteSheetWidth / 4 - 70, spriteSheetHeight / 4 - 20),
    position: Vector2(25, 10))
  ..collisionType = CollisionType.active;

foot = RectangleHitbox(
  size: Vector2(50, 10),
  position: Vector2(70, spriteSheetWidth / 4 - 70),
)..collisionType = CollisionType.passive;
```

lib\components\meteor_component.dart

```
hitbox.collisionType = CollisionType.passive;
```

lib\components\ground.dart

```
class Ground extends PositionComponent {
  Ground({required size, required position})
      : super(size: size, position: position) {
    debugMode = true;
    add(RectangleHitbox()..collisionType = CollisionType.active);
  }
}
```

With this configuration, the player's **foot** hitbox and the meteorite, being both passive, will not collide with each other, but the meteorites will collide with the hitbox of the player's **body**. With this, we solve the problem of the detection of double collisions with the meteorites, and the counter should count only the collisions with the **body** hitbox.

Important

If after making the preceding changes you do not count the impacts on the body, it is likely that the property

```
body.isColliding
```

is marking false. If so, you can remove the check on that property from the condition:

```
if (other is MeteorComponent /*&& body.isColliding*/) {
  game.collisionMeteors++;
  game.overlays.remove('Statistics');
  game.overlays.add('Statistics');
}
```

In the player, we have two hitboxes, and one of the hitboxes (the one with the feet) is defined as passive, just like the meteorite, and so they cannot collide with each other. So, as long as the collision functions are executed of type callback on the player, the collision will occur in the **body** hitbox.

Update the position Property with Delta Time

One problem that currently exists in the app is with the player moving, as currently implemented, the **position** vector is modified when the keys are pressed:

```
lib / components / player_component.dart

@override
bool onKeyEvent(RawKeyEvent event, Set<LogicalKeyboardKey> keysPressed) {
  ***

  switch (movementType) {
    case MovementType.walkingright:
```

```
    case MovementType.runright:
        position.x += jumpForceXY *
            (movementType == MovementType.walkingright ? 1 : 2);
      break;
    case MovementType.walkingleft:
    case MovementType.runleft:
        position.x -= jumpForceXY *
            (movementType == MovementType.walkingright ? 1 : 2);
    case MovementType.jump:
    case MovementType.jumpright:
    case MovementType.jumpleft:
      position.y -= jumpForceXY;
      if (movementType == MovementType.jumpright) {
        if (!collisionXRight)
          position.x += jumpForceXY;
      } else if (movementType == MovementType.jumpleft) {
        if (!collisionXLeft)
          position.x -= jumpForceXY;
      }
    }
  }
}
```

This is incorrect since, for the calculations to apply to the position (**position** property), size (**size** property), and similar attributes (other properties to perform geometric transformations), we must apply the value of the **deltaTime** available from the **update()** function. Currently, if you run the application on other devices with different processing speeds, you will have a different movement both at the level of the jumps and when walking/running. So the implementation should look like the following:

lib/components/ player_component.dart

```
class PlayerComponent extends Character {
  ***

  @override
  bool onKeyEvent(RawKeyEvent event, Set<LogicalKeyboardKey> keysPressed) {
```

```
if (keysPressed.isEmpty) {
  animation = idleAnimation;
  movementType = MovementType.idle;
  velocity = Vector2.all(0);
}
***
  switch (movementType) {
    case MovementType.walkingright:
    case MovementType.runright:
      if (!right) flipHorizontally();
      right = true;

      if (!collisionXRight) {
        animation = (movementType == MovementType.walkingright
            ? walkAnimation
            : runAnimation);
        velocity.x = jumpForceUp *
            (movementType == MovementType.walkingright ? 1 : 2);
        // position.x += jumpForceXY *
        //     (movementType == MovementType.walkingright ? 1 : 2);
      } else {
        animation = walkSlowAnimation;
      }
      break;
    case MovementType.walkingleft:
    case MovementType.runleft:
      if (right) flipHorizontally();
      right = false;

      if (!collisionXLeft) {
        animation = (movementType == MovementType.walkingleft
            ? walkAnimation
            : runAnimation);
        // posX--;
        velocity.x = -jumpForceUp *
            (movementType == MovementType.walkingleft ? 1 : 2);
```

```
    // position.x -= jumpForceXY *
    //     (movementType == MovementType.walkingright ? 1 : 2);
  } else {
    animation = walkSlowAnimation;
  }

  break;
case MovementType.jump:
case MovementType.jumpright:
case MovementType.jumpleft:
  velocity.y = -jumpForceUp;
  // position.y -= jumpForceXY;
  inGround = false;
  jumpUp = true;
  animation = jumpAnimation;
  if (movementType == MovementType.jumpright) {
    if (!right) flipHorizontally();
    right = true;

    if (!collisionXRight) {
      velocity.x = jumpForceSide;
      // position.x += jumpForceXY;
    }
  } else if (movementType == MovementType.jumpleft) {
    if (right) flipHorizontally();
    right = false;

    if (!collisionXLeft) {
      velocity.x = -jumpForceSide;
      // position.x -= jumpForceXY;
    }
  }

  break;
case MovementType.idle:
  break;
  }
}
```

223

```
      return true;
   }

   @override
   void update(double dt) {

      if (!inGround) {
         // in the air

         if (velocity.y * dt > 0 && jumpUp) {
            jumpUp = false;
         }

         velocity.y += gravity;
         //
      } else {
         velocity.y = 0;
      }

      position += velocity * dt;

      super.update(dt);
   }
}
```

With this implementation, movement will be the same on any device running the game.

Block Player Movement by Time

Another function that we must implement is to block the player 's movement, that is, jumping, running, or walking, for a configurable period of time; for this, we will use three properties.

The first property indicates if the player's movements are blocked or not:

```
bool blockPlayer = false;
```

The second property indicates how long to block the player's movement:

```
double blockPlayerTime = 2.0;
```

The third property is the counter:

```
double blockPlayerElapsedTime = 0;
```

This is a function that we want to implement in the player, so we won't implement it in the **Character** class. In other types of components, such as an enemy, you don't have to implement the blocking function, which, at least in most cases, would not make sense to implement.

To block the player's movements, all we have to do is block the movements from the **onKeyEvent()** function depending on whether the blocking is active or not:

```
@override
bool onKeyEvent(RawKeyEvent event, Set<LogicalKeyboardKey> keysPressed) {
  if (blockPlayer) {
    return true;
  }
  ***
}
```

From the **update()** function, we set the timer to re-enable movement at the specified time. The interesting thing about this implementation is that the blocking time can vary according to the needs of the game; in this implementation, it is two seconds. This implementation is the same as the one used in the **main.dart** to add the meteorites:

```
void update(double dt) {

  if (blockPlayer) {
    if (blockPlayerElapsedTime > blockPlayerTime) {
      blockPlayer = false;
      blockPlayerElapsedTime = 0.0;
    }
    blockPlayerElapsedTime +=dt;
  }
  ***
}
```

Finally, we want to use the movement lock every time the game is restarted, which corresponds to using the **reset()** function:

```
void reset({bool dead = false}) {

  blockPlayer = true;
  ***

}
```

Finally, here's the complete code:

`lib/components/ player_component.dart`

```
class PlayerComponent extends Character {
  Vector2 mapSize;
  MyGame game;

  bool blockPlayer = false;
  double blockPlayerTime = 2.0;
  double blockPlayerElapsedTime = 0;

  @override
  bool onKeyEvent(RawKeyEvent event, Set<LogicalKeyboardKey> keysPressed) {
    if (blockPlayer) {
      return true;
    }
    ***

  }

  @override
  void update(double dt) {

    if (blockPlayer) {
      if (blockPlayerElapsedTime > blockPlayerTime) {
        blockPlayer = false;
        blockPlayerElapsedTime = 0.0;
      }
      blockPlayerElapsedTime +=dt;
    }
```

```
    ***
  }
  void reset({bool dead = false}) {
    blockPlayer = true;
    ***
  }
}
```

Invincibility

To implement the function that the user is invincible for a certain time, we can follow the same logic as the one used for the previous section to block the movement, but applying in the collision between the player and the meteorites:

lib/components/ player_component.dart

```
class PlayerComponent extends Character {
  bool invinciblePlayer = false;
  double invinciblePlayerTime = 10.0;
  double invinciblePlayerElapsedTime = 0;

  @override
  void update(double dt) {
    if (blockPlayer) {
      if (blockPlayerElapsedTime > blockPlayerTime) {
        blockPlayer = false;
        blockPlayerElapsedTime = 0.0;
      }
      blockPlayerElapsedTime += dt;
    }

    if (invinciblePlayer) {
      if (invinciblePlayerElapsedTime > invinciblePlayerTime) {
        invinciblePlayer = false;
        invinciblePlayerElapsedTime = 0.0;
      }
```

```
    invinciblePlayerElapsedTime += dt;
  }
  ***
  super.update(dt);
}

@override
void onCollision(Set<Vector2> points, PositionComponent other) {
  ***

  if (game.collisionMeteors >= 3 && !invinciblePlayer) {
    reset(dead: true);
  }

  super.onCollision(points, other);
}

@override
void onCollisionEnd(PositionComponent other) {
  collisionXLeft = collisionXRight = false;

  if (other is Ground) {
    inGround = false;
  }

  if (other is MeteorComponent && !invinciblePlayer /*&& body.
  isColliding*/) {
    game.collisionMeteors++;
    game.overlays.remove('Statistics');
    game.overlays.add('Statistics');
  }

  super.onCollisionEnd(other);
 }
}
```

Consumables on the Map

We are going to update the previous map to add references to many objects, where we want to place consumables. In this example, the game is about the player being able to collect these consumables; we will create as many layers of object type as there are types of consumables we want them to have. For this game, they will be the following:

1. *consumable_food*: To recover a heart

2. *consumable_invincible*: So that the player is invincible for a certain time

3. *consumable_end*: To end the game

In each of the layers, you must draw a small box where you will place the consumable from the Flutter project. The map that we are going to use looks like the following.

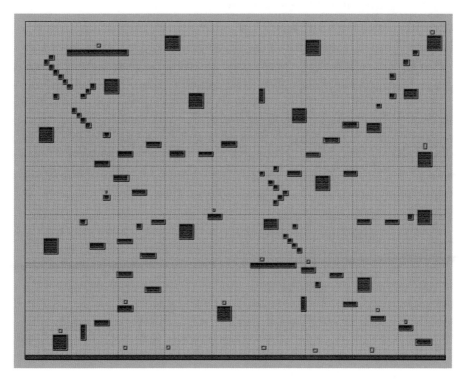

Figure 7-17. *Layers for consumables on the map*

And the layers are as follows.

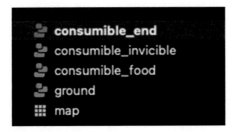

Figure 7-18. *Layers for consumables*

We will use these throughout the player component, every time it is necessary to reload the statistics overlay.

Render Consumables on the Map

In this section, we are going to create the consumables defined on the preceding map; for this, we will use the following images:

Win lives:

www.flaticon.es/icono-gratis/filete_4056243?term=steak&page=1&position=1 &origin=search&related_id=4056243

End of the game:

www.flaticon.es/icono-gratis/estrella_561238?term=star&page=1&position=5 &origin=search&related_id=561238

Icon for invincibility:

www.flaticon.com/free-icon/shield_929429?term=shield&page=1&position=16& origin=search&related_id=929429

You have to import the images to the project and register:

pubspec.yaml

```
assets:
    - assets/images/shield.png
    - assets/images/star.png
    - assets/images/steak.png
    ***
```

Now, a component of type **SpriteComponent** is created for each consumable:
To earn a life:

lib/consumibles/life.dart

```dart
import 'package:flame/collisions.dart';
import 'package:flame/components.dart';

class Life extends SpriteComponent {
  Life({required position}) : super(position: position) {
    debugMode = true;
    add(RectangleHitbox()..collisionType = CollisionType.passive);
  }

  @override
  void onLoad() async {
    sprite = await Sprite.load('steak.png');
    size = Vector2.all(40);
  }
}
```

For timed invincible mode:

lib/consumibles/shield.dart

```dart
import 'package:flame/collisions.dart';
import 'package:flame/components.dart';

class Shield extends SpriteComponent {
  Shield({required position}) : super(position: position) {
    debugMode = true;
    add(RectangleHitbox()..collisionType = CollisionType.passive);
  }

  @override
  void onLoad() async {
    sprite = await Sprite.load('shield.png');
    size = Vector2.all(40);
  }
}
```

To win the game:

lib/consumibles/win.dart

```dart
import 'package:flame/collisions.dart';
import 'package:flame/components.dart';

class Win extends SpriteComponent {
  Win({required position}) : super(position: position) {
    debugMode = true;
    add(RectangleHitbox()..collisionType = CollisionType.passive);
  }

  @override
  void onLoad() async {
    sprite = await Sprite.load('star.png');
    size = Vector2.all(40);
  }
}
```

Its structure is very simple, in which we define a fixed size and the image/sprite that we want to use as a consumable. You can also create a class and reuse the structure since it is exactly the same in the three preceding components.

Once registered, we are going to go to the map component and create the functions to create a sprite of the consumables given their position:

lib/components/tile_map_component.dart

```dart
//import 'package:tiled/tiled.dart';
import 'package:dinojump03/consumibles/shield.dart';
import 'package:dinojump03/consumibles/win.dart';
import 'package:dinojump03/consumibles/life.dart';
import 'package:dinojump03/components/ground.dart';

import 'package:flame/components.dart';
import 'package:flame_tiled/flame_tiled.dart';

class TileMapComponent extends PositionComponent {
  late TiledComponent tiledMap;
```

```dart
@override
void onLoad() async {
  ***
  addConsumables();
}

void addConsumables() {

  //** LIFES */
  final lifeGroup =
      tiledMap.tileMap.getLayer<ObjectGroup>('consumable_food');

  for (var lifeObj in lifeGroup!.objects) {
    add(Life(position: Vector2(lifeObj.x, lifeObj.y)));
  }
  //** WIN */
  final winGroup =
      tiledMap.tileMap.getLayer<ObjectGroup>('consumable_end');

  for (var winObj in winGroup!.objects) {
    add(Win(position: Vector2(winObj.x, winObj.y)));
  }
  //** Shield */
  final shieldGroup =
      tiledMap.tileMap.getLayer<ObjectGroup>('consumible_invicible');

  for (var shieldObj in shieldGroup!.objects) {
    add(Shield(position: Vector2(shieldObj.x, shieldObj.y)));
  }
  }
}
```

The approach applied is exactly the same as the one used for the **ground** layer, only this time a sprite is drawn and not just a hitbox. When running the game, we will see the following.

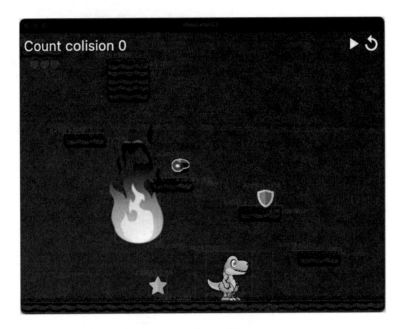

Figure 7-19. *Consumables on the map from Flame*

Recover a Life

The logic to recover a life is very simple. It is enough that the player is missing at least one life, so that when they collide, the sprite is consumed and a life is added to the player (an impact is removed):

lib/components/player_component.dart

```
class PlayerComponent extends Character {
  ***
  @override
  void onCollision(Set<Vector2> points, PositionComponent other) {
    ***
    if (game.collisionMeteors >= 3 && !invinciblePlayer) {
      reset(dead: true);
    }

    super.onCollision(points, other);
  }
}
```

Problem When Restarting the Game

An important factor is that, when restarting the game, the consumed components must be loaded again; for this, the player component and the tile component must communicate. However, since they are sibling components, it is not so easy to carry out this communication directly; therefore, said communication will go through the Game-type class, that is, the parent. To do this, we convert the **background** variable into a property and create a function to add the consumables from the Game-type class:

lib/components/player_component.dart

```
class MyGame extends FlameGame
    with HasKeyboardHandlerComponents, HasCollisionDetection {
  late TileMapComponent background;

  @override
  void onLoad() {
    background = TileMapComponent();
    add(background);
    ***

  }

  void addConsumables() {
    background.addConsumables();
  }
}
```

Now, from the player, we add the consumables from the game reset:

lib/components/player_component.dart

```
class PlayerComponent extends Character {
  void reset({bool dead = false}) {
    ***
    game.addConsumables();
  }
}
```

The first component that is loaded in the game is the background, then the **reset()** method is invoked to load the consumables and with this, the rest of the game components.

Overwrite Consumables at Reboot

The problem left by the preceding solution is that, when executing the **addConsumables()** function, it will register consumables again and, if there were **consumables that were not consumed by the player, the consumables will overlap.** They will continue to overlap as long as there are consumables not consumed and the game is restarted. To avoid this, we will create a list with which we can remove all the instances previously added before the reboot; for this, we will use a list for each consumable. With this, we will have direct control over the added consumables, and therefore, when restarting the game, we first remove all the consumables from said lists:

lib\components\tile_map_component.dart

```
class TileMapComponent extends PositionComponent {
  late TiledComponent tiledMap;

  List<Life> lifes = [];
  List<Shield> shields = [];
  List<Win> win = [];

  @override
  void onLoad() async {
    tiledMap = await TiledComponent.load('map2.tmx', Vector2.all(32));
    add(tiledMap);

    final objGroup = tiledMap.tileMap.getLayer<ObjectGroup>("ground");

    for (final obj in objGroup!.objects) {
      add(Ground(
          size: Vector2(obj.width, 20), position: Vector2(obj.x, obj.y)));
    }

  }
```

```
void addConsumables() {
  //** LIFES */
  final lifeGroup = tiledMap.tileMap.getLayer<ObjectGroup>('consumab
  le_food');

  // removes consumables
  lifes.forEach((l) => l.removeFromParent());
  lifes.clear();

  for (var lifeObj in lifeGroup!.objects) {
    lifes.add(Life(position: Vector2(lifeObj.x, lifeObj.y)));
    add(lifes.last);
  }

  //** WIN */

  // removes consumibles
  win.forEach((w) => w.removeFromParent());
  win.clear();

  final winGroup = tiledMap.tileMap.getLayer<ObjectGroup>('consumi
  ble_end');

  for (var winObj in winGroup!.objects) {
    win.add(Win(position: Vector2(winObj.x, winObj.y)));
    add(win.last);
  }

  //** Shields */
  // removes consumables
  shields.forEach((s) => s.removeFromParent());
  shields.clear();
  final shieldGroup =
      tiledMap.tileMap.getLayer<ObjectGroup>('consumible_invicible');
```

```
    for (var shieldObj in shieldGroup!.objects) {
      shield.add(Shield(position: Vector2(shieldObj.x, shieldObj.y)));
      add(shield.last);
    }
  }
}
```

The lists are also used to add the consumables:

```
win.add(Win(position: Vector2(winObj.x, winObj.y)));
```

And from them, add it to the game:

```
add(win.last);
```

Invincibility

To activate momentary invincibility, it's just as easy as consuming a life; all you have to do is detect the collision and implement the logic. Remember that we have a property to indicate if the user is in invincible mode or not:

lib/components/player_component.dart

```
@override
void onCollision(Set<Vector2> points, PositionComponent other) {
  ***
  if (other is Shield) {
    invinciblePlayer = true;
    other.removeFromParent();
  }
  if (game.collisionMeteors >= 3 && !invinciblePlayer) {
    reset(dead: true);
  }

  super.onCollision(points, other);
}
```

Game Over

For this implementation, the player only has to select one of the star consumables defined throughout the entire game. Upon detecting the collision with one of these consumables, we end the game. For the implementation, we pause the game and show the end of game overlay:

lib/components/player_component.dart

```dart
@override
void onCollision(Set<Vector2> points, PositionComponent other) {
  ***

  if (other is Win) {
    game.paused = true;
    game.overlays.add('GameOver');
  }

  if (game.collisionMeteors >= 3 && !invinciblePlayer) {
    reset(dead: true);
  }

  super.onCollision(points, other);
}
```

For the end of game overlay, we reset it and remove the end of game overlay:

lib/overlays/game_over.dart

```dart
child: ElevatedButton(
  onPressed: () {
    widget.game.player.reset();
    widget.game.overlays.remove('GameOver');
  },
);
```

In the **reset()** function, we indicate that the game is no longer paused:

lib/components/player_component.dart

```
void reset({bool dead = false}) {
    game.paused=false;
    ***
}
```

You can take different approaches based on this implementation, for example, have the player consume (collide) all star-type consumables to end the game; you can keep track of star-type consumables consumed and display them in an overlay.

Chapter source code:
https://github.com/libredesarrollo/flame-curso-libro-dinojump03/releases/tag/v0.2

CHAPTER 8

Game 2: Many Experiments

In this chapter, we are going to perform many experiments for the game defined in the previous chapter.

Unlike other application developments such as blogs, notes, or administrative applications in general, where there is always a pattern to follow in terms of business logic (e.g., in a blog application, we have a management module with CRUD for POSTs and a user query module), in game development, we have complete creative freedom and are not limited by the same rules as these traditional applications. This is why I wanted to separate the previous chapter from this chapter, to be able to experiment more with our game and learn about other possible variants and, with this, show other implementations that may be of interest to you.

Vary the Jump

Throughout the previous chapters, we have seen several variants on the player's movement. We are going to know another possible variant on the jump, which will be that the player can vary the position in the air by pressing the left (A) and right (D) direction arrows.

The change is extremely simple. If we go to the **onKeyEvent()** function, we see that any movement of the player happens when they are on the ground, but, for this change, we need that when the player is in the air, they can move to the sides:

lib/components/player_component.dart

```
@override
bool onKeyEvent(RawKeyEvent event, Set<LogicalKeyboardKey> keysPressed) {
```

© Andrés Cruz Yoris 2024
A. Cruz Yoris, *Flame Game Development*, https://doi.org/10.1007/979-8-8688-0063-4_8

```
if (blockPlayer) {
  return true;
}

if (keysPressed.isEmpty) {
  animation = idleAnimation;
  movementType = MovementType.idle;
  velocity = Vector2.all(0);
}

if (inGround) {
  // RIGHT
  if (keysPressed.contains(LogicalKeyboardKey.arrowRight) ||
      keysPressed.contains(LogicalKeyboardKey.keyD)) {
    if (keysPressed.contains(LogicalKeyboardKey.shiftLeft)) {
      // RUN
      movementType = MovementType.runright;
    } else {
      // WALKING
      movementType = MovementType.walkingright;
    }
  }
  // LEFT
  if (keysPressed.contains(LogicalKeyboardKey.arrowLeft) ||
      keysPressed.contains(LogicalKeyboardKey.keyA)) {
    if (keysPressed.contains(LogicalKeyboardKey.shiftLeft)) {
      // RUN
      movementType = MovementType.runleft;
    } else {
      // WALKING
      movementType = MovementType.walkingleft;
    }
  }
  // JUMP
  if (keysPressed.contains(LogicalKeyboardKey.arrowUp) ||
      keysPressed.contains(LogicalKeyboardKey.keyW)) {
```

```
      movementType = MovementType.jump;
    }
  } else {
    if (keysPressed.contains(LogicalKeyboardKey.arrowRight) ||
        keysPressed.contains(LogicalKeyboardKey.keyD)) {
      // RIGHT
      movementType = MovementType.jumpright;
    } else if (keysPressed.contains(LogicalKeyboardKey.arrowLeft) ||
        keysPressed.contains(LogicalKeyboardKey.keyA)) {
      // LEFT
      movementType = MovementType.jumpleft;
    }
  }

  switch (movementType) {
    case MovementType.walkingright:
    case MovementType.runright:
      if (!right) flipHorizontally();
      right = true;

      if (!collisionXRight) {
        animation = (movementType == MovementType.walkingright
            ? walkAnimation
            : runAnimation);
        velocity.x =
            jumpForceUp * (movementType == MovementType.walkingright
            ? 1 : 2);
        // position.x += jumpForceXY *
        //     (movementType == MovementType.walkingright ? 1 : 2);
      } else {
        animation = walkSlowAnimation;
      }
      break;
    case MovementType.walkingleft:
    case MovementType.runleft:
      if (right) flipHorizontally();
      right = false;
```

```
      if (!collisionXLeft) {
        animation = (movementType == MovementType.walkingleft
            ? walkAnimation
            : runAnimation);
        // posX--;
        velocity.x =
            -jumpForceUp * (movementType == MovementType.walkingleft
? 1 : 2);
        // position.x -= jumpForceXY *
        //      (movementType == MovementType.walkingright ? 1 : 2);
      } else {
        animation = walkSlowAnimation;
      }
      break;
    case MovementType.jump:
    case MovementType.jumpright:
    case MovementType.jumpleft:
      if (inGround) {
        velocity.y = -jumpForceUp;
      }
      // position.y -= jumpForceXY;
      inGround = false;
      jumpUp = true;
      animation = jumpAnimation;
      if (movementType == MovementType.jumpright) {
        if (!right) flipHorizontally();
        right = true;

        if (!collisionXRight) {
          velocity.x = jumpForceSide;
          // position.x += jumpForceXY;
        }
      } else if (movementType == MovementType.jumpleft) {
        if (right) flipHorizontally();
        right = false;
```

```
      if (!collisionXLeft) {
        velocity.x = -jumpForceSide;
        // position.x -= jumpForceXY;
      }
    }

    break;
  case MovementType.idle:
    break;
  }

  return true;
}
```

In practice, when the player jumps, they can move to the sides, giving better control over the jump, and it's not as limited a scheme as the arched jump we presented before, which is ideal to be able to move in the tiles.

Also, we'll increase the jump and gravity a bit to make the player fall faster:

lib/components/player_component.dart

```
class Character extends SpriteAnimationComponent
    with KeyboardHandler, CollisionCallbacks {
  ***

  double gravity = 15;
  final double spriteSheetWidth = 680;
}
```

As we mentioned at the beginning, this is just one possible variant. The arched jump is not a bad implementation, and you can use it together with this type of jump. Also, you can disable/enable any of them according to some game condition, like when some consumable has been consumed, the level you are at, or other variations in the game.

Background Image

As we have seen up to this point, the main elements of the game consist of components; for the current game, we have a component for the player, tiles, and meteorites. Therefore, and as we saw in the previous project, we can use another component to draw a background image; for this game, we'll be using the same background used in the previous app. So once it's copied into the project, we import it:

pubspec.yaml

```
  assets:
    - assets/images/background.jpg
  ***
```

And we create the component to place a background image:

lib\components\sky.dart

```
import 'package:flame/components.dart';
import 'package:flutter/widgets.dart';

class Sky extends SpriteComponent {

  @override

  void onLoad() async {
    position = Vector2(0, 0);

    sprite = await Sprite.load('background.jpg');
    size = sprite!.originalSize;
  }
}
```

In the **FlameGame** class, we have

lib\main.dart

```
@override
void onLoad() {
  world.add(Sky());
  ***
}
```

And we will have the following.

Figure 8-1. *Set a background image*

Map Size and Player Movement

In this section, we will know a couple of ways so that the player does not leave the screen on the right and left sides.

Alternative 1

The first implementation is using the borders of the screen; for this, the **ScreenHitbox** component is used. Currently, there are already a couple of properties that allow you to block the player's movement to the right

```
bool collisionXRight = false;
```

and left:

```
bool collisionXLeft = false;
```

And they block the movement of the player on the corresponding axis, for example:

```
case MovementType.walkingright:
case MovementType.runright:
   if (!right) flipHorizontally();
      right = true;
      if (!collisionXRight) {//***}
```

So, in the collision, we check the position of the player on the screen:

1.   If it's close to zero, then it's on the left edge side.

2.   If it's close to the width of the map, then it's on the right edge side.

```
@override
void onCollision(Set<Vector2> points, PositionComponent other) {
   if (other is ScreenHitbox) {
     if (points.first[0] <= 0.0) {
       // left
       collisionXLeft = true;
     } else if (points.first[0] >= mapSize.x
         //gameRef.size.y

       ) {
       // right
       collisionXRight = true;
     }
   }
}
```

And at the end of the collision with the screen, we reset the corresponding properties:

```
lib\components\player_component.dart
```

```
@override
void onCollisionEnd(PositionComponent other) {
```

```
if (other is ScreenHitbox) {
  collisionXLeft = collisionXRight = false;
}
***
}
```

It is important to note that we can only apply this implementation in the player, since the camera moves along with the player and, therefore, the sides of the screen also move until reaching the limits specified in the camera.

Another important point is that we can have race conditions between the **update()** function, which is the one that updates the **position** property for the player to move, and the **onCollision()** function, which is the one used to implement the preceding logic for locking the player position; therefore, if the **position** property updates very fast (which can happen if the player is close to the edge of the screen and runs), you can escape the map and thus run into a void, so this implementation as defined may have problems.

Alternative 2

The following implementation is using the size of the map exclusively; it is not necessary to use the collision functions. So, at the time of movement, check if the player does not go off the map following the same principles that we saw before:

```
@override
bool onKeyEvent(RawKeyEvent event, Set<LogicalKeyboardKey> keysPressed) {
  ***

  switch (movementType) {
    case MovementType.walkingright:
    case MovementType.runright:
      if (!right) flipHorizontally();
      right = true;

      if (!collisionXRight && position.x < mapSize.x) {
        animation = (movementType == MovementType.walkingright
            ? walkAnimation
            : runAnimation);
        velocity.x =
```

249

```
            jumpForceUp * (movementType == MovementType.walkingright
? 1 : 2);
    } else {
      animation = walkSlowAnimation;
    }
    break;
  case MovementType.walkingleft:
  case MovementType.runleft:
    if (right) flipHorizontally();
    right = false;

    if (!collisionXLeft && position.x > 0) {
      animation = (movementType == MovementType.walkingleft
          ? walkAnimation
          : runAnimation);
      velocity.x =
          -jumpForceUp * (movementType == MovementType.walkingleft
? 1 : 2);
    } else {
      animation = walkSlowAnimation;
    }

    break;
  case MovementType.jump:
  case MovementType.jumpright:
  case MovementType.jumpleft:
    if (inGround) {
      velocity.y = -jumpForceUp;
    }

    inGround = false;
    jumpUp = true;
    animation = jumpAnimation;
    if (movementType == MovementType.jumpright) {
      if (!right) flipHorizontally();
      right = true;
```

```
    if (!collisionXRight  && position.x < mapSize.x) {
      velocity.x = jumpForceSide;
    }
  } else if (movementType == MovementType.jumpleft) {
    if (right) flipHorizontally();
    right = false;

    if (!collisionXLeft && position.x > 0) {
      velocity.x = -jumpForceSide;
    }
  }

  break;
 case MovementType.idle:
   break;
}

return true;
}
```

In this way, the race condition seen before does not exist, but, even so, since the comparison is so limited (comparing only the values of the extremes), it may be that, when executing the update on the **position** property, the player leaves the map and therefore falls into the void.

Conclusion

In both implementations, we have a similar approach, but using different mechanisms. It is worth mentioning that depending on the update of the game and the update of the **position** property, the player may or may not escape from the screen as we mentioned before. If we try several collisions on the screen, we will see that there are times that it goes into the edge.

Figure 8-2. *Player at the edge of the screen*

Other times it is blocked and other times it just escapes.

You can handle a constant value to have a larger range in the comparison and reduce the margin of errors, for example:

```
if (!collisionXLeft && position.x > 50) {
    velocity.x = -jumpForceSide;
}
```

And this can be accompanied by an image on the sides of the screen, like some rocks.

Correct Unevenness Between Player Positioning and Tiles

In this section, we are going to correct the unevenness that exists between the player and the tiles. Surely, as you have developed the application and when interacting with the player, you have seen the unevenness many times.

Figure 8-3. *Unevenness of the player with the tiles*

This mostly happens when the player falls from jumping or lands on another tile. The problem is typical in this type of games, since there are no instant updates; they are processes that are executed in an infinite cycle, as it happens with the **update()** function and the collision functions, where variants often exist in the collisions as they are detected. This happens especially when the **position** property is updated very quickly that by varying the same (as a result of the player 's movement), it will collide with the objects.

To avoid this problem, from the collision function, we are going to place a fixed positioning when the player is positioned on a tile, taking as parameters

- The position of the tile, which can be obtained by using the **other** argument

- The size of the player sprite – being aligned in the middle through **Anchor.center**, we take half the size of the player

- The height of the **foot** hitbox, which is ten pixels

With these variants, we implement the following logic:

lib/components/player_component.dart

```
@override
void onCollision(Set<Vector2> points, PositionComponent other) {
    ***
  if (other is Ground && !jumpUp && foot.isColliding && !inGround) {
```

```
    inGround = true;
    position.y = other.position.y - size.y / 2 + 10;
  }
}
```

With the preceding code, we will always have the player positioning at the same level in all the tiles.

Prevent the Player from Falling at a Very High Speed

If the player falls from a great height, for the implementation of gravity, it will progressively accelerate the player, a situation that is a problem since it becomes very difficult to control the player. Due to the speed at which the player falls, there may be problems in the detection of collisions with the floor, resulting in the player going through the tiles and falling into the void. To avoid this, we can use the **clamp()** function that allows us to keep a number in a certain range and, therefore, control the drop, for example:

```
var result = 10.5.clamp(5, 10.0); // 10.0
result = 0.75.clamp(5, 10.0); // 5
result = (-10).clamp(-5, 5.0); // -5
result = (-0.0).clamp(-5, 5.0); // -0.0
```

And we will use it to calculate the speed on the Y axis:

```
final double terminalVelocity = 150;
***

@override
void update(double dt) {
  ***
  // Prevents the player from falling too fast
  velocity.y = velocity.y.clamp(-jumpForceUp, terminalVelocity);
  position += velocity * dt;
  ***
}
```

Mathematical Formulas for Collision Detection

At the moment, we have not used too many mathematical formulas for our game, the use mathematical operations to calculate different measures such as the direction of the collision between the player and the tile/floor, the collision normal, calculation for gravity collisions with objects in certain angles among others, are some common operations in this type of games in which gravity and the collision between components are implemented; specifically, our case of interest for this section, between the player and the floor/tiles, since it is the one that we must implement the most logic to position the player on top of the floor/tiles and avoid behaviors such as those presented before, such as the player remaining suspended on detecting tile collision as shown in Figure 7-1.

Cases that would happen if we don't implement additional logic to handle these situations; we have made several implementations that may be considered unusual such as adding a player foot hitbox to handle collisions in a small area and avoid this unrealistic behavior.

These types of operations are usually performed using only the same hitbox, the so-called **body** in our case, that is, over the entire body; but, to determine exactly where the collision occurred and act accordingly, mathematical calculations are used on the vectors that we can either consult or generate based on the positions of the components; for this, a vector is calculated to calculate the collision normal and from this vector, the distance between the player and the floor/tiles; doing calculations on vectors such as generating normals, normalization, magnitudes, among others, are concepts that may not seem easy to process for everyone and therefore, this type of implementation was avoided, but in this section we are going to learn about some of these calculations in the application to follow a more traditional game development.

Implementation

Let's start by removing any reference to the property called **foot** from the application:

```
class Character extends *** {
  ***
  late RectangleHitbox body /*, foot*/;
}
```

Now, to detect collisions, we'll use the body component, which we'll adjust to look like the following:

lib\components\player_component.dart

```
@override
Future<void>? onLoad() async {
  ***

  body = RectangleHitbox(
    size: Vector2(spriteSheetWidth / 4 - 70, spriteSheetHeight / 4 - 20),
    position: Vector2(25, 10),
  )
    // ..debugMode = true
    // ..debugColor = Colors.orange
    ..collisionType = CollisionType.active;
}
```

And it would be much more adjusted than how we had it before.

Figure 8-4. *Adjust the player hitbox*

We changed the debug color to make it easier to know the hitbox values displayed on the interface. The only changes we are going to make are in the player component, specifically in the collision function, leaving the code as follows:

lib\components\player_component.dart

```
class PlayerComponent extends Character {
  final Vector2 fromAbove = Vector2(0, -1);
  ***
  @override
  void onCollision(Set<Vector2> points, PositionComponent other) {
    if (other is ScreenHitbox) {
      if (points.first[0] <= 0.0) {
```

```
      // left
      collisionXLeft = true;
    } else if (points.first[0] >= mapSize.x) {
      // right
      collisionXRight = true;
    }
  }
}

if (other is Ground && !jumpUp && !inGround) {
  if (points.length == 2) {

    // separation distance
    // point Ground + point Player / 2
    final mid = (points.elementAt(0) + points.elementAt(1))/2;

    //distance between the center of the collision and the center of
      the component
    final collisionNormal = absoluteCenter - mid;
    // collisionNormal.length returns the magnitude of the vector, it
      is used to know
    // that is to say, the length of the vector, that is, how
      long is it
    // that is to say, how much is there from one end to the other end
    // that is to say, from one point to the other point
    final separationDistance = (size.y / 2) - collisionNormal.
    length - 10;
    collisionNormal.normalize(); //convert to a unit vector

    // If collision normal is almost upwards,
    final v = fromAbove.dot(collisionNormal);
    if (v > 0.9) {
      inGround = true;
```

257

```
        // Resolve collision by moving player along
        position += collisionNormal.scaled(separationDistance);
      }
    }
    ***

  }
}
```

As you can see, these are quite specific changes, about 11 new lines of code to replace what we had before:

```
if (points.length == 2) {
  final mid = (points.elementAt(0) + points.elementAt(1))/2;
  final collisionNormal = absoluteCenter - mid;
  final separationDistance = (size.x / 2) - collisionNormal.length;
  collisionNormal.normalize();
  final v = fromAbove.dot(collisionNormal);
  if (v > 0.9) {
    inGround = true;
    position += collisionNormal.scaled(separationDistance);
  }
}
```

In the following sections, we will see in detail what each line of the preceding code is used for.

Collision Centers

The first thing that is calculated is the **midpoint of the collision** or center of the collision, which is necessary to calculate the collision normal that we will talk about a little later. To calculate the midpoint of the collision, the interception points at the moment of the collision are used:

```
final mid = (points.elementAt(0) + points.elementAt(1))
```

To understand these values more clearly, let's look at a couple of possible scenarios.

Figure 8-5. *Intersection points example 1*

In this first example, the collision occurs at the top of the **ground** component's container.

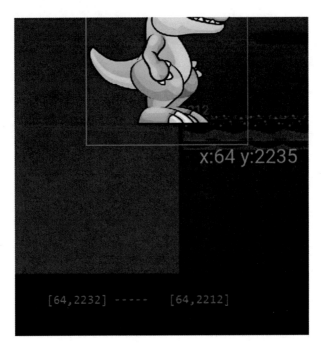

Figure 8-6. *Intersection points example 2*

In this second example, the collision occurs at the bottom of the **ground** component's container.

The numbers that you can see in the preceding images correspond to two points, which are the intersection points between the player component and the floor.

Let's remember that, when executing the application in a cycle (game loop) through the **update()** function, the updates can occur a little before (first image) or a little after (second image), and for this reason doing additional calculations for the position is as natural as possible always regardless of the update rate.

Regardless of the case, we have the vector to obtain the center of the collision. In the first image it would be the position occupied by the white circle.

Figure 8-7. *Breakpoints example 1 in more detail*

And in the second it would be the following.

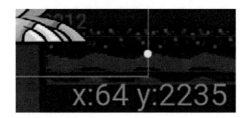

Figure 8-8. *Breakpoints example 2 in more detail*

And for this, we do the operation:

```
final mid = (points.elementAt(0) + points.elementAt(1)) / 2
```

This is nothing more than the calculation of an average between two numbers, but, in the case of our game, it is two points:

```
(10 + 15) / 2 = 12.5
```

But being points, the result is a value in X and Y.

Since they are collisions between rectangular-type hitboxes, we are interested in calculating the center of the collision when there are two interception points for a component of type **ground**:

```
if (other is Ground ***)
   if (points.length == 2)
```

For example, for the image of example 1, the two collisions would be those marked with a red X.

Figure 8-9. *Showing hitbox breakpoints, example 1*

And here are the collisions for image 2.

Figure 8-10. *Showing hitbox breakpoints, example 2*

And from there is the preceding operation to calculate the center of the collision. We need to know the center of the player component. For this, we use the **absoluteCenter** property; it returns the absolute center of the component. Therefore, depending on which part on the map the player component is, the value will change.

Figure 8-11. *absoluteCenter of the player with respect to the world*

In the image above, the player is located in the lower left corner of the map:

- (4 in X)

- (2144 in Y)

Therefore, this value is updated as the player moves around the map and does not correspond to a fixed value like the **size** and **anchor** properties but to a variable value like the **position** property.

Normal Collision

There are many ways to calculate the collision normal, and it depends a lot on the context, such as if you are using circles or spheres or if it is a 2D or 3D world or even if you are using other types of tools like Unity or Unreal Engine that have methods to simplify the operation and therefore the procedure can change. In this section, we are going to show a common implementation in this type of game.

It also depends on the implementation that you want to give it. For example, in this scenario we have two well-defined bodies, the one for the player and the one for the floor/tiles, but nothing prevents situations like the following:

- It is about equal bodies, for example, those of the player and an enemy, or it is a clash of three or more bodies of the same type. In these cases, each of the bodies can calculate its own normal based on the collision that occurred.

- There are several points of intersection; therefore, in these cases you can select one of these points to have an approximation or select the point of intersection closest to the collision or do an average (as we do).

- The contact surfaces are not uniform; therefore, you could have several normals, and you can choose one based on some criteria.

Therefore, in order to not complicate the development, we are going to know a possible implementation that we can use for what we need, which is to position the player correctly on the floor/tiles.

As possible definitions of collision normal, we have the following:

The collision normal refers to a vector perpendicular to the plane of impact between two colliding objects.

The collision normal is just the direction vector between the objects.

The normal allows to determine the magnitude and direction in which the impact force is produced, as well as to determine the trajectory after the collision. When two objects collide, the normal of the collision indicates the direction in which the force resulting from the impact is produced.

We already have both centers of the collided objects (player component and floor/tiles), so now we can calculate the collision normal.

The collision normal is nothing more than the difference (subtraction) between the centers of the normalized components.

As we already have both centers (component center and collision center), therefore, we subtract these vectors:

```
collisionNormal = absoluteCenter - mid;
```

Usually when we subtract vectors in game development, we do it to get distances; in our specific case, it is the distance between the center of the component and the collision center of the tiles/floor, which results in a vector called the collision normal.

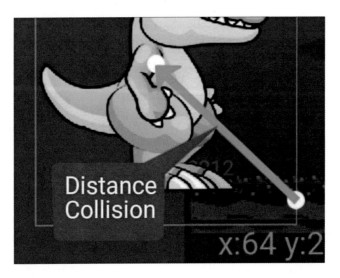

Figure 8-12. *Collision distance*

And this is (almost, since we need to normalize the vector) our collision normal, which is nothing more than a vector, with a certain direction; this vector can be used for many operations, for example, to calculate impulses after the collision, although in our case it will help us detect and control the collision between both components (player and floor/tiles).

The next step we need to do is to normalize the vector (the vector collision normal). Following the concept of collision normal, we have the following:

The normal of the collision is nothing more than the difference (subtraction) between the centers of the normalized components.

As we can see, the preceding vector (the collision normal) has a variable length other than one. So that we can operate correctly with the following methods that we are going to see, it is necessary that it will have a length of one (unit vector) but maintaining the same sense, which is essentially the concept of normalization of a vector.

Normalizing a vector means transforming it into a vector with the same direction but with a module equal to 1.

Vector
module = 4

Vector
module = 1

Figure 8-13. *Normalization of a vector*

To do this, we do

```
collisionNormal.normalize();
```

Magnitude

With

```
collisionNormal.length
```

the magnitude of the vector is calculated. It is used to know what the length of the vector is, that is, how much it measures (how much a vector measures from end to end or point to point).

The rest of the values in the operation are as follows:

```
final separationDistance = (size.y / 2) - collisionNormal.length - 10;
```

They are nothing more than constants to calculate the position of the player on the floor. **These values will be used to calculate the exact position of the player with respect to the floor.** Since we are using a sprite for the irregular player, with many white spaces around it (the dinosaur image), when we want to position the player in a particular location that depends on its size, it is necessary to use these constant values; therefore, depending on the image used, you may need to adjust these values. If you see that at the moment of executing the game, there is a kind of automatic jump, it means that there is a problem when positioning the player on the floor/tile and you should try other constant values. Specifically, the automatic jump occurs when updating the position of the player from the **onCollision()** function:

```
position += collisionNormal.scaled(separationDistance);
```

This calculation causes the player to not come into contact with the floor/tiles, and due to the condition we have when updating the **inGround** property at the end of the collision

```
@override
void onCollisionEnd(PositionComponent other) {
  ***

  if (other is Ground) {
    inGround = false;
  }
}
```

it makes the player not be in contact with the floor/tiles again, and therefore, gravity is activated again and it falls again and collides with the floor/tiles, doing all the previous calculation again and entering an infinite cycle.

Scalar Product

The next operation we do is

```
if (fromAbove.dot(collisionNormal) > 0.9) ***
```

With dot() we calculate the dot product of a vector, for our game, we will use the dot product between the collision vector of the normal and the "up" world (specifically this vector is implicitly defined in the floor and tiles) and It's normal in this type of games:

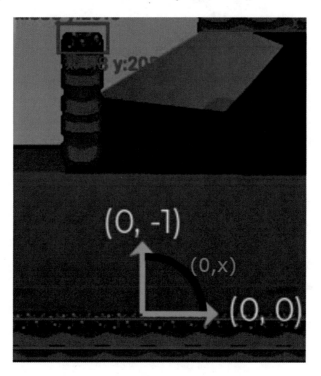

Figure 8-14. *"From above" of the world*

Defined in the variable

```
final Vector2 fromAbove = Vector2(0, -1);
```

With the dot product of two unit vectors (normalized), the direction in which both vectors point is calculated, that is, the dot product returns a floating-point value between –1 and 1 that can be used to determine some properties of the angle between two vectors. In game development it has several implementations, but what you need to know is that if the value is a positive one, both vectors are parallel and have the same direction. Therefore, we can deduce that if their value is close to 1 (in our example 0.9), it means that it is an acceptable value in which the player fell correctly on the floor/tiles and the player remains on the floor.

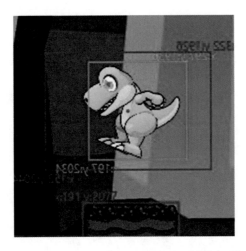

Figure 8-15. *Acceptable positioning of the player on the tile*

On the contrary, if the jump comes from below or from the side, the jump becomes very inclined, and therefore the player did not fall correctly on the floor/tiles and will continue falling. This can happen when the player steps too close to the edge of the tiles or just makes contact on the ends of the tiles.

Figure 8-16. *Incorrect positioning of the player on the tile*

In our case, being the normal vector to which we are going to apply the dot product, we can determine how inclined the collision normal vector is, which indicates the collision angle of the player component with respect to the world, which has a fixed vector of $(0,-1)$.

Finally, the distance to position the player is calculated; for the moment, we have is a vector that we can use to indicate the position but of module 1, that is, its values in X and Y are between -1 and 1; for example:

```
Vector2 ([0.2584250044858353,-0.9660313230203749])
```

And now, using the **scaled()** function, what it does is multiply the X and Y components by a fixed value, which represents the separation between the centers of the collisions (the player component and the center of the collision) resulting in the vector that we have to add to the position of the player so that it settles on top of the floor/tiles:

```
position += collisionNormal.scaled(separationDistance);
```

To understand this more clearly, you can see that when the player makes contact with the corners of the tiles, the dot product is very far from 0.9 (e.g., 0.4) as shown in Figure 8-15.

And therefore the preceding condition is not triggered and gravity is not suspended (**inGround = true**), this is due to the inclination of the normal vector; on the other hand, if the player falling in a straight line on top of the floor/tile, the value obtained would be approximately 1 and therefore it is handled as a valid collision with the **Ground** component and therefore the player is positioned on the floor:

```
inGround = true;
```

In conclusion, two main calculations are made:

1. The collision normal, to obtain the angle of incidence on the player and the floor/tiles

2. The position that the player should have on the floor/tiles

These changes were adapted from one of the sample applications that you can find in the official documentation:

```
https://docs.flame-engine.org/latest/tutorials/platformer/step_5.
html#collisions
```

As a recommendation to you, place a breakpoint in your editor when detecting the collision:

```
if (points.length == 2) {}
```

And evaluate the new changes made in this section.

Implement the Game on Small Screens

So that you can use the game on multiple platforms, such as desktop, web, and mobile devices, where the factor that changes is the size of the screen, you can scale the game when the application detects a small screen:

lib/components/player_component.dart

```
PlayerComponent({required this.mapSize, required this.game}) : super() {
  ***
  scale = Vector2.all(0.5);
}
```

lib/components/meteor_component.dart

```
MeteorComponent({required this.cameraPosition}) : super() {
  ***
  scale = Vector2.all(0.5);
}
```

And for the background, you can create multiple backgrounds (e.g., two) for the same level, where you change the size of the tile used, which in this example is 32 pixels. You can use 24 pixels or less to create a smaller background. You can also rescale the current background, but we will talk about this in detail in game 4.

This would be done to have a better visualization of the game in general on small screens.

Chapter source code:

https://github.com/libredesarrollo/flame-curso-libro-dinojump03/releases/tag/v0.3

CHAPTER 9

Game 3: Move XY

2D games, where there is a main player who can move, are generally of two types:

1. The ones where the player can only move left and right, like the one we created earlier

Figure 9-1. *Game type 1, moving horizontally and jumping*

2. Those where the player has a freedom to move not only to the right and left but also up and down

© Andrés Cruz Yoris 2024
A. Cruz Yoris, *Flame Game Development*, https://doi.org/10.1007/979-8-8688-0063-4_9

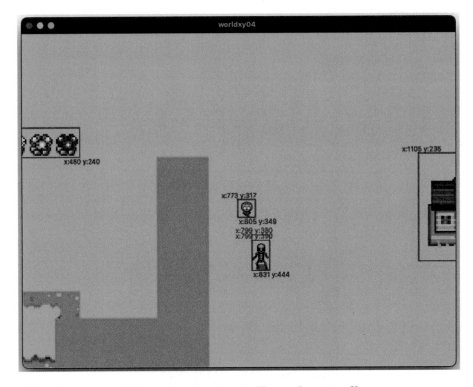

Figure 9-2. *Game type 2, moving horizontally and vertically*

Of course, from these two types, there may be variants to create other types such as runner-type games, games like *Flappy Bird*, etc. Mainly what changes here is how the camera looks at the scene. In the first image, the camera is looking from the side; therefore, the player's allowed movements are limited to moving to the sides or jumping. In the second image, the camera sees from above; therefore, the character has complete freedom to move to the sides, forward, or backward.

The type of games that we are going to implement in this chapter is easier to carry out in terms of player movements, since there is no need to implement logic for jumps, gravity, and the like.

Creating the Bases of the Game

For this chapter, we'll create a project called **worldxy04**. As we are going to see in the following implementations, it has a very similar structure to the one presented in the previous project, but much simpler, since the movement consists of moving up, down, right, and left with a constant speed; in other words, there is no need to use velocity vectors nor to implement jumps.

Let's start with the important helper function to create the **SpriteAnimationComponent** created in the previous project:

`lib/utils/create_animation_by_limit.dart`

We import the resources that we are going to use, the player's.

Figure 9-3. *Sprite for the player (https://pipoya.itch.io/pipoya-free-rpg-character-sprites-nekonin)*

Creating the Map

For the new map that we are going to use in this project, we are going to use the same principles that we applied in the map of the third project. However, as we mentioned before, the type of games that we are going to develop in this chapter tends to have richer maps, with more options, and with this we can create maps with a higher level of customization, so we will use some additional layers to be able to personalize the same. For the map, we will use a tileset from

`https://limezu.itch.io/serenevillagerevamped`

The one with 48 pixels is called as

`Serene_Village_48x48.png`

which we will rename as

`tile.png`

This was chosen for the large number of options and objects in general that we can use to create our map.

Create

We will create a map whose suggested dimensions are as follows.

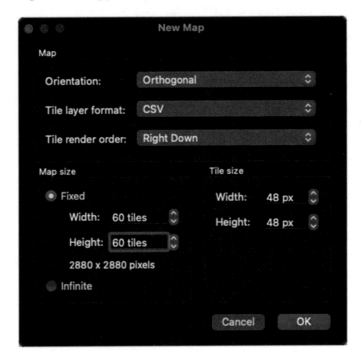

Figure 9-4. *Settings for the new map*

Design

We will use two layers to render the map layout. The first layer we will call as

base

We will use it to define the base tile, which in this case will be that of the grass, since it is the most prevalent on the map, resulting in the following.

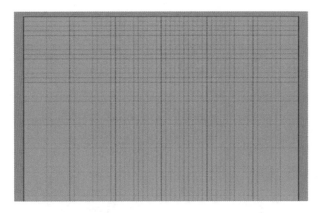

Figure 9-5. *Base layer in Tiled Map Editor*

The other layer

others

we will use to add the objects and details in general. You can customize it as you see fit, and the more objects you add, the better tests you can perform, but at least add some houses, poles as objects, and water with a bridge for the player to interact with. Our map will look like the following.

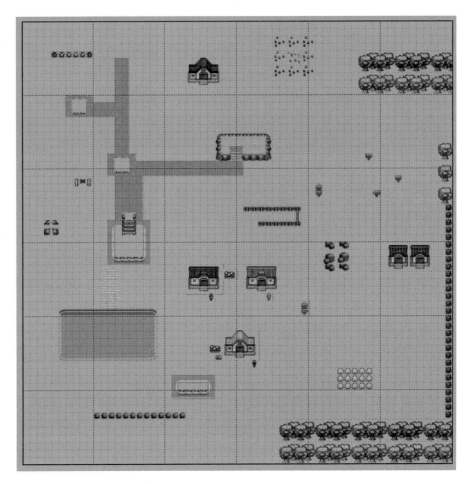

Figure 9-6. *Map created in Tiled Map Editor*

Object Layer

In this second layer called others, all are objects through which our player cannot move, except for the bridge over the water.

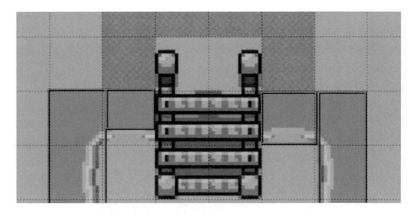

Figure 9-7. *Object layer with water in Tiled Map Editor*

Therefore, we must add at least one layer of type object to indicate these regions; in the book, we'll use two object layers, one to select the regions with water and another layer for the rest of the objects:

1. obstacles_object

2. water_object

With these layers of objects, the map is as follows.

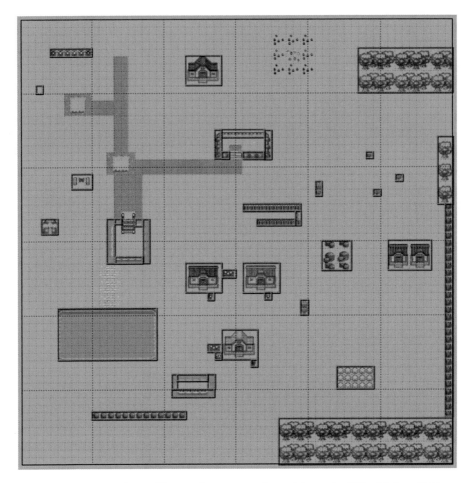

Figure 9-8. *Map with the collision layers on the objects in Tiled Map Editor*

To avoid placing the player in a position that is not valid and to be able to customize the place where we want the player to be for each map we design, we are going to add another layer of objects to indicate the position of the player:

    player_object

For the preceding map, we will place it as follows.

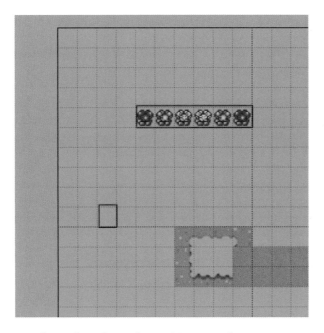

Figure 9-9. *Layer to place the player's position on the map*

Import into the Project

Now with this, we import the tmx and tsx together with the tileset in the project:

pubspec.yaml

```
assets:
  - assets/images/player.png
  - assets/images/tile.png
  - assets/tiles/map.tmx
  - assets/tiles/map.tsx
```

We change the references of the files:

assets\tiles\map.tsx

```
<?xml version="1.0" encoding="UTF-8"?>
<tileset version="1.9" tiledversion="1.9.2" name="tile" tilewidth="48"
tileheight="48" tilecount="855" columns="19">
 <image source="../images/tile.png" width="912" height="2160"/>
</tileset>
```

Finally, we create the class to load the map and add the camera to follow the player component:

lib\maps\tile_map_component.dart

```dart
import 'package:flame/collisions.dart';
import 'package:flame/components.dart';

import 'package:flame_tiled/flame_tiled.dart';

import 'package:tiled/tiled.dart';
import 'package:worldxy04/maps/tile/object_component.dart';
import 'package:worldxy04/maps/tile/water_component.dart';

class TileMapComponent extends PositionComponent {
  late TiledComponent tiledMap;

  @override
  void onLoad() async {
    tiledMap = await TiledComponent.load('map.tmx', Vector2.all(48));
    add(tiledMap);
  }
}
```

And from the main.dart, we have

lib/main.dart

```dart
import 'package:flame/collisions.dart';

import 'package:flame/game.dart';
import 'package:flame/input.dart';
import 'package:flutter/material.dart';
import 'package:flame/experimental.dart';
import 'package:flutter/material.dart';

import 'package:flame/game.dart';
import 'package:flame/input.dart';

import 'package:flame/components.dart';

import 'package:worldxy04/components/playerComponent.dart';
import 'package:worldxy04/maps/tile_map_component.dart';
```

```dart
class MyGame extends FlameGame
    with HasKeyboardHandlerComponents, HasCollisionDetection {
  final world = World();
  late final CameraComponent cameraComponent;

  @override
  void onLoad() {
    add(world);

    var background = TileMapComponent();
    world.add(background);

    background.loaded.then(
      (value) {
        cameraComponent = CameraComponent(world: world);
        cameraComponent.follow(player);
        cameraComponent.setBounds(Rectangle.fromLTRB(
            0, 0, background.tiledMap.size.x, background.tiledMap.size.y));
        cameraComponent.viewfinder.anchor = Anchor.center;

        add(cameraComponent);

        world.add(player);

      },
    );

  @override
  Color backgroundColor() {
    super.backgroundColor();
    return Colors.purple;
  }
}

void main() {
  runApp(GameWidget(
    game: MyGame(),
  ));
}
```

Base Class

In this section, we are going to create the basic classes for the player, which would be of two types. First is the **Character** base class, which we inherit and modify from the previous project to define aspects such as types of movement and animations, among other basic properties:

lib\components\character.dart

```
import 'package:flame/collisions.dart';
import 'package:flame/components.dart';

enum MovementType {
  idle,
  walkingright,
  walkingleft,
  walkingup,
  walkingdown,
  runright,
  runleft,
  runup,
  rundown,
}

class Character extends SpriteAnimationComponent
    with KeyboardHandler, CollisionCallbacks {
  MovementType movementType = MovementType.idle;

  double speed = 40;
  bool isMoving = false;

  double spriteSheetWidth = 32;
  double spriteSheetHeight = 32;

  late SpriteAnimation idleAnimation,
      leftAnimation,
      rightAnimation,
      upAnimation,
      downAnimation;
```

```
    late RectangleHitbox body;
}
```

Second is the player class, which inherits from the previous class:

```
lib\components\player_component.dart
class PlayerComponent extends Character {
  MyGame game;
  PlayerComponent({required this.game}) : super() {
    debugMode = true;
  }
}
```

Finally, we register both components in the Game class:

```
lib\main.dart

class MyGame extends ***;

  @override
  void onLoad() {
    add(world);

    var background = TileMapComponent();
    world.add(background);

    background.loaded.then(
      (value) {
        var player = PlayerComponent(
            game: this,
            mapSize: background.tiledMap.size,
            posPlayer: background.posPlayer);

        cameraComponent = CameraComponent(world: world);
        cameraComponent.follow(player);
        cameraComponent.setBounds(Rectangle.fromLTRB(
            0, 0, background.tiledMap.size.x, background.tiledMap.size.y));
        cameraComponent.viewfinder.anchor = Anchor.center;

        add(cameraComponent);
```

```
    world.add(player);
  },
 );
}
```

Animations

Based on the sprite sheet of the player used for this project, we see that it has the fragments to walk to the right and left and to walk up and down. We could use the other half of the player sprite sheet for another purpose, like throwing some power, but for now, we are interested in the implementation of the movement:

lib\components\player_component.dart

```
import 'package:flame/extensions.dart';
import 'package:flame/flame.dart';
import 'package:flame/sprite.dart';
import 'package:worldxy04/main.dart';
import 'package:worldxy04/components/character.dart';
import 'package:worldxy04/utils/create_animation_by_limit.dart';

class PlayerComponent extends Character {
  MyGame game;

  PlayerComponent({required this.game}) : super() {
    debugMode = true;
  }

  @override
  void onLoad() async {
    final spriteImage = await Flame.images.load('player.png');
    final spriteSheet = SpriteSheet(
        image: spriteImage,
        srcSize: Vector2(spriteSheetWidth, spriteSheetHeight));

    idleAnimation = spriteSheet.createAnimationByLimit(
        xInit: 0, yInit: 1, step: 1, sizeX: 3, stepTime: .2);
```

```
   downAnimation = spriteSheet.createAnimationByLimit(
      xInit: 0, yInit: 0, step: 3, sizeX: 3, stepTime: .2);
   leftAnimation = spriteSheet.createAnimationByLimit(
      xInit: 1, yInit: 0, step: 3, sizeX: 3, stepTime: .2);
   rightAnimation = spriteSheet.createAnimationByLimit(
      xInit: 2, yInit: 0, step: 3, sizeX: 3, stepTime: .2);
   upAnimation = spriteSheet.createAnimationByLimit(
      xInit: 3, yInit: 0, step: 3, sizeX: 3, stepTime: .2);

   reset();
 }

 void reset() {
   animation = idleAnimation;
   position = Vector2(spriteSheetWidth, spriteSheetHeight);
   size = Vector2(spriteSheetWidth, spriteSheetHeight);
   movementType = MovementType.idle;
 }
}
```

We keep an animation for the idle state, for which, since it doesn't exist in the sprite sheet, we use one of the walking animations instead.

Movement

For one of the most important parts of the game, we are going to vary the movement scheme, to show another implementation that is more suited to the type of game we are playing.

We implement a mobility based on fixed values when pressing the corresponding keys. For the key listener event, as in the previous project, depending on the keys or combination of keys pressed, we indicate the direction of movement; furthermore, we use an additional property called **isMoving** that indicates whether or not the player is moving. However, as we also show in the implementation, we can use the **movementType** property with the value of **MovementType.idle** and the **onKeyEvent()** function to set the type of movement:

lib\components\player_component.dart

```
@override
bool onKeyEvent(RawKeyEvent event, Set<LogicalKeyboardKey> keysPressed) {
  if (keysPressed.isEmpty) {
    movementType = MovementType.idle;
    // isMoving = false;
  }
  // else {
  //   isMoving = true;
  // }

  //**** RIGHT
  if (keysPressed.contains(LogicalKeyboardKey.arrowRight) ||
      keysPressed.contains(LogicalKeyboardKey.keyD)) {
    if (keysPressed.contains(LogicalKeyboardKey.shiftLeft)) {
      // RUN
      movementType = MovementType.runright;
    } else {
      // WALKING
      movementType = MovementType.walkingright;
    }
  } else if (keysPressed.contains(LogicalKeyboardKey.arrowLeft) ||
  //**** LEFT
      keysPressed.contains(LogicalKeyboardKey.keyA)) {
    if (keysPressed.contains(LogicalKeyboardKey.shiftLeft)) {
      // RUN
      movementType = MovementType.runleft;
    } else {
      // WALKING
      movementType = MovementType.walkingleft;
    }
  } else if (keysPressed.contains(LogicalKeyboardKey.arrowUp) || //**** TOP
      keysPressed.contains(LogicalKeyboardKey.keyW)) {
    if (keysPressed.contains(LogicalKeyboardKey.shiftLeft)) {
      // RUN
```

```
      movementType = MovementType.runup;
    } else {
      // WALKING
      movementType = MovementType.walkingup;
    }
  } else if (keysPressed
          .contains(LogicalKeyboardKey.arrowDown) || //**** BOTTOM
      keysPressed.contains(LogicalKeyboardKey.keyS)) {
    if (keysPressed.contains(LogicalKeyboardKey.shiftLeft)) {
      // RUN
      movementType = MovementType.rundown;
    } else {
      // WALKING
      movementType = MovementType.walkingdown;
    }
  }

  return true;
}
```

The following function, based on the key pressed, changes the animation of the player. Here, there is no need to rotate or flip the player using the **flipHorizontally()** function, since there is an animation for each direction the player can take:

lib\components\player_component.dart

```
void moveAnimation(double delta) {
  // if (!isMoving) return;

  movePlayer(delta);

  switch (movementType) {
    case MovementType.walkingright:
    case MovementType.runright:
      animation = rightAnimation;
      break;
    case MovementType.walkingleft:
    case MovementType.runleft:
```

```
      animation = leftAnimation;
      break;
    case MovementType.walkingup:
    case MovementType.runup:
      animation = upAnimation;
      break;
    case MovementType.walkingdown:
    case MovementType.rundown:
      animation = downAnimation;
      break;
    default: // idle
      animation = idleAnimation;
  }
}
```

Additionally, the function **moveAnimation()** invokes the function called **movePlayer()**, which is in charge of making the movement of the player on the corresponding axis:

lib\components\player_component.dart

```
void movePlayer(double delta) {
  switch (movementType) {
    case MovementType.walkingright:
    case MovementType.runright:
      position.add(Vector2(delta * speed, 0));
      break;
    case MovementType.walkingleft:
    case MovementType.runleft:
      position.add(Vector2(delta * -speed, 0));
      break;
    case MovementType.walkingup:
    case MovementType.runup:
      position.add(Vector2(0, delta * -speed));
      break;
    case MovementType.walkingdown:
    case MovementType.rundown:
```

```
    position.add(Vector2(0, delta * speed));
    break;
  case MovementType.idle:
    break;
  }
}
```

The **update()** function is in charge of calling the function **moveAnimation()**, which is in charge of calling the **movePlayer()** function that establishes the movement whenever **animation** is not **idleAnimation**:

lib\components\player_component.dart

```
@override
void update(double delta) {
  moveAnimation(delta);
  super.update(delta);
}
```

The previous cycle can be summarized in two processes, that of the **update()** function that is always being executed and updating the position of the player in case it is necessary through the **movePlayer()** function and that of the **onKeyEvent()** function that is in charge of keeping the state of the player updated, that is, if it is being moved and the direction.

In preceding implementations, there are sections of code that reference the **isMoving** property, which has the same use as using the **movementType** property, that is to say:

- If the player is moving, **isMoving** is **true**, and the value of **movementType** is other than **MovementType.idle**.

- If the player is not moving, **isMoving** is **false**, and the value of **movementType** is **MovementType.idle**.

Therefore, you can use one scheme or another according to the needs of the project.

Changes in Movement

One of the possible problems that we can have in the preceding implementation is that, even though the player is not moved and should be at rest, it always keeps moving at its current position since the animation continues to run; additionally, when finishing scrolling, the player always faces in the same direction, regardless of the direction in which they are walking; for example, if we are walking from bottom to top, when finished, the player looks like the following.

Figure 9-10. *Player, state after walking*

The same happens if you are walking from right to left or left to right.

To avoid this, we can pause the animation, although there is no method or property to do such an operation. However, we can stop the animation by setting the loop to false. Finally, the implementation looks like this:

lib\components\player_component.dart

```
class PlayerComponent extends Character {
  ***

  void moveAnimation(double delta) {
    movePlayer(delta);

    switch (movementType) {
      case MovementType.walkingright:
      case MovementType.runright:
        animation = rightAnimation;
        _resetAnimation();

        break;
      case MovementType.walkingleft:
      case MovementType.runleft:
        animation = leftAnimation;
        _resetAnimation();
```

```dart
      break;
    case MovementType.walkingtop:
    case MovementType.runtop:
      animation = topAnimation;
      _resetAnimation();

      break;
    case MovementType.walkingbottom:
    case MovementType.runbottom:
      animation = bottomAnimation;
      _resetAnimation();

      break;

    case MovementType.idle:
      animation?.loop = false;
      break;
    default:
      break;
  }
}

void _resetAnimation() {
  if (!animation!.loop) {
    animation?.loop = true;
  }
}

void movePlayer(double delta) {
  // if (!isMoving) {
  //   return;
  // }
    ***
  }
}
```

```
@override
bool onKeyEvent(RawKeyEvent event, Set<LogicalKeyboardKey> keysPressed) {
  if (keysPressed.isEmpty) {
    movementType = MovementType.idle;
    //   isMoving = false;
    // } else {
    //   isMoving = true;
  }
  ***
  }
}
```

Additionally, for when the player is idle, the animation stops, disabling the loop:

```
animation?.loop = false;
```

When starting the scroll and only at the moment of starting the scroll (that's why there's the conditional if (**!animation!.loop) {}**), the animation is looped. Finally, the animation is cloned to restart it:

```
if (!animation!.loop) {
    animation?.loop = true;
    animation = animation?.clone();
}
```

With these changes, when the player walks, the corresponding animation is activated, and when they stop pressing any key, the animation stops.

Map and Initial Collidables

In this section, we are going to use the previous map in the game; for this, apart from loading it as we showed before, we are going to specify the parts where the player cannot walk, which for the map would be the sections that have water, stones, and other objects. The player can only move where there are dirt or grass roads. For this, as we did with the tiles, we are going to create collidable-type **PositionComponents**, and in this way, coming into contact with these components prevents the player from being able to continue scrolling. Let's start by creating the components:

lib\maps\tile\water_component.dart

```dart
import 'package:flame/collisions.dart';
import 'package:flame/components.dart';

class WaterComponent extends PositionComponent {
  WaterComponent({required size, required position})
      : super(size: size, position: position) {
    debugMode = true;
    add(RectangleHitbox()..collisionType = CollisionType.passive);
  }
}
```

and

lib\maps\tile\object_component.dart

```dart
import 'package:flame/collisions.dart';
import 'package:flame/components.dart';

class ObjectComponent extends PositionComponent {
  ObjectComponent({required size, required position})
      : super(size: size, position: position) {
    debugMode = true;
    add(RectangleHitbox()..collisionType = CollisionType.passive);
  }
}
```

And we iterate through the map layers:

lib\maps\tile_map_component.dart

```dart
import 'package:worldxy04/maps/tile/object_component.dart';
import 'package:worldxy04/maps/tile/water_component.dart';

class TileMapComponent extends PositionComponent {
  late TiledComponent tiledMap;

  @override
  void onLoad() async {
    tiledMap = await TiledComponent.load('map.tmx', Vector2.all(48));
    add(tiledMap);
```

```
final objWater = tiledMap.tileMap.getLayer<ObjectGroup>("water_
object");

for (final obj in objWater!.objects) {
  add(WaterComponent(
      size: Vector2(obj.width, obj.height),
      position: Vector2(obj.x, obj.y)));
}

final objObs = tiledMap.tileMap.getLayer<ObjectGroup>("obstacles_
object");

for (final obj in objObs!.objects) {
  add(ObjectComponent(
      size: Vector2(obj.width, obj.height),
      position: Vector2(obj.x, obj.y)));
}
}
}
```

Collisions Between the Player and Objects

To handle collisions with objects and water on the map, we'll use some additional properties that

- Will let you know if there is a collision

- Will let you know what the address of the player is or what the player's direction was in the collision, that is, when the player collides with some of the objects on the map, we record the direction

We'll use an additional enum to handle addresses:

```
enum PlayerDirection { up, right, left, down }
```

You might wonder why we don't use the enum of type **MovementType** by the **movementType** property; the reason is that, with this enumeration, more than just the direction that the player faces is handled, as if they are walking or running, this would cause more problems to handle the direction. Finally, here's the code with the additional properties:

294

lib/main.dart

```
enum PlayerDirection { up, right, left, down }

class Character extends SpriteAnimationComponent
    with KeyboardHandler, CollisionCallbacks {

  PlayerDirection playerDirection = PlayerDirection.down;
  PlayerDirection? playerCollisionDirection = null;
}
```

It is important to note that the **playerCollisionDirection** property can be null; the reason for this will be explained later.

By pressing the keys, we update the **playerDirection** property and, with this, know the direction of the player:

lib\components\player_component.dart

```
@override
bool onKeyEvent(RawKeyEvent event, Set<LogicalKeyboardKey> keysPressed) {
  if (keysPressed.isEmpty) {
    movementType = MovementType.idle;
    //   isMoving = false;
    // } else {
    //   isMoving = true;
  }

  // RIGHT
  if (keysPressed.contains(LogicalKeyboardKey.arrowRight) ||
      keysPressed.contains(LogicalKeyboardKey.keyD)) {
    playerDirection = PlayerDirection.right;
    ***
  } else
  // LEFT
  if (keysPressed.contains(LogicalKeyboardKey.arrowLeft) ||
      keysPressed.contains(LogicalKeyboardKey.keyA)) {
```

```
    playerDirection = PlayerDirection.left;
    ***
  } else if (keysPressed.contains(LogicalKeyboardKey.arrowDown) ||
      keysPressed.contains(LogicalKeyboardKey.keyS)) {
    playerDirection = PlayerDirection.down;
    ***
  } else
  // LEFT
  if (keysPressed.contains(LogicalKeyboardKey.arrowUp) ||
      keysPressed.contains(LogicalKeyboardKey.keyW)) {
    playerDirection = PlayerDirection.up;
    ***
  }
  return true;
}
```

In a collision with water or an object, the current position of the player is recorded in the **playerCollisionDirection** property, which means that it is different from null and, therefore, there is a collision:

lib\components\player_component.dart

```
@override
void onCollision(Set<Vector2> points, PositionComponent other) {

  if (other is WaterComponent || other is ObjectComponent) {
    playerCollisionDirection = playerDirection;
  }

  super.onCollision(points, other);
}
```

The **playerCollisionDirection** property is reset indicating a null value. With this, we know that if **playerCollisionDirection** is null, then there is no collision and if it is different from null, then there is a collision:

```
@override
void onCollisionEnd(PositionComponent other) {

  if (other is WaterComponent || other is ObjectComponent) {
    playerCollisionDirection = null;
  }

  super.onCollisionEnd(other);
}
```

From the **movePlayer()** function, if **playerDirection** is equal to **playerCollisionDirection,** it means that there is a collision, and therefore, we interrupt the player movements:

```
void movePlayer(double delta) {
  if (playerDirection == playerCollisionDirection) {
    return;
  }
  ***
}
```

The problem with this implementation is that if the player collides on one of its sides, then movement is blocked on all sides, for example, refer to the following image.

Figure 9-11. *Collisions of the player with objects*

The player collided on the left side and therefore, the player's movements are blocked; this does not mean that the player cannot move since, pressing a different direction key in which the collision is maintained, causes the **playerCollisionDirection** property to be updated with the direction of the pressed key (and the player moves one step); for example, in the previous image, if you press the left arrow/A the player does not move, but if you press the down arrow/S or up arrow/W the player moves one step, but that movement makes it stay the collision according to the aforementioned considerations:

297

Figure 9-12. *Problems in collision with the player and objects*

But, if the key is pressed, it removes the collision; in this case, it would be the left arrow/A, so the player can move freely.

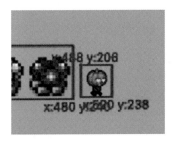

Figure 9-13. *Free yourself from the collision of the player and the object*

Another problem that exists with the preceding implementation is that, if there is a collision like the preceding one and you alternately press the left arrow/A and up arrow/W keys, the player will move and go down into the component with the collision.

Figure 9-14. *Player entering the collidable object*

Second Implementation

We are going to carry out some more tests to understand in a more practical way how the implementation should be to handle collisions between the player and the objects.

A simple way to correct the preceding problem is to convert the **playerCollisionDirection** property to a list and add the collision directions of the player:

lib\components\character.dart

```
class Character extends SpriteAnimationComponent
    with KeyboardHandler, CollisionCallbacks {
  ***
  List<PlayerDirection> playerCollisionDirection = [];
}
```

lib\components\player_component.dart

```
class PlayerComponent extends Character {
  ***

  @override
  void onCollision(Set<Vector2> points, PositionComponent other) {

    if (other is WaterComponent || other is ObjectComponent) {
      //playerCollisionDirection = playerDirection;
      if (!playerCollisionDirection.contains(playerDirection)) {
        playerCollisionDirection.add(playerDirection);
      }
    }

    super.onCollision(points, other);
  }

  @override
  void onCollisionEnd(PositionComponent other) {
    if (other is WaterComponent || other is ObjectComponent) {
      playerCollisionDirection = [];
    }
```

```
    super.onCollisionEnd(other);
  }

  void movePlayer(double delta) {
    // if (playerDirection == playerCollisionDirection) {
    if (playerCollisionDirection.contains(playerDirection)) {
      return;
    }
    ***

  }
}
```

However, this may not solve the problem that when in collision, the player can get stuck, since this largely depends on the speed of your processor as the slower it is, the less times the **onCollision()** function will be called, and with this the player hitbox can get deeper into the object in the collision.

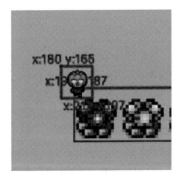

Figure 9-15. *Player entering the collidable object for the second implementation*

Therefore, the player can get stuck, because regardless of the direction it takes from the preceding collision, it will always be in collision; therefore, they will be set in the **playerCollisionDirection** list, making any player movement impossible.

To avoid this, we could evaluate each of the cases one by one when making the movement:

```
void movePlayer(double delta) {
  switch (movementType) {
    case MovementType.walkingright:
    case MovementType.runright:
```

```
    if (playerCollisionDirection.isNotEmpty &&
        playerCollisionDirection[0] == PlayerDirection.right) {
    } else {
      position.add(Vector2(delta * speed, 0));
    }

    break;
  case MovementType.walkingleft:
  case MovementType.runleft:
    if (playerCollisionDirection.isNotEmpty &&
        playerCollisionDirection[0] == PlayerDirection.left) {
    } else {
      position.add(Vector2(delta * -speed, 0));
    }

    break;
  case MovementType.walkingup:
  case MovementType.runup:
    if (playerCollisionDirection.isNotEmpty &&
        playerCollisionDirection[0] == PlayerDirection.up) {
    } else {
      position.add(Vector2(0, delta * -speed));
    }

    break;
  case MovementType.walkingdown:
  case MovementType.rundown:
    if (playerCollisionDirection.isNotEmpty &&
        playerCollisionDirection[0] == PlayerDirection.down) {
    } else {
      position.add(Vector2(0, delta * speed));
    }
    break;
  default:
    break;
  }
}
```

In the preceding implementation, to avoid asking for null values, the check for playerCollisionDirection is used beforehand:

```
playerCollisionDirection.isNotEmpty
```

With this, we can know if it contains at least one registered collision. An important factor is that the zero position is always asked in the collisions; this is because the collision in the zero position refers to the initial collision, which is what we are interested in evaluating. With the preceding implementation, some problems we had before are corrected, for example, the problem that when we alternately press the right arrow/D and down arrow/S keys, the player is inserted into the collision object.

This implementation is not perfect either, since it incorporates several problems when colliding with objects; for example, when there are two or more objects colliding with the player's hitbox, since only the first collision is taken into account (**playerCollisionDirection[0]**), we can pass over other objects attached to the object with the collision with the player.

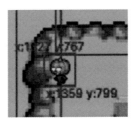

Figure 9-16. *Problems with double collision*

You are recommended to try the implementations we made before one by one and evaluate the result.

Third Implementation

As another implementation, we are going to detect the initial collision, since, as we saw in the previous implementations, it is the most important one. For this reason, we pass from a list to an **enum**:

```
lib\components\character.dart
```

```
class Character extends SpriteAnimationComponent
    with KeyboardHandler, CollisionCallbacks {
  MovementType movementType = MovementType.idle;
```

```
PlayerDirection playerDirection = PlayerDirection.down;
PlayerDirection? playerCollisionDirection = null;

double speed = 120;
bool objectCollision = false;
***
}
```

Apart from the fact that with the **objectCollision** Boolean we handle when a collision exists or not, in this implementation, it is only necessary to record when the main collision occurs:

lib\components\player_component.dart

```
class PlayerComponent extends Character {
  @override
  void onCollision(Set<Vector2> points, PositionComponent other) {

    if (other is WaterComponent || other is ObjectComponent) {
      if (!objectCollision) {
        playerCollisionDirection = playerDirection;
        objectCollision = true;
      }
    }

    super.onCollision(points, other);
  }
}
```

When the collision ends, the previous properties are restored:

lib\components\player_component.dart

```
@override
void onCollisionEnd(PositionComponent other) {
  if (other is WaterComponent || other is ObjectComponent) {
    playerCollisionDirection = null;
    objectCollision = false;
  }
```

```
    super.onCollisionEnd(other);
}
```

Finally, from the function that updates the **position** property depending on the key pressed, we are not going to allow updating said vector if the collision is maintained (**objectCollision** property) and if the direction of the collision is maintained (**playerCollisionDirection** property). It is important that, in this implementation, the **playerCollisionDirection** enum is not updated until the collision ends, and this is the fundamental difference we have from the previous implementations:

lib\components\player_component.dart

```
void movePlayer(double delta) {

  if (!(objectCollision && playerCollisionDirection == playerDirection)) {
    switch (movementType) {
      case MovementType.walkingright:
      case MovementType.runright:
        position.add(Vector2(delta * speed, 0));
        break;
      case MovementType.walkingleft:
      case MovementType.runleft:
        position.add(Vector2(delta * -speed, 0));
        break;
      case MovementType.walkingup:
      case MovementType.runup:
        position.add(Vector2(0, delta * -speed));
        break;
      case MovementType.walkingdown:
      case MovementType.rundown:
        position.add(Vector2(0, delta * speed));
        break;
      default:
        break;
    }
  }
}
```

With this implementation, in practice, when a collision occurs, the player can move freely in the other three directions, giving a better gaming experience; this implementation is one of the simplest and also the one that works best in this type of game since, for example, when the player crashes as follows

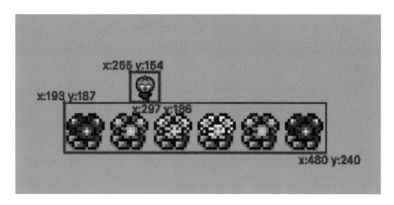

Figure 9-17. *Player collision, third scheme*

the player is allowed to scroll sideways or backward.

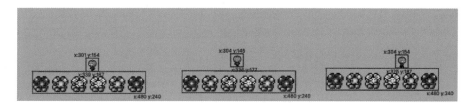

Figure 9-18. *Player collision, third scheme, operation*

And the same logic happens if the main collision happens from above, the right, or the left.

This implementation maintains the problem that, when there is a double collision, the player can traverse the second object with which it collided, as you can see in the following image.

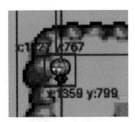

Figure 9-19. *Problem of the third implementation in handling double collision*

This is because only **the first collision is tracked**, blocking the direction of said collision, but leaving the rest of the directions free. For example, in the preceding image, the collision occurs when the player walks up, which is the one that is blocked with the following conditional:

```
if (!(playerCollisionDirection == playerDirection)) {
  ***
}
```

But, since the second object is not tracked, the result is that the player passes through the object; we will see the solution to this problem in the "fifth implementation."

Fourth Implementation

For this implementation we are not going to use the **objectCollision** property since, to know if there is a collision or not, we can use the **playerCollisionDirection**. If it is null, then there is no collision; otherwise, there is a collision:

```
import 'package:flame/collisions.dart';
import 'package:flame/components.dart';
import 'package:flame/extensions.dart';
import 'package:flame/flame.dart';
import 'package:flame/sprite.dart';
import 'package:flutter/material.dart';
import 'package:flutter/services.dart';
import 'package:worldxy04/main.dart';
import 'package:worldxy04/components/character.dart';
import 'package:worldxy04/maps/tile/object_component.dart';
import 'package:worldxy04/maps/tile/water_component.dart';
```

```
import 'package:worldxy04/utils/create_animation_by_limit.dart';

class PlayerComponent extends Character {
  ***

  void movePlayer(double delta) {
    if (!(playerCollisionDirection == playerDirection)) {
      ***
    }
  }
}
***

  @override
  void onCollision(Set<Vector2> points, PositionComponent other) {
    if (other is WaterComponent || other is ObjectComponent) {
      if (playerCollisionDirection == null) {
        playerCollisionDirection = playerDirection;
        //objectCollision = true;
      }
    }

    super.onCollision(points, other);
  }

  @override
  void onCollisionEnd(PositionComponent other) {
    if (other is WaterComponent || other is ObjectComponent) {
      playerCollisionDirection = null;
      //objectCollision = false;
    }

    super.onCollisionEnd(other);
  }
}
```

The operation is the same as that of the third implementation, but simpler since we do without a property. We can use this scheme to solve the problem of the double collision that we have pending.

Fifth Implementation: Double Collision

As a final implementation, we are going to solve the double collision problem. It is important to note that if you design the map so that the player can only collide with a single object at any time, there is no need to use the following implementation.

For the following implementation, we are going to track for two collisions. Since there is no property in the Flame API to check how many objects are colliding with the player and uniquely identify a collidable object, we are going to create an implementation from scratch.

We are going to need to handle the following properties:

lib\components\character.dart

```
PlayerDirection? playerCollisionDirection = null;
PlayerDirection? playerCollisionDirectionTwo = null;

double objectCollisionId = -1;
double objectCollisionTwoId = -1;
```

The properties

```
PlayerDirection? playerCollisionDirection = null;
PlayerDirection? playerCollisionDirectionTwo = null;
```

are going to capture the direction of the first collision and of a second collision in case it exists; if they are defined as null, there is no collision; otherwise, there is a collision.

The properties

```
double objectCollisionId = -1;
double objectCollisionTwoId = -1;
```

will capture the IDs of the objects with which the player collided, which can be of the **WaterComponent** or **ObjectComponent** type. Since there is no ID for the collision objects, we can use any other property that allows this type of behavior to be performed, for example, the position; each of these objects has a unique position on the map, since they do not overlap each other. Therefore, we can use the position of the collision object on the X or Y axis to know if the object with which the player is colliding is the same or another. If they are defined as −1, then there is no collision; if they have a positive value, then there is a collision.

In the collision function, first, we check if there is no longer a registered collision:

```
if (objectCollisionId == -1)
```

The following refers to the first collision; if there is a collision, then the ID (position) and the direction of the player at the time of the collision are recorded:

```
if (objectCollisionId == -1) {
  playerCollisionDirection = playerDirection;
  objectCollisionId = other.position.x;
}
```

If there is another collision, it is verified if it is not the one as the first collision and if a second collision has not been registered:

```
else if (objectCollisionTwoId == -1 && objectCollisionId != other.
position.x)
```

If the preceding conditional is fulfilled, it means that the player collided with two objects at the same time, like what we see in the following image.

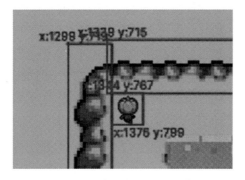

Figure 9-20. *Implementation of the fifth scheme in handling collisions with objects and the player*

So the second collision is logged:

```
else if (objectCollisionTwoId == -1 &&
      objectCollisionId != other.position.x) {
    playerCollisionDirectionTwo = playerDirection;
    objectCollisionTwoId = other.position.x;
}
```

Finally, the implementation looks like the following:

lib\components\player_component.dart

```dart
@override
void onCollision(Set<Vector2> points, PositionComponent other) {
  if (other is WaterComponent || other is ObjectComponent) {
    //fifth double collision implementation
    if (objectCollisionId == -1) {
      // first collision
      playerCollisionDirection = playerDirection;
      objectCollisionId = other.position.x;
      print(
          "First collision ${playerCollisionDirection}
          ${playerCollisionDirectionTwo} ${objectCollisionId}
          ${objectCollisionTwoId}");
    } else if (objectCollisionTwoId == -1 &&
        objectCollisionId != other.position.x) {
      playerCollisionDirectionTwo = playerDirection;
      objectCollisionTwoId = other.position.x;
      print(
          "Second collision ${playerCollisionDirection}
          ${playerCollisionDirectionTwo} ${objectCollisionId}
          ${objectCollisionTwoId}");
    }
  }

  super.onCollision(points, other);
}
```

Now, it is necessary to release the collisions. For this, we have to keep in mind that the following scenarios can occur if the player collides with two objects:

1. The second collision terminates, but the first collision remains.
   In this scenario, it is enough to reinitialize the properties that
   track the second collision, thus indicating that there is no second
   collision:

```
    if (objectCollisionTwoId == other.position.x) {
        // the second collision is ended
        playerCollisionDirectionTwo = null;
        objectCollisionTwoId = -1;
        print(
            "The second collision is ended
            ${playerCollisionDirection}
            ${playerCollisionDirectionTwo} ${objectCollisionId}
            ${objectCollisionTwoId}");
    }
```

2. The first collision terminates, but the second collision remains.
   In this scenario, the properties that track the first collision should
   track the second collision:

```
    if (objectCollisionId == other.position.x) {
        // the first collision is ended
        objectCollisionId  = objectCollisionTwoId;
        playerCollisionDirection = playerCollisionDirectionTwo;

        // the second collision is ended
        playerCollisionDirectionTwo = null;
        objectCollisionTwoId = -1;
    }
```

This is because if there is a single collision, the **playerCollisionDirection** and
objectCollisionId properties are tracked.

Having this clear, we have the following implementation:

lib\components\player_component.dart

```
@override
void onCollisionEnd(PositionComponent other) {
  if (other is WaterComponent || other is ObjectComponent) {
    playerCollisionDirection = null;
    //objectCollision = false;
    //playerCollisionDirection = [];
```

```dart
    if (objectCollisionId == other.position.x) {
      // the first collision ended
      objectCollisionId = objectCollisionTwoId;
      playerCollisionDirection = playerCollisionDirectionTwo;

      // the second collision ended
      playerCollisionDirectionTwo = null;
      objectCollisionTwoId = -1;
    print(
          "The first collision left ${playerCollisionDirection}
          ${playerCollisionDirectionTwo} ${objectCollisionId}
          ${objectCollisionTwoId}");
    } else if (objectCollisionTwoId == other.position.x) {
      // the second collision was gone
      playerCollisionDirectionTwo = null;
      objectCollisionTwoId = -1;
      print(
          "The second collision is gone ${playerCollisionDirection}
          ${playerCollisionDirectionTwo} ${objectCollisionId}
          ${objectCollisionTwoId}");
    }
  }

  super.onCollisionEnd(other);
}
```

Finally, at the moment of scrolling, the movement of the player is blocked by evaluating the values of the properties **playerCollisionDirection** and **playerCollisionDirectionTwo** with the direction of the player:

lib\components\player_component.dart

```dart
void movePlayer(double delta) {

  if (!(playerCollisionDirection == playerDirection ||
      playerCollisionDirectionTwo == playerDirection)) {
```

With this, the player will not be able to go through the collision objects as it happened before when two collisions occur at the same time. As you can see, the logic applied is the same as the one used in the "fourth implementation" but duplicating the tracking logic, that is, if we had two properties to track a collision

```
PlayerDirection? playerCollisionDirection = null;
double objectCollisionId = -1;
```

to handle two collisions, we would duplicate the preceding properties:

```
PlayerDirection? playerCollisionDirection = null;
PlayerDirection? playerCollisionDirectionTwo = null;

double objectCollisionId = -1;
double objectCollisionTwoId = -1;
```

And finally, in case it is necessary to handle the tracking of three collisions simultaneously, you simply have to create another pair of properties

```
PlayerDirection? playerCollisionDirection = null;
PlayerDirection? playerCollisionDirectionTwo = null;
PlayerDirection? playerCollisionDirectionThree = null;

double objectCollisionId = -1;
double objectCollisionTwoId = -1;
double objectCollisionThreeId = -1;
```

and adapt the preceding logic in the collision functions.

Limit Player Movement to the Map

In this section, we are going to limit the player's movements to the map, so that the player cannot move outside of it; to do this, we must pass the size of the map to the player component:

lib\main.dart

```
player = PlayerComponent(mapSize: background.tiledMap.size, game: this);
```

And every time the position property is going to be updated, we verify that it is in range:

lib\components\player_component.dart

```
class PlayerComponent extends Character {
  MyGame game;
  Vector2 mapSize;

  PlayerComponent({required this.game, required this.mapSize}) : super() {
    debugMode = true;
  }

  void movePlayer(double delta) {

    if (!(playerCollisionDirection == playerDirection ||
        playerCollisionDirectionTwo == playerDirection)) {
      switch (movementType) {
        case MovementType.walkingright:
        case MovementType.runright:
          if (position.x < mapSize.x - size.x) {
            position.add(Vector2(delta * speed, 0));
          }

          break;
        case MovementType.walkingleft:
        case MovementType.runleft:
          if (position.x > 0) {
            position.add(Vector2(delta * -speed, 0));
          }

          break;
        case MovementType.walkingup:
        case MovementType.runup:
          if (position.y > 0) {
            position.add(Vector2(0, delta * -speed));
          }
```

```
      break;
    case MovementType.walkingdown:
    case MovementType.rundown:
      if (position.y < mapSize.y - size.y) {
        position.add(Vector2(0, delta * speed));
      }
      break;
    case MovementType.idle:
      break;
    }
  }
 }
}
```

Player Position

Remember that we created a layer of objects on the map to be able to position the player; from the tile component, we create a property to record the position:

lib\maps\tile_map_component.dart

```
class TileMapComponent extends PositionComponent {
  late TiledComponent tiledMap;
  late Vector2 posPlayer;

  @override
  void onLoad() async {
    ***
    final objPlayer = tiledMap.tileMap.getLayer<ObjectGroup>("player_
    object");
    posPlayer = Vector2(objPlayer!.objects[0].x, objPlayer.objects[0].y);
  }
}
```

Once the map is loaded, the position that must be established in the player is passed:

lib\main.dart

```
background.loaded.then(
  (value) {
    player = PlayerComponent(
        mapSize: background.tiledMap.size,
        game: this,
        posPlayer: background.posPlayer);
      ***
  },
);
```

And it is set from the player component:

lib\components\player_component.dart

```
class PlayerComponent extends Character {
  MyGame game;
  Vector2 mapSize;
  Vector2 posPlayer;

  PlayerComponent(
      {required this.mapSize, required this.game, required this.posPlayer})
      : super() {
    debugMode = true;
    position = posPlayer;
  }
  void reset({bool dead = false}) {
    // position = Vector2(0, 0);
    ***
  }
}
```

Hitbox Size

For this sprite, it is not necessary to make adjustments to the player hitbox, but if you use another sprite, you can adjust it:

```
body = RectangleHitbox(size: Vector2(spriteSheetWidth,
spriteSheetHeight))..collisionType = CollisionType.active;
```

And we will have the following.

Figure 9-21. *Player hitbox*

Run

For the jogging functionality, simply increase the speed:

lib\components\player_component.dart

```
void movePlayer(double delta) {
  if (!(playerCollisionDirection == playerDirection ||
      playerCollisionDirectionTwo == playerDirection)) {
    switch (movementType) {
      case MovementType.walkingright:
      case MovementType.runright:

        if (position.x < mapSize.x - size.x) {
          position.add(Vector2(delta * speed * (movementType ==
          MovementType.runright ? 3 : 1), 0));
        }

        break;
      case MovementType.walkingleft:
      case MovementType.runleft:
```

```dart
    if (position.x > 0) {
      position.add(Vector2(delta * -speed * (movementType ==
      MovementType.runleft ? 3 : 1), 0));
    }

    break;
  case MovementType.walkingup:
  case MovementType.runup:

    if (position.y > 0) {
      position.add(Vector2(0, delta * -speed * (movementType ==
      MovementType.runup ? 3 : 1)));
    }

    break;
  case MovementType.walkingdown:
  case MovementType.rundown:
    if (position.y < mapSize.y - size.y) {
      position.add(Vector2(0, delta * speed * (movementType ==
      MovementType.rundown ? 3 : 1)));
    }
    break;
  case MovementType.idle:
    break;
  }
 }
}
```

Chapter source code:

https://github.com/libredesarrollo/flame-curso-libro-world-xy-4/ releases/tag/v0.1

CHAPTER 10

Game 3: Enemies

In this chapter, we are going to incorporate some enemies on the map. For this, they will have a mobility like that of the player; therefore, we will use the **Character** class as a base.

We are going to define the following class, where we will incorporate the necessary functionalities for the different enemies that we are going to need. For now, it will be a class with which the enemy will change movement randomly:

lib/components/eneminy_character.dart

```
import 'dart:math';

import 'package:worldxy04/components/character.dart';

class EnemyCharacter extends Character{

  void changeDirection(){
    Random random = Random();

    int newDirection = random.nextInt(4); // 0 1 2 3

    if(newDirection == 0){
      animation = downAnimation;
      playerDirection = PlayerDirection.down;
    } else if(newDirection == 1){
      animation = upAnimation;
      playerDirection = PlayerDirection.up;
    } else if(newDirection == 2) {
      animation = leftAnimation;
      playerDirection = PlayerDirection.left;
    } else if (newDirection == 3){
      animation = rightAnimation;
```

© Andrés Cruz Yoris 2024
A. Cruz Yoris, *Flame Game Development*, https://doi.org/10.1007/979-8-8688-0063-4_10

```
    playerDirection = PlayerDirection.right;
  }
 }
}
```

The preceding class inherits from **Character**; therefore, we already have the bases to manage a sprite similar to the player. The preceding class can implement other functionalities such as moving. One factor to take into account is that we can have different types of enemies such as zombies, skeletons, or soldiers, and therefore, we can make them inherit from the preceding class and vary the sprites, among other properties that you consider to customize the experience. In this example, we have a zombie enemy type:

lib/components/zombie_component.dart

```
import 'package:flame/collisions.dart';
import 'package:flame/extensions.dart';
import 'package:flame/flame.dart';
import 'package:flame/sprite.dart';

import 'package:worldxy04/components/character.dart';
import 'package:worldxy04/components/eneminy_character.dart';
import 'package:worldxy04/utils/create_animation_by_limit.dart';

class ZombieComponent extends EnemyCharacter {
  double elapseTime = 0;

  @override
  void onLoad() async {
    final spriteImage = await Flame.images.load('player.png');
    final spriteSheet = SpriteSheet(
        image: spriteImage,
        srcSize: Vector2(spriteSheetWidth, spriteSheetHeight));

    idleAnimation = spriteSheet.createAnimationByLimit(
        xInit: 0, yInit: 0, step: 4, sizeX: 8, stepTime: .2);
    downAnimation = spriteSheet.createAnimationByLimit(
        xInit: 0, yInit: 0, step: 4, sizeX: 8, stepTime: .2);
```

```
    leftAnimation = spriteSheet.createAnimationByLimit(
        xInit: 1, yInit: 0, step: 4, sizeX: 8, stepTime: .2);
    rightAnimation = spriteSheet.createAnimationByLimit(
        xInit: 2, yInit: 0, step: 4, sizeX: 8, stepTime: .2);
    upAnimation = spriteSheet.createAnimationByLimit(
        xInit: 3, yInit: 0, step: 4, sizeX: 8, stepTime: .2);

    body = RectangleHitbox(
        size: Vector2(spriteSheetWidth - 60, spriteSheetHeight - 40),
        position: Vector2(30, 20))
      ..collisionType = CollisionType.active;

    add(body);
    reset();
    //
}

void reset() {
    animation = idleAnimation;
    position = Vector2(spriteSheetWidth, spriteSheetHeight - 130);

    size = Vector2(spriteSheetWidth, spriteSheetHeight);
    // size = Vector2.all(30);
    movementType = MovementType.idle;
}

@override
void update(double dt) {
    elapseTime += dt;

    if (elapseTime > 2.0) {
        changeDirection();
        elapseTime = 0;
    }

    switch (playerDirection) {
        case PlayerDirection.down:
            position.y += speed * dt;
            break;
```

```
      case PlayerDirection.up:
        position.y -= speed * dt;
        break;
      case PlayerDirection.left:
        position.x -= speed * dt;
        break;
      case PlayerDirection.right:
        position.x += speed * dt;
        break;
    }

    super.update(dt);
  }
}
```

From the Game-type class, we add the enemy:

lib/main.dart

```
void onLoad() {
    ***
    world.add(ZombieComponent());
}
```

As you can see, the enemy has a free and random movement for a certain time of about two seconds.

The preceding implementation is far from perfect since there is only one enemy, and with the movement of the enemy being random, it can leave the map or pass over the collision objects.

Refresh the Sprite

For the sprite of the zombie component, we are going to use the following:

```
https://opengameart.org/content/zombie-and-skeleton-32x48
```

We import it:

pubspec.yaml

```
assets:
  - assets/images/zombie.png
  ***
```

And for it to have a different size than that of the player sprite, we are going to vary the size; to do this, we remove the **final** type from the **spriteSheetWidth** and **spriteSheetHeight** properties:

lib\components\character.dart

```
class Character extends SpriteAnimationComponent
    with KeyboardHandler, CollisionCallbacks {
  MovementType movementType = MovementType.idle;
  double spriteSheetWidth = 128, spriteSheetHeight = 128;
}
```

The sprite defined has a size of 32 × 64, so the previous properties are overwritten and the zombie sprite is loaded:

lib\components\zombie_component.dart

```
@override
void onLoad() async {
  spriteSheetWidth = 32;
  spriteSheetHeight = 64;
  final spriteImage = await Flame.images.load('zombie.png');

  ZombieComponent({required this.mapSize}) : super() {
    debugMode = true;
  }

  final spriteSheet = SpriteSheet(
      image: spriteImage,
      srcSize: Vector2(spriteSheetWidth, spriteSheetHeight));
```

```
    idleAnimation = spriteSheet.createAnimationByLimit(
        xInit: 0, yInit: 0, step: 3, sizeX: 3, stepTime: .2);
    downAnimation = spriteSheet.createAnimationByLimit(
        xInit: 0, yInit: 0, step: 3, sizeX: 3, stepTime: .2);
    leftAnimation = spriteSheet.createAnimationByLimit(
        xInit: 1, yInit: 0, step: 3, sizeX: 3, stepTime: .2);
    rightAnimation = spriteSheet.createAnimationByLimit(
        xInit: 2, yInit: 0, step: 3, sizeX: 3, stepTime: .2);
    upAnimation = spriteSheet.createAnimationByLimit(
        xInit: 3, yInit: 0, step: 3, sizeX: 3, stepTime: .2);
  ***

  body = RectangleHitbox(
      size: Vector2(
        spriteSheetWidth,
        spriteSheetHeight - 30,
      ),
      position: Vector2(0, 30))
    ..collisionType = CollisionType.active;
}
```

The hitbox is also updated to encompass only the sprite figure.

Collisions Between Objects and Boundaries for the Map

To handle collisions between objects and the enemy being able to leave the map, we are going to implement the same logic used for the player component. In the case of collisions, we will use the "fourth implementation":

```
class ZombieComponent extends EnemyCharacter {
  Vector2 mapSize;

  ***
  ZombieComponent({required this.mapSize}) : super() {
    debugMode = true;
  }
```

```
@override
void update(double dt) {
  elapsedTime += dt;

  if (elapsedTime > 3.0) {
    changeDirection();
    elapsedTime = 0.0;
  }

  if (playerCollisionDirection != playerDirection) {
    switch (playerDirection) {
      case PlayerDirection.down:
        if (position.y < mapSize.y - size.y) {
          position.y += speed * dt;
        }
        break;
      case PlayerDirection.left:
        if (position.x > 0) {
          position.x -= speed * dt;
        }
        break;
      case PlayerDirection.up:
        if (position.y > 0) {
          position.y -= speed * dt;
        }
        break;
      case PlayerDirection.right:
        if (position.x < mapSize.x - size.x) {
          position.x += speed * dt;
        }
        break;
    }
  }

  super.update(dt);
}
```

```
  @override
  void onCollision(Set<Vector2> points, PositionComponent other) {
    if (other is WaterComponent || other is ObjectComponent) {
      if (playerCollisionDirection == null) {
        // ??=
        playerCollisionDirection = playerDirection;
      }
    }

    super.onCollision(points, other);
  }

  @override
  void onCollisionEnd(PositionComponent other) {
    if (other is WaterComponent || other is ObjectComponent) {
      playerCollisionDirection = null;
    }

    super.onCollisionEnd(other);
  }
}
```

You can adapt the behavior of the preceding script to customize, for example, when the enemy collides with objects or map boundaries, prevent the enemy from continuing to walk and divert the direction. Finally, we pass the size of the map to the enemy component:

lib\main.dart

```
@override
void onLoad() {
  ***

  background.loaded.then(
    (value) {
      player = PlayerComponent(
          mapSize: background.tiledMap.size,
          game: this,
          posPlayer: background.posPlayer);
```

```
        world.add(ZombieComponent(mapSize: background.tiledMap.size));
        ***
    },
  );
}
```

You can place the layers in any location and in any amount you want; remember that at the end of the chapter, you have access to the source code so you can see the details of the map.

Change the Position Based on a Pattern

Apart from changing the direction of the enemy randomly, we can further customize the experience, so that it repeats based on a pattern; that is, we are going to define an array with the positions that we want the enemy to be able to move.

We begin by creating a new file with which we will manage the necessary structure to indicate the type of movement of the enemies.

We will have an enum to indicate the type of enemy:

```
enum TypeEnemy { zombie, skeleton }
```

We will have another **enum** to indicate the type of movement to use, if it is random or by pattern:

```
enum TypeEnemyMovement { random, pattern }
```

Finally, we have a list of enemies by map; this is a suggested order that you can use for your games if you have multiple maps. Based on an array of enemies, you keep the behavior that each enemy specified in the map should have; in this array that demonstratively is called **enemiesMap1** whose name refers to the enemies of map 1, they are specified based on the instance of the **BehaviorEnemy** class, the type of movement, and, in the case of patterns, the movements that the enemy must have; each element of the **enemiesMap1** array refers to an enemy on the map. Finally, here's the complete code:

`lib/helpers/enemy/movements.dart`

```dart
import 'package:worldxy04/components/character.dart';

enum TypeEnemy { zombie, skeleton }

enum TypeEnemyMovement { random, pattern }

class BehaviorEnemy {
  BehaviorEnemy(
      {this.movementEnemies = const [],
      required this.typeEnemyMovement,
      required this.typeEnemy});

  List<PlayerDirection> movementEnemies;
  TypeEnemyMovement typeEnemyMovement;
  TypeEnemy typeEnemy;
}

List<BehaviorEnemy> enemiesMap1 = [
  BehaviorEnemy(
      typeEnemyMovement: TypeEnemyMovement.random, typeEnemy: TypeEnemy.
      zombie),
  BehaviorEnemy(
      typeEnemyMovement: TypeEnemyMovement.pattern,
      typeEnemy: TypeEnemy.zombie,
      movementEnemies: [
        PlayerDirection.right,
        PlayerDirection.right,
        PlayerDirection.down,
        PlayerDirection.left,
        PlayerDirection.down,
        PlayerDirection.up,
      ]),
  BehaviorEnemy(
      typeEnemyMovement: TypeEnemyMovement.pattern,
      typeEnemy: TypeEnemy.zombie,
```

```
    movementEnemies: [
      PlayerDirection.right,
      PlayerDirection.left
    ]),
];
```

In the class of enemies, we will apply some changes indicating a property to specify the array of movements called as **movementTypes** and the type of movement that we will call as **typeEnemyMovement**:

lib/components/enemy_character.dart

```
import 'dart:math';

import 'package:worldxy04/components/character.dart';
import 'package:worldxy04/helpers/enemy/movements.dart';

class EnemyCharacter extends Character {
  EnemyCharacter(this.typeEnemyMovement, this.movementTypes);

  TypeEnemyMovement typeEnemyMovement;
  List<PlayerDirection> movementTypes;
  int newDirection = -1;

  void changeDirection() {
    if(typeEnemyMovement == TypeEnemyMovement.random){
      _changeDirectionRandom();
    }else{
      _changeDirectionPattern();
    }
  }

  void _changeDirectionRandom() {
    Random random = Random();

    newDirection = random.nextInt(4); // 0 1 2 3

    if (newDirection == 0) {
      animation = downAnimation;
```

```
      playerDirection = PlayerDirection.down;
    } else if (newDirection == 1) {
      animation = upAnimation;
      playerDirection = PlayerDirection.up;
    } else if (newDirection == 2) {
      animation = leftAnimation;
      playerDirection = PlayerDirection.left;
    } else if (newDirection == 3) {
      animation = rightAnimation;
      playerDirection = PlayerDirection.right;
    }
  }

  void _changeDirectionPattern() {
    newDirection++;

    if (newDirection >= movementTypes.length) {
      newDirection = 0;
    }

    playerDirection = movementTypes[newDirection];

    if (playerDirection == PlayerDirection.up) {
      animation = upAnimation;
    } else if (playerDirection == PlayerDirection.down) {
      animation = downAnimation;
    } else if (playerDirection == PlayerDirection.right) {
      animation = rightAnimation;
    } else if (playerDirection == PlayerDirection.left) {
      animation = leftAnimation;
    }
  }
}
```

As you can see in the preceding code, we have a new function called
_changeDirectionPattern() so that the enemy can move based on patterns, and the
original function called as **changeDirection()** is renamed as **_changeDirectionRandom()**.

Depending on the type of movement the enemy is going to have, the random or pattern movement function is called using the **changeDirection** function.

From the zombie component, we supply the two new properties of the **EnemyCharacter** base class:

lib/components/zombie_component.dart

```
class ZombieComponent extends EnemyCharacter {
  Vector2 mapSize;
  double elapsedTime = 0;

  ZombieComponent(
      {required this.mapSize,
      required movementTypes,
      required typeEnemyMovement})
      : super(typeEnemyMovement, movementTypes) {
    debugMode = true;
  }
  ***
}
```

And from main, we iterate over all the enemies for map 1 using the property called **enemiesMap1**:

lib/main.dart

```
@override
void onLoad() {
  ***

  background.loaded.then(
    (value) {
      player = PlayerComponent(
          mapSize: background.tiledMap.size,
          game: this,
          posPlayer: background.posPlayer);
      ***
```

```
    // map 1
    enemiesMap1.forEach((e) => world.add(ZombieComponent(
        mapSize: background.tiledMap.size,
        typeEnemyMovement: e.typeEnemyMovement,
        movementTypes: e.movementEnemies)
      ..position = Vector2.all(50)));
  },
  ***
);
}
```

You can customize the number of enemies as well as their behavior through the **movements.dart** file; this is an easy scheme to use for other maps, customize the experience with more enemies, or include other types of enemies. For the two enemies we have in the file

lib/helpers/enemy/movements.dart

we will have the following.

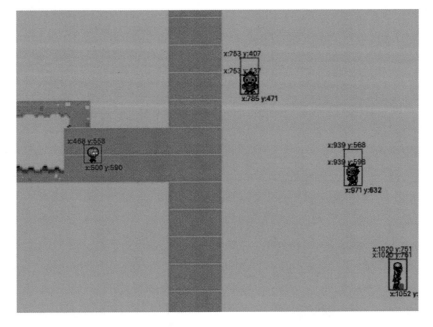

Figure 10-1. *Include enemies on the map*

Set the Object Layer for Enemies

For our map, we define the object layer in which we indicate the position of the enemies; to do this, you must edit the current map and create the enemies layer called **enemies_object**. You can create as many enemies as you want in the positions you consider.

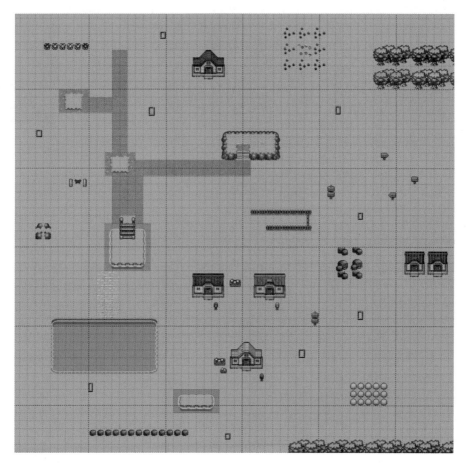

Figure 10-2. *Layer of enemies on the map*

Skeleton Class

As we mentioned before, we can have multiple classes of enemies. In the case of the sprite that we loaded earlier for the zombie, it also has a section for a skeleton that we will use in this class; otherwise, it will be exactly the same as the zombie component:

lib/components/skeleton_component.dart

```dart
import 'package:flame/collisions.dart';
import 'package:flame/components.dart';
import 'package:flame/extensions.dart';
import 'package:flame/flame.dart';
import 'package:flame/sprite.dart';

import 'package:worldxy04/components/character.dart';
import 'package:worldxy04/components/enemy_character.dart';
import 'package:worldxy04/maps/tile/object_component.dart';
import 'package:worldxy04/maps/tile/water_component.dart';
import 'package:worldxy04/utils/create_animation_by_limit.dart';

class SkeletonComponent extends EnemyCharacter {
  double elapseTime = 0;
  Vector2 mapSize;

  SkeletonComponent({required this.mapSize, required typeEnemyMovement,
  required movementTypes}) : super(typeEnemyMovement, movementTypes) {
    debugMode = true;
  }

  @override
  void onLoad() async {
    spriteSheetWidth = 32;
    spriteSheetHeight = 64;
    final spriteImage = await Flame.images
        .load('zombie_skeleton.png'); //288×256    - 288/9 = 32 x 256/4 64
    final spriteSheet = SpriteSheet(
        image: spriteImage,
        srcSize: Vector2(spriteSheetWidth, spriteSheetHeight));

    idleAnimation = spriteSheet.createAnimationByLimit(
        xInit: 0, yInit: 3, step: 6, sizeX: 9, stepTime: .2);
    downAnimation = spriteSheet.createAnimationByLimit(
        xInit: 0, yInit: 3, step: 6, sizeX: 9, stepTime: .2);
    leftAnimation = spriteSheet.createAnimationByLimit(
        xInit: 1, yInit: 3, step: 6, sizeX: 9, stepTime: .2);
```

```
  rightAnimation = spriteSheet.createAnimationByLimit(
      xInit: 2, yInit: 3, step: 6, sizeX: 9, stepTime: .2);
  upAnimation = spriteSheet.createAnimationByLimit(
      xInit: 3, yInit: 3, step: 6, sizeX: 9, stepTime: .2);

  body = RectangleHitbox(
      size: Vector2(
        spriteSheetWidth,
        spriteSheetHeight - 10,
      ),
      position: Vector2(0, 10))
    ..collisionType = CollisionType.active;

  add(body);
  reset();
}

void reset() {
  animation = idleAnimation;

  size = Vector2(spriteSheetWidth, spriteSheetHeight);
  // size = Vector2.all(30);
  movementType = MovementType.idle;
}

@override
void update(double dt) {
  elapsedTime += dt;

  if (elapsedTime > 2.0) {
    changeDirection();
    elapsedTime = 0;
  }
  if (playerCollisionDirection != playerDirection) {
    switch (playerDirection) {
      case PlayerDirection.down:
        if (position.y < mapSize.y) {
          position.y += speed * dt;
        }
```

```
          break;
        case PlayerDirection.up:
          if (position.y > 0) {
            position.y -= speed * dt;
          }
          break;
        case PlayerDirection.left:
          if (position.x > 0) {
            position.x -= speed * dt;
          }
          break;
        case PlayerDirection.right:
          if (position.x < mapSize.x) {
            position.x += speed * dt;
          }
          break;
      }
    }
    super.update(dt);
  }

  @override
  void onCollision(Set<Vector2> points, PositionComponent other) {
    if (other is WaterComponent || other is ObjectComponent) {
      if (playerCollisionDirection == null) {
        playerCollisionDirection = playerDirection;
      }
    }

    super.onCollision(points, other);
  }

  @override
  void onCollisionEnd(PositionComponent other) {
    if (other is WaterComponent || other is ObjectComponent) {
      playerCollisionDirection = null;
    }
```

```
    super.onCollisionEnd(other);
  }
}
```

Load Enemies Based on the Map

From the map component, we iterate the layer for the enemies, and we add each of the enemies according to the type in the position established on the map:

lib/map/tile_map_component.dart

```
@override
void onLoad() async {
  ***

  final objenemies = tiledMap.tileMap.getLayer<ObjectGroup>('enemies_
  object');

  for (var i = 0; i < objenemies!.objects.length; i++) {
    var e = enemiesMap1[i];
    if(e.typeEnemy == TypeEnemy.zombie){
      add(ZombieComponent(
        mapSize: tiledMap.size,
        movementTypes: e.movementEnemies,
        typeEnemyMovement: e.typeEnemyMovement)
      ..position = Vector2(objenemies.objects[i].x, objenemies.
      objects[i].y));
    }else{
      add(SkeletonComponent(
        mapSize: tiledMap.size,
        movementTypes: e.movementEnemies,
        typeEnemyMovement: e.typeEnemyMovement)
      ..position = Vector2(objenemies.objects[i].x, objenemies.
      objects[i].y));
    }
  }
}
```

Remember to remove the initialization of the position property in the enemy classes:

```
void reset() {
  // position = Vector2(300, 300);
  ***
}
```

And depending on how many objects you will place on the map for the enemies layer, place its equivalent in the **enemiesMap1** variable. That is, in the preceding example, we have nine objects defined in the enemies layer; therefore, we place nine enemies:

lib/helpers/enemy/movements.dart

```
List<BehaviorEnemy> enemiesMap1 = [
  BehaviorEnemy(
      typeEnemyMovement: TypeEnemyMovement.random, typeEnemy: TypeEnemy.
      zombie),
  BehaviorEnemy(
      typeEnemyMovement: TypeEnemyMovement.random, typeEnemy: TypeEnemy.
      skeleton),
  BehaviorEnemy(
      typeEnemyMovement: TypeEnemyMovement.random, typeEnemy: TypeEnemy.
      zombie),
  BehaviorEnemy(
      typeEnemyMovement: TypeEnemyMovement.random, typeEnemy: TypeEnemy.
      skeleton),
  BehaviorEnemy(
      typeEnemyMovement: TypeEnemyMovement.random, typeEnemy: TypeEnemy.
      skeleton),
  BehaviorEnemy(
      typeEnemyMovement: TypeEnemyMovement.random, typeEnemy: TypeEnemy.
      zombie),
  BehaviorEnemy(
      typeEnemyMovement: TypeEnemyMovement.random, typeEnemy: TypeEnemy.
      skeleton),
```

```
BehaviorEnemy(
    typeEnemyMovement: TypeEnemyMovement.pattern,
    typeEnemy: TypeEnemy.zombie,
    movementEnemies: [
      PlayerDirection.right,
      PlayerDirection.right,
      PlayerDirection.down,
      PlayerDirection.left,
      PlayerDirection.down,
      PlayerDirection.up,
    ]),
  BehaviorEnemy(
    typeEnemyMovement: TypeEnemyMovement.pattern,
    typeEnemy: TypeEnemy.skeleton,
    movementEnemies: [
      PlayerDirection.right,
      PlayerDirection.left
    ]),
];
```

Chapter source code:

https://github.com/libredesarrollo/flame-curso-libro-world-xy-4/releases/tag/v0.2

CHAPTER 11

Game 4: Plants vs. Zombies

This game is based on the famous game called *Plants vs. Zombies*, in which we will see the main characteristics that this game has:

- Different types of collisions between

  - Zombies and plants

  - Zombies with the projectiles ejected from the plants

- Placing objects (for this game it would be the **SpriteComponent** represented by the plants) at specific locations on the map

In case you don't know it, I recommend that you install it on your Android and/or iOS device and play the game.

Map

Let's start the game by defining the map that we are going to use; as with the other projects, we'll be using Tiled Map Editor for the map.

Define the Map

It is time to create a map for our game; for its design, we must understand that we must separate the map into two parts:

- On the left side is where our plants will be.

- On the right side is where the zombies will come out.

© Andrés Cruz Yoris 2024
A. Cruz Yoris, *Flame Game Development*, https://doi.org/10.1007/979-8-8688-0063-4_11

We create a new map like the following.

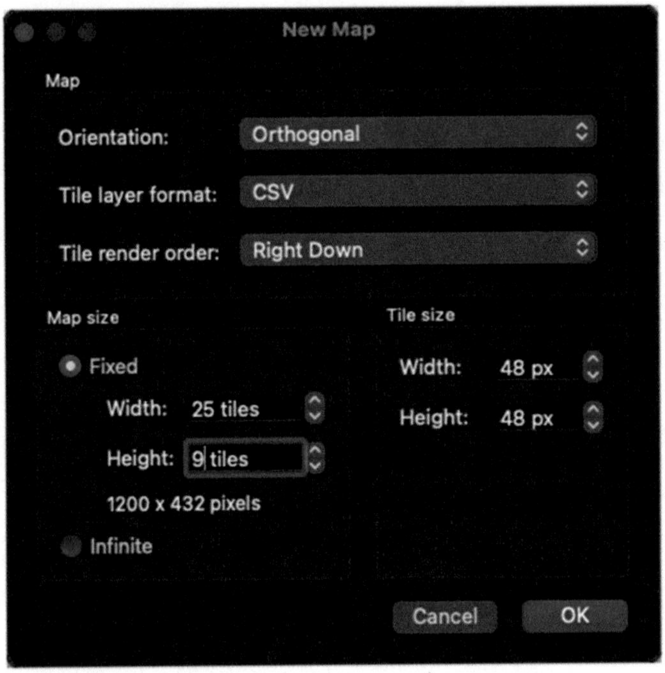

Figure 11-1. *Settings for the new map*

In this map, we will use the same tileset from the previous project:

`https://limezu.itch.io/serenevillagerevamped`

The map is going to be divided into sections, which are the places where we can sow or place our plants. Of course, we can place obstacles so that there are sections in which plants cannot be placed and other objects can be placed and, with this, customize the experience on each map. Let's start by renaming the current layer of type pattern to **floor** and placing the whole tile in green.

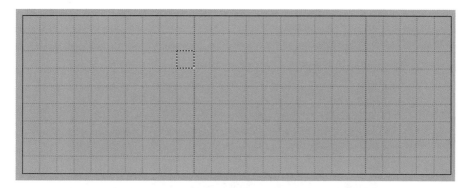

Figure 11-2. *Base layer for the map in Tiled Map Editor*

We create another layer of type pattern to place the objects called **objects.**

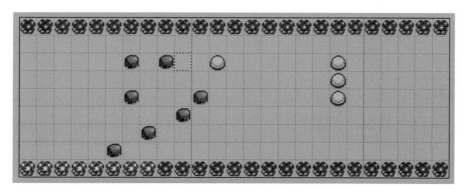

Figure 11-3. *Objects on the map in Tiled Map Editor*

We create a layer of type object called **seed** that indicates the sections where it is possible to sow and place the plants. Finally, the map looks like the following.

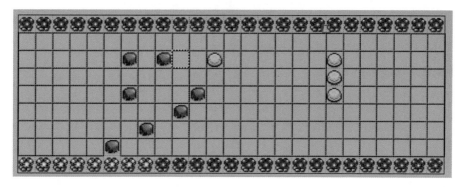

Figure 11-4. *Seed layer on the map*

To make the objects completely aligned and the same size, hold down the Ctrl key when making the selection.

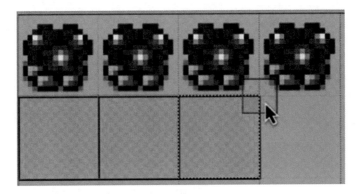

Figure 11-5. *Draw the seed layer on the map*

Add the **flame_tiled** package and reference the files:

pubspec.yaml

```
dependencies:
  flutter:
    sdk: flutter

  ***
  flame:
  flame_tiled:
```

***

```
  assets:
    - assets/images/PlantPeashooter.png
    - assets/images/PlantCactus.png
    - assets/images/tile.png
    - assets/tiles/map.tmx
    - assets/tiles/map.tsx
```

Load the Map

As in previous projects, we load the map into the game:

lib/map/tile_map_component.dart

```
import 'dart:async';

import 'package:flame/components.dart';
import 'package:flame_tiled/flame_tiled.dart';

class TileMapComponent extends PositionComponent {
  late TiledComponent tiledMap;

  @override
  void onLoad() async {

    tiledMap = await TiledComponent.load('map.tmx', Vector2.all(48));
    add(tiledMap);
  }
}
```

And we add from the main:

lib/main.dart

```
void onLoad() {
  var background = TileMapComponent();
  add(background);
  super.onLoad();
}
```

If we run the application, we will see the map in the window.

Plants

In this section, we will develop the most important layer of the game, which would be that of the plants; we will create a flexible scheme in which we can use multiple types of plants for the game.

Sprites

Let's start by creating a project called **plantvszombie05** into which we import the following sprites

- www.freepik.es/vector-gratis/caritas-mazana_869533.htm
- www.freepik.com/free-vector/hand-drawn-emotes-elements-collection_34305334.htm

which, respectively, we will call as

- PlantCactus.png
- PlantPeashooter.png

The images whose name begins with the prefix "Plant" are for plants. We chose plants with linear movements (no catapults) since they have an easier implementation in the attack that will be carried out.

The preceding sprites have unused background colors and states that are recommended to be removed using an image editing program such as GIMP; you can check the source code and get the edited images of the project in case you don't want to do the process. Also remember that you can use any other type of sprite in case the ones presented are not to your liking and adjust the sizes of the images used.

We import them into the project:

pubspec.yaml

```
assets:
  - assets/images/PlantPeashooter.png
  - assets/images/PlantCactus.png
```

Base Classes

We are going to create a base class for the plants, which need to have two states: at rest and when they fire. We also define the ticker to control the firing animation and its update in the **update()** function:

lib/components/plants/plant_component.dart

```
import 'package:flame/collisions.dart';
import 'package:flame/components.dart';
```

346

```dart
class PlantComponent extends SpriteAnimationComponent with
CollisionCallbacks {
  double spriteSheetWidth = 50;
  double spriteSheetHeight = 50;

  late SpriteAnimationTicker shootAnimationTicker;

  late SpriteAnimation idleAnimation;
  late SpriteAnimation shootAnimation;

  late RectangleHitbox body;

  PlantComponent() : super() {
    debugMode = true;
    // scale = Vector2.all(3);
  }

  @override
  void update(double dt) {
   shootAnimationTicker.update(dt);
   super.update(dt);
  }

}
```

Logically the plants do not need to move nor handle collisions, and that is why this class is much simpler than the one of previous projects.

We implement two classes for plants, in which we have the initialization of the animations and the collision box. The peashooter class looks like the following:

lib/components/plants/peashooter_component.dart

```dart
import 'package:flame/collisions.dart';
import 'package:flame/extensions.dart';
import 'package:flame/flame.dart';
import 'package:flame/sprite.dart';

import 'package:plantvszombie05/components/plants/plant_component.dart';
import 'package:plantvszombie05/utils/create_animation_by_limit.dart';
```

```
class PeashooterComponent extends PlantComponent {

  PeashooterComponent({required sizeMap, required position})
      : super(sizeMap, position) {
    spriteSheetWidth = 433;
    spriteSheetHeight = 433;
    size = Vector2(30, 30);
  }

  @override
  void onLoad() async {

    final spriteImage = await Flame.images.load('PlantPeashooter.png');
    final spriteSheetIdle = SpriteSheet(
        image: spriteImage,
        srcSize: Vector2(spriteSheetWidth, spriteSheetHeight));

    idleAnimation = spriteSheetIdle.createAnimationByLimit(
        xInit: 0, yInit: 0, step: 3, sizeX: 3, stepTime: .2);
    shootAnimation = spriteSheetIdle.createAnimationByLimit(
        xInit: 1, yInit: 0, step: 3, sizeX: 3, stepTime: .8);

    animation = idleAnimation;

    shootAnimationTicker = shootAnimation.createTicker();

    body = RectangleHitbox();
    add(body);

    super.onLoad();
  }
}
```

For the sprite sheet, a different size is used (**spriteSheetWidth-2**), and therefore the shoot state is loaded using another variable. Also remember to copy the utility file called **create_animation_by_limit.dart** to load the animations.

Here's the code for the cactus component:

lib/components/plants/cactus_component.dart

```dart
import 'package:flame/collisions.dart';
import 'package:flame/extensions.dart';
import 'package:flame/flame.dart';
import 'package:flame/sprite.dart';

import 'package:plantvszombie05/components/plants/plant_component.dart';
import 'package:plantvszombie05/utils/create_animation_by_limit.dart';

class CactusComponent extends PlantComponent {
  CactusComponent({required sizeMap, required position})
      : super(sizeMap, position) {
    spriteSheetWidth = 1000;
    spriteSheetHeight = 1000;
    size = Vector2(40, 40);
  }

  @override
  void onLoad() async {

    final spriteImage = await Flame.images.load('PlantCactus.png');
    final spriteSheet = SpriteSheet(
        image: spriteImage,
        srcSize: Vector2(spriteSheetWidth, spriteSheetHeight));

    idleAnimation = spriteSheet.createAnimationByLimit(
        xInit: 0, yInit: 0, step: 3, sizeX: 3, stepTime: .2);
    shootAnimation = spriteSheet.createAnimationByLimit(
        xInit: 0, yInit: 1, step: 3, sizeX: 3, stepTime: .8);
    animation = shootAnimation;

    body = RectangleHitbox(/*size: Vector2(spriteSheetWidth,
    spriteSheetHeight)*/);
    add(body);

    super.onLoad();
  }
}
```

And here's for the Game-type class:

`lib/main.dart`

```dart
import 'package:flame/input.dart';
import 'package:flutter/material.dart';

import 'package:flame/game.dart';

import 'package:plantvszombie05/components/plants/cactus_component.dart';
import 'package:plantvszombie05/components/plants/peashooter_
component.dart';

class MyGame extends FlameGame with HasCollisionDetection{
  @override
  void onLoad() {
    super.onLoad();
    addPlant();
  }

  void addPlant() {
    // add(PeashooterComponent());
    add(CactusComponent()..position = Vector2(position.dx, position.dy));
  }

  @override
  Color backgroundColor() {
    super.backgroundColor();
    return Colors.purple;
  }
}

void main() {
  runApp(GameWidget(game: MyGame()));
}
```

FlameGame: Add One Plant by Tap

One of the features that the game has is that by tapping an empty space on the screen, a plant is added. For now, let's implement the logic in the Game-type class. When tapping on the screen, a plant is added in the position where the tap was made:

lib/main.dart

```
class MyGame extends FlameGame with HasCollisionDetection, TapDetector {
  ***

  void addPlant(Offset position) {
    // add(PeashooterComponent());
    add(CactusComponent()..position = Vector2(position.dx, position.dy));
  }

  @override
  void onLoad() {
    super.onLoad();
  }

  @override
  void onTapDown(TapDownInfo info) {
    addPlant(info.raw.localPosition);
    super.onTapDown(info);
  }
}
```

As you can see, in the **info** argument, we have information about the touch such as the position; you can place a breakpoint and evaluate the **onTapDown** property.

Tap on the screen, and you see something like the following.

Figure 11-6. *Plant added with a touch*

Component: Add a Plant by Tap

With the map already defined and the layers available to plant the plants, the next goal is to be able to add the plants in the grids defined on the map.

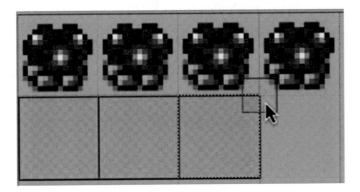

Figure 11-7. *Parts for planting plants*

For this, the idea is that the user can tap anywhere in the grids and the plant is always aligned and that the plant can only be added in these grids.

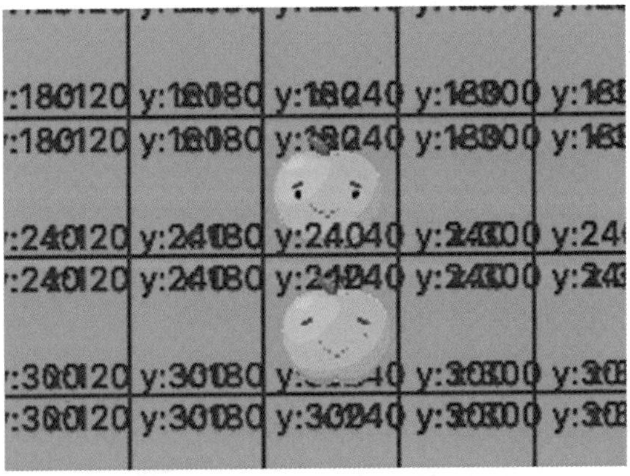

Figure 11-8. *Planted plants*

For this, we can use a Flame component to facilitate this entire process and detect the tap event in said components; for each grid defined in the **seed** layer of our map, we are going to place a component like the following:

lib/map/seed_component.dart

```
import 'package:flame/collisions.dart';
import 'package:flame/components.dart';

import 'package:flame/events.dart';
import 'package:plantvszombie05/main.dart';

class SeedComponent extends PositionComponent with TapCallbacks {
  MyGame game;
  SeedComponent({required size, required position, required this.game})
      : super(size: size, position: position) {
    debugMode = true;

    add(RectangleHitbox()..collisionType = CollisionType.passive);
  }

  @override
  void onTapDown(TapDownEvent event) {
    //info.raw.localPosition
    game.addPlant(position);
    super.onTapDown(event);
  }
}
```

In the implementation, we change from

```
info.raw.localPosition
```

to

```
game.addPlant(position);
```

so that, when adding the plant, it is completely aligned and is not placed in the position where the tap was made.

From the **seed** object layer, add the preceding component:

lib/map/tile_map_component.dart

```
import 'dart:async';
import 'package:flame/components.dart';
```

```dart
import 'package:flame_tiled/flame_tiled.dart';
import 'package:plantvszombie05/main.dart';
import 'package:plantvszombie05/map/seed_component.dart';

class TileMapComponent extends PositionComponent {
  late TiledComponent tiledMap;
  MyGame game;

  TileMapComponent({required this.game});

  @override
  void onLoad() async {

    tiledMap = await TiledComponent.load('map.tmx', Vector2.all(48));
    add(tiledMap);

    final objSeed = tiledMap.tileMap.getLayer<ObjectGroup>('seed');

    for (var obj in objSeed!.objects) {
      add(SeedComponent(
          size: Vector2(obj.width, obj.height),
          position: Vector2(obj.x, obj.y),
          game: game
          ));
    }

  }
}
```

As you can see, the preceding instances (the **TileMapComponent** and **SeedComponent** components) receive an instance of the Game class, which is necessary to be able to call the **addPlant()** function defined in the **FlameGame** class. So from main we have

lib/main.dart

```dart
class MyGame extends FlameGame
    with HasCollisionDetection, HasTappablesBridge /*TapDetector*/ {
  @override
```

```
void onLoad() {
  var background = TileMapComponent(game: this);
  add(background);
  super.onLoad();
}

void addPlant(Vector2 position, Vector2 sizeSeed) {
  add(CactusComponent()..position = Vector2(position.x, position.y));
}

// @override
// void onTapDown(TapDownInfo info) {
//   addPlant(info.raw.localPosition);
//   super.onTapDown(info);
// }
}
```

It is also important to note that we removed the **TapDetector** mixin to be able to use tap at the component level and added the **HasTappablesBridge** mixin to allow the tap event to be used from components.

Seed Size

Another problem to fix is that the size of the plant sprites does not match the size of the grids, that is, the size of the **SeedComponent**. To solve this, we can pass the size of the component:

lib/map/seed_component.dart

```
import 'package:flame/collisions.dart';
import 'package:flame/components.dart';
import 'package:flame/events.dart';
import 'package:plantvszombie05/main.dart';

class SeedComponent extends PositionComponent with TapCallbacks {
  ***
```

```
  @override
  void onTapDown(TapDownEvent event) {
    game.addPlant(position, size);
    super.onTapDown(event);
  }
}
```

And from the **main.dart**, we calculate the factor to know by how much we need to scale the plant:

lib/main.dart

```
void addPlant(Vector2 position, Vector2 sizeSeed) {
  var p = PeashooterComponent()..position = Vector2(position.x,
  position.y);

  var fac = sizeSeed.y / p.size.y;
  p.size *= fac;
  add(p);
}
```

This is a problem that exists with the image sprites that we are using, which have different sizes and are smaller than the size of the map grid. In order to have a better visualization, a calculation is made like the following:

Suppose that the size of the tile is 50 and the floor is 25, that is, the tile is twice the size of the image. To make this calculation, we must perform the following division:

$$50/25 = 2$$

And we already have the scale factor that we use to resize the image, and it is applied to the **size** property.

Avoid Adding Several Plants in One Place

To avoid planting multiple plants in one place, we'll create a Boolean property on the SeedComponent that we set to **true** when placing a plant and check the state of that property before adding a plant:

`lib\maps\seed_component.dart`

```
class SeedComponent extends PositionComponent with TapCallbacks {
  ***
  bool sown = false;

  @override
  void onTapDown(TapDownEvent event) {
    if (!sown) {
      ***
      if (game.addPlant(position, size)) {
        sown = true;
      }
    }
    super.onTapDown(event);
  }
}
```

There can be multiple reasons it is not possible to add more plants; they depend on the logic that you want to implement. In the original game, you can't add more plants if you don't have enough suns; this logic will be done in the **FlameGame** class. Therefore, if the function returns **true**, the plant is added; otherwise, it is not added:

`lib/ main.dart`

```
void addPlant(Vector2 position, Vector2 sizeSeed) {
 ***
 return true;
}
```

As you can see in the implementation in the **SeedComponent**, the **sown** property, which indicates that a plant was seeded, is set to **true** if the **addPlant()** function returns **true**, which means that the plant was added.

Zombies

In this section, we will implement the second crucial element in the game (besides the plants), which is the zombies; just like with plants, we'll use more than one type of zombie in order to create a flexible scheme where we can easily adapt it with other zombie types.

We will use the following sprites for the zombies

- www.gameart2d.com/the-zombies-free-sprites.html

which, respectively, we will call as

- ZombieMale.png

- ZombieFemale.png

The preceding images were modified to add an extra state for when the zombie is injured as well as generate a sprite sheet. You can use any other sprite in case this one is not to your liking.

And we import them into the project:

pubspec.lock

```
assets:
  - assets/images/ZombieMale.png
  - assets/images/ZombieFemale.png
```

Base Classes

As with the plants, we'll create a base class that defines the zombie's base properties and functions:

lib\components\zombies\zombie_component.dart

```
import 'package:flame/collisions.dart';
import 'package:flame/components.dart';

class ZombieComponent extends SpriteAnimationComponent {
  late SpriteAnimation walkingAnimation;
  double speed = 15;
  double spriteSheetWidth = 430;
```

```dart
double spriteSheetHeight = 519;

late RectangleHitbox body;

ZombieComponent(position) : super(position: position) {
  debugMode = true;
  scale = Vector2.all(1);
}

@override
void update(double dt) {
  position.add(Vector2(-dt * speed, 0));
  super.update(dt);
}
}
```

The preceding class defines properties for the walking animation, sprite size, and zombie movement whose speed factor is the **speed** property that you can customize for each zombie. The implementation is similar to the one used in the sprites in previous projects, and the fundamental difference is the movement, which only moves on the X axis in a single direction:

```dart
position.add(Vector2(-dt * speed, 0));
```

Here are the zombie classes for the sprites defined previously:

lib\components\zombies\zombie_male_component.dart

```dart
import 'dart:async';

import 'package:flame/collisions.dart';
import 'package:flame/flame.dart';
import 'package:flame/input.dart';
import 'package:flame/sprite.dart';

import 'package:plantvszombie05/components/zombies/zombie_component.dart';
import 'package:plantvszombie05/utils/create_animation_by_limit.dart';
class ZombieMaleComponent extends ZombieComponent {
  ZombieMaleComponent({required position}) : super(position) {
    spriteSheetWidth = 430;
```

```
    spriteSheetHeight = 519;
    size = Vector2(37, 56);

    speed = 15;
  }

  @override
  void onLoad() async{

    final spriteImage = await Flame.images.load('ZombieMale.png');

    final spriteSheet = SpriteSheet(image: spriteImage,
    srcSize: Vector2(spriteSheetWidth,spriteSheetHeight));

    walkingAnimation = spriteSheet.createAnimationByLimit(
        xInit: 2, yInit: 0, step: 8, sizeX: 4, stepTime: .2);

    animation = walkingAnimation;

    body = RectangleHitbox()..collisionType = CollisionType.active;
    add(body);
  }
}
```

and

lib\components\zombies\zombie_female_component.dart

```
import 'dart:async';

import 'package:flame/collisions.dart';
import 'package:flame/flame.dart';
import 'package:flame/input.dart';
import 'package:flame/sprite.dart';

import 'package:plantvszombie05/components/zombies/zombie_component.dart';
import 'package:plantvszombie05/utils/create_animation_by_limit.dart';

class ZombieFemaleComponent extends ZombieComponent {
  ZombieFemaleComponent({required position}) : super(position) {
    spriteSheetWidth = 521;
```

```
    spriteSheetHeight = 576;
    size = Vector2(37, 56);
  }

@override
void onLoad() async{

  final spriteImage = await Flame.images.load('ZombieFemale.png');

  final spriteSheet = SpriteSheet(image: spriteImage,
  srcSize: Vector2(spriteSheetWidth,spriteSheetHeight));

  eatingAnimation = spriteSheet.createAnimationByLimit(
      xInit: 0, yInit: 0, step: 8, sizeX: 3, stepTime: .2);
  walkingAnimation = spriteSheet.createAnimationByLimit(
      xInit: 3, yInit: 3, step: 10, sizeX: 3, stepTime: .2);
  walkingHurtAnimation = spriteSheet.createAnimationByLimit(
      xInit: 6, yInit: 0, step: 9, sizeX: 3, stepTime: .2);
  animation = walkingAnimation;

  body = RectangleHitbox()..collisionType = CollisionType.active;
  add(body);
  }
}
```

Level Enemies/Zombies

In this section, we are going to define the zombies that will appear in each of the levels, that is, by map. To do this, we will follow the same organization that we did with the enemies in the previous project, but adapted to this project.

We will create an enum to handle the types of zombies, which are only two, the male and the female:

```
enum TypeEnemy { zombie1, zombie2 }
```

You can customize the preceding names. Now, here's the class, with the necessary properties to create a zombie enemy, which would be the position and the type:

```
class BehaviorEnemy {
  int position;
  TypeEnemy typeEnemy;
  BehaviorEnemy({required this.position, required this.typeEnemy});
}
```

The position is a very important factor since, depending on the map, we are going to have more or fewer places where the zombies appear. The map we are using in the book has seven channels where zombies can walk.

Figure 11-9. *Channels on the map where the zombies pass*

Each of these channels measures 48 pixels according to the tileset used to generate the map. So thinking about this, first, we create a property with which the size of each tile is indicated:

```
const sizeTileMap = 48;
```

With this, you can create the property with which we are going to have all the enemies. Finally, here's the complete code:

```
lib\helpers\enemies\movements.dart
```

```dart
enum TypeEnemy { zombie1, zombie2 }

const sizeTileMap = 48;

class BehaviorEnemy {
  int position;
  TypeEnemy typeEnemy;
  BehaviorEnemy({required this.position, required this.typeEnemy});
}

List<BehaviorEnemy> enemiesMap1 = [
  BehaviorEnemy(typeEnemy: TypeEnemy.zombie1, position: 4 * sizeTileMap),
  BehaviorEnemy(typeEnemy: TypeEnemy.zombie2, position: 1 * sizeTileMap),
  BehaviorEnemy(typeEnemy: TypeEnemy.zombie1, position: 2 * sizeTileMap),
  BehaviorEnemy(typeEnemy: TypeEnemy.zombie1, position: 3 * sizeTileMap),
  BehaviorEnemy(typeEnemy: TypeEnemy.zombie2, position: 4 * sizeTileMap),
  BehaviorEnemy(typeEnemy: TypeEnemy.zombie1, position: 5 * sizeTileMap),
  BehaviorEnemy(typeEnemy: TypeEnemy.zombie2, position: 6 * sizeTileMap),
  BehaviorEnemy(typeEnemy: TypeEnemy.zombie2, position: 7 * sizeTileMap),
];
```

From the main, every so often (in this example, every three seconds) a zombie is added to the map (you could also establish one more option in the preceding list to indicate how long you want to add the zombie):

```
lib/main.dart
```

```dart
double elapsedTime = 0.0;
int zombieI = 0;
```

```
@override
void update(double dt) {
  if (elapsedTime > 3.0) {
    if (zombieI < enemiesMap1.length) {
      if (enemiesMap1[zombieI].typeEnemy == TypeEnemy.zombie1) {
        add(ZombieMaleComponent(
            position: Vector2(background.tiledMap.size.x,
                enemiesMap1[zombieI].position - alignZombie)));
      } else {
        add(ZombieFemaleComponent(
            position: Vector2(background.tiledMap.size.x,
                enemiesMap1[zombieI].position - alignZombie)));
      }
      zombieI++;
    }
    elapsedTime = 0.0;
  }
  elapsedTime += dt;
  super.update(dt);
}
```

The **alignZombie** variable is defined in the zombie component:

lib\components\zombies\zombie_component.dart

```
const double alignZombie = 20;
class ZombieComponent{***}
```

It is important to note that the width of the map is used to locate the initial position of the zombie, which is on the right side; also, a constant number is subtracted, in this case 20 defined by the **alignZombie** variable set in the base class for the zombie that allows repositioning the zombie since the zombie is bigger than the tile. Finally we will have the following.

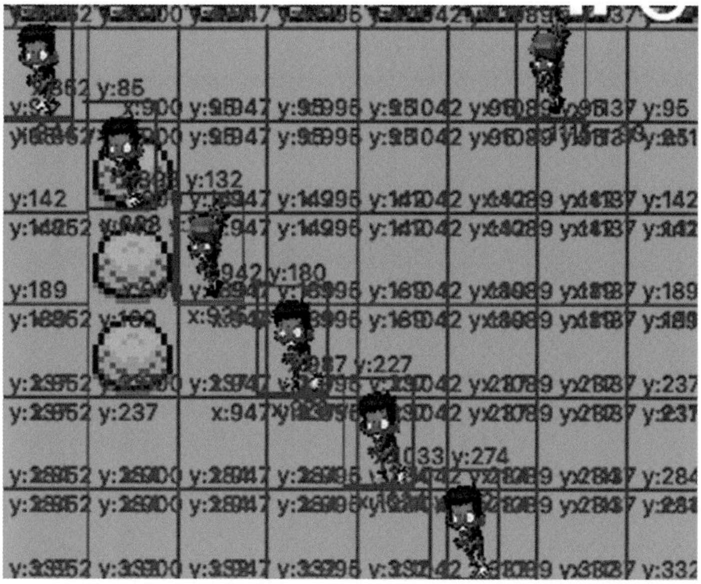

Figure 11-10. *Zombies in the channel*

One factor that you have to take into account is the position of the zombie. As we indicated before, each zombie is in a channel, and the plants that are in that channel, upon detecting that there is a zombie, begin to attack. These implementations will be carried out in the following sections.

Define Logic for Channels

In this section, we are going to divide the map into channels. As we presented previously, we must divide the map into channels through which we must detect when there are zombies so that the plants start the attack, keeping in mind the division we made for the channels in Figure 11-9.

This division will be logical; therefore, through code we will determine when there are zombies present in the channels and it will not be necessary to make any changes to the map.

In the **ZombieComponent** base class, we'll create a function called **_setChannel()** with which we'll check what the zombie's position is and then occupy or free the channel depending on whether there are zombies in the channel or not; in this simple way, we can determine when a channel is taken:

lib\components\zombies\zombie_component.dart

```
class ZombieComponent extends SpriteAnimationComponent with
CollisionCallbacks {
  ***

  @override
  void update(double dt) {
    position.add(Vector2(-dt * speed, 0));

    if (position.x <= -size.x) {
      print(position.x.toString());
      // the zombie reaches the end
      _setChannel(false);
      removeFromParent();
    }
    super.update(dt);
  }

  @override
  void onCollision(Set<Vector2> intersectionPoints, PositionComponent other) {
    if (other is SeedComponent) _setChannel(true);
    super.onCollision(intersectionPoints, other);
  }

  _setChannel(bool value) {
    if (position.y + alignZombie == 48) {
      enemiesInChannel[0] = value;
    } else if (position.y + alignZombie == 96) {
      enemiesInChannel[1] = value;
    } else if (position.y + alignZombie == 144) {
      enemiesInChannel[2] = value;
    } else if (position.y + alignZombie == 192) {
      enemiesInChannel[3] = value;
    } else if (position.y + alignZombie == 240) {
      enemiesInChannel[4] = value;
    } else if (position.y + alignZombie == 288) {
      enemiesInChannel[5] = value;
```

```
  } else if (position.y + alignZombie == 336) {
    enemiesInChannel[6] = value;
  }

  print(enemiesInChannel.toString());
}

@override
void onRemove() {
  _setChannel(false);
  super.onRemove();
}
}
```

The _**setChannel()** function sets a channel as taken/free:

- When there is a collision between the zombie and the tile/**SeedComponent**, the channel is taken (**onCollision()** function).

- When the collision between the channel and the zombie no longer exists, the channel is set to released; when the zombie crosses the map without being killed (**position.x <= -size.x**), the channel is released. The size of the zombie is used as a factor to know when the zombie is no longer in contact with the channel (function **update()**).

Regarding the **onCollisionEnd()** function, since a channel is made up of multiple tiles assigned to the **SeedComponent**, which are used to detect collisions and, with this, for the control of the channels specified before, in practice, when exiting a tile, a collision would end, but if next to that tile there is another tile, the zombie would be in collision again; in practice, you will be updating the channel incorrectly.

Finally, the updating of the channels is done in a variable called **enemiesInChannel**; this variable is essential to know at all times if the channel is occupied or not and with this determine the control of the plants. Finally, we define **enemiesInChannel** within the base component of the zombie:

lib\helpers\enemies\movements.dart

***

```
const channelsMap1 = 7;
List enemiesInChannel = List.generate(channelsMap1, (index) => false);
```

Therefore, by consulting the variable, the status of the channel is known, whether it is busy or not.

It is important to note that, when removing the zombie using the function

```
removeFromParent();
```

the **OnRemove()** function is called, so we can use it to reset the channel:

```
@override
void onRemove() {
  _setChannel(false);
  super.onRemove();
}
```

Attacks

In this section, we are going to work on the attack of the plants. We vary the animation when detecting at least one zombie in the channel in which the plant is planted, where it goes into attack mode.

Figure 11-11. *The plant attacks the zombie*

In addition, we implement the following functionalities:

- Shoot the projectile from the plant.

- Handle collisions between the projectile and zombie.

- Handle collisions between the zombie and the plants.

- Reduce the life of the zombie and the plant.

Change Animation of Plants in Attack Mode

Let's start by implementing the functionality to change the animation when detecting a zombie in the channel where the plant is planted. For this, in the **PlantComponent** we will implement the revision of the **enemiesInChannel** array that we implemented in the previous section to know in which channels there are zombies:

lib/components/plants/plant_component.dart

```
enum State { idle, shoot }

class PlantComponent extends Plant {
  double elapsedTime = 0;

  State state = State.idle;

  ***

  @override
  void update(double dt) {
    if (enemiesInChannel[(y / sizeTileMap).toInt() - 1]) {
      // hay enemigos en en canal
      if (state != State.shoot) {
        animation = shootAnimation;
      }
      state = State.shoot;
    } else {
      if (state != State.idle) {
        animation = idleAnimation;
      }
      state = State.idle;
    }
}
```

Since the **PlantComponent** class is a component that inherits from **PositionComponent**, you can directly access the position with

x

y

instead of accessing through

```
position.x
position.y
```

Projectile: Create Structure

In this section we are going to implement the plant projectiles, which are ejected from the plants when they are in attack mode as we show in Figure 11-11.

Let's start by defining the logic to handle a projectile, which will be a sprite handled from a **SpriteComponent** in order to handle collision logic as well as movement:

```
lib\components\plants\projectile_component.dart

import 'package:flame/components.dart';

class ProjectileComponent extends SpriteComponent {
  final Sprite projectile;
  final double speed;
  final Vector2 sizeMap;

  ProjectileComponent(
      {required this.projectile, required this.sizeMap, this.speed = 120})
      : super(size: Vector2.all(20), sprite: projectile) {
    add(RectangleHitbox());
  }
}
```

In the preceding code, there are properties to handle the sprite of the projectile, the speed, as well as the size of the map, respectively. We will use the following projectiles.

Figure 11-12. *Projectiles*

These were taken from the following resource:

`www.freepik.com/free-vector/set-different-nuts_37677350.htm`

And we load the images:

lib/components/plants/plant_component.dart

```
assets:
- assets/images/PlantPeashooterProjectile.png
- assets/images/PlantCactusProjectile.png
```

With this, we can easily handle these projectiles from the plant components without navigating the original sprite sheet.

Projectile: Shoot

Once the projectile component has been created, the next step is to use it, that is, add the projectile when the plants are in attack mode, and it is projected toward the zombies in the channel to then count the collision with the zombie. It seems complex, but it is quite simple.

Let's start by adapting the projectile component to enable movement of the projectile on the X axis. It is the same implementation as the one made in the zombie component, only using the positive X:

lib\components\plants\projectile_component.dart

```dart
import 'package:flame/collisions.dart';
import 'package:flame/components.dart';

class ProjectileComponent extends SpriteComponent {
  final Sprite projectile;
  final double speed;
  final Vector2 sizeMap;

  ProjectileComponent(
      {required this.projectile, required this.sizeMap, this.speed = 120})
      : super(size: Vector2.all(20), sprite: projectile) {
    add(RectangleHitbox());
  }
```

```
  @override
  void update(double dt) {
    position.add(Vector2(dt * speed, 0));

    if (position.x >= sizeMap.x) {
      removeFromParent();
    }

    super.update(dt);
  }
}
```

Also, you can see that when the screen limit is reached, the sprite is removed:

```
if (position.x >= sizeMap.x) {
  removeFromParent();
}
```

Remember that the position of the projectile is relative to the plant that added the projectile, as you can see in the following image.

Figure 11-13. *Aligned projectile*

The projectile's position is **Vector2(0,0)**.

For the plants, we use the **onFrame()** function checking for the last frame (the **onComplete()** function is not used as it is not executed when the animation is set to loop) for the **AnimationTicker** that will fire when the animation completes. We add a projectile:

lib\components\plants\plant_component.dart

```
void shoot(String sprite) {
    shootAnimationTicker.onFrame = (value) async {
      if (shootAnimationTicker.isLastFrame) {
```

```
      if (state == State.shoot) {
        add(ProjectileComponent(
            projectile: await Sprite.load(sprite), sizeMap: sizeMap));
      }
    }
  };
}
```

This is why we see that in the **shoot()** function defined, we use the **reset()** function of the animation, and it is to start the animation again and have the loop in the attack phase. Also, as you can see, we set the animation to run more slowly, changing the **stepTime**, to prevent it from firing many projectiles in the same amount of time (you can apply another type of logic to this, for example, once fired, the plant will pass to idle mode for a few seconds and then switch to attack mode).

This function will only be called once in the **onLoad()** function of each of the plant components:

lib\components\plants\peashooter_component.dart

```
@override
void onLoad() async {
  ***
  shootAnimation = spriteSheetIdle.createAnimationByLimit(
      xInit: 1, yInit: 0, step: 3, sizeX: 3, stepTime: .8);
  shoot('PlantPeashooterProjectile.png');
}
```

and

lib\components\plants\cactus_component.dart

```
@override
void onLoad() async {
  ***
    shootAnimation = spriteSheet.createAnimationByLimit(
        xInit: 0, yInit: 4, step: 2, sizeX: 6, stepTime: .8);
    shoot('PlantCactusProjectile.png');
}
```

The great thing about the preceding implementation is that, when passing the animation to attack, the **onComplete()** function of said animation is automatically started, resulting in the projectile being added with the **ProjectileComponent()** and, with this, the projectile's offset.

Finally, in the zombie component, in the **onCollision()** function, when the projectile is colliding with the zombie, the projectile is removed:

lib\components\zombies\zombie_component.dart

```
@override
void onCollision(Set<Vector2> intersectionPoints, PositionComponent
other) {
  if (other is SeedComponent) _setChannel(true);

  if (other is ProjectileComponent) {
    other.removeFromParent();
  }
  super.onCollision(intersectionPoints, other);
}
```

At the moment, this will only be the behavior, but, as you can suppose, in this function we will also kill the zombie, but we will do this implementation later.

Also remember to update the plant components to receive the new argument, the size of the map:

lib\components\plants\plant_component.dart

```
class PlantComponent extends Plant {
  Vector2 sizeMap;
  PlantComponent(this.sizeMap)
  ***
}
```

lib\components\plants\cactus_component.dart

```
class CactusComponent extends PlantComponent {
  CactusComponent({required sizeMap}) : super(sizeMap)
  ***
}
```

lib\components\plants\peashooter_component.dart

```
class PeashooterComponent extends PlantComponent {
  PeashooterComponent({required sizeMap}) : super(sizeMap)
  ***
}
```

Finally, we will have something like what is shown in Figure 11-11.

As you can see, the channels that have zombies activate the attack mode of the plants, which launch the projectiles; in the channels that do not have zombies, the plants remain in a state of rest.

Projectile: Starting Position

Currently, the projectile is appearing on the side of the plant sprite like the one shown in Figure 11-12. To improve the appearance of the attack, we are going to place an initial position where the projectile should appear when adding it, like the following.

Figure 11-14. *Aligned projectile*

For that, we add a new argument in the constructor of the collision component:

lib/components/plants/projectile_component.dart

```
class ProjectileComponent extends SpriteComponent {
  final Sprite projectile;
  final double speed;
  final Vector2 sizeMap;
```

```
ProjectileComponent(
    {required this.projectile, required this.sizeMap, required position,
    this.speed = 120})
    : super(size: Vector2.all(20), sprite: projectile, position:
    position) {
  add(RectangleHitbox());
  }
}
```

We add the same in the **shoot()** function:

lib/components/plants/plant_component.dart

```
void shoot(String sprite, Vector2 position) {
  shootAnimationTicker.onFrame = (value) async {
    if (shootAnimationTicker.isLastFrame) {
      if (state == State.shoot) {
        add(ProjectileComponent(
            projectile: await Sprite.load(sprite),
            sizeMap: sizeMap,
            position: position));
      }
    }
  };
}
```

Finally, from each of the plant components, we place the position of the projectile that we consider to be the best:

lib/components/plants/peashooter_component.dart

```
shoot('PlantPeashooterProjectile.png', Vector2(27, 20));
```

lib/components/plants/cactus_component.dart

```
shoot('PlantCactusProjectile.png', Vector2(30, 12));
```

CHAPTER 11   GAME 4: PLANTS VS. ZOMBIES

Life and Collisions

In this section, we are going to complete the main flow between the attack of the plants toward the zombies and the zombies toward the plants; for this, we are going to implement the logic to define the life of each character as well as the level of attack and remove those characters that lost their lives.

Health and Damage

We'll define a couple of properties to handle the health of the characters and the damage that zombies and plants can do.

Let's start by defining the life and attack of plants. In the case of plants, the attack must be passed to the projectile, which is the one that inflicts the damage on the zombie, since the plant does not directly do damage to the zombie; as for life, it is defined directly in the plant component.

Let's start by placing a couple of properties to handle the health and damage that plants can cause in the base component:

lib/components/plants/plant_component.dart

```
class PlantComponent *** {
  int life = 100;
  int damage = 10;
  ***
  void shoot(String sprite, Vector2 position) {
    shootAnimationTicker.onFrame = (value) async {
      if (shootAnimationTicker.isLastFrame) {
        if (state == State.shoot) {
          add(ProjectileComponent(
              projectile: await Sprite.load(sprite),
              sizeMap: sizeMap,
              position: position,
              damage: damage));
        }
      }
    };
  ***
}
```

Of course, these properties can be customized in the classes that inherit from **PlantComponent** to vary the life and capacity of the attack.

From the projectile, we receive the new argument, the damage:

lib/components/plants/projectile_component.dart

```
class ProjectileComponent extends SpriteComponent {
  ***
  int damage;
  ProjectileComponent(
      {required this.projectile,
      required this.sizeMap,
      position,
      this.damage = 10,
      this.speed = 120})
      : super(size: Vector2.all(20), sprite: projectile, position:
      position) {
    add(RectangleHitbox());
  }
}
```

For the zombie, we also define the same properties to handle life and damage in its base component, although, since the zombie is the one that attacks directly without using projectiles, both properties are handled directly in the zombie's base class:

lib/components/zombies/zombie_component.dart

```
class ZombieComponent *** {
  int life = 100;
  int damage = 20;
  ***
}
```

The Plant Attacks the Zombies

Completing the implementation of the plant attack by projectiles, we are going to implement the life reduction of the zombie that receives a projectile hit and removal of the zombie when the life is zero:

```
@override
void onCollision(Set<Vector2> intersectionPoints, PositionComponent
other) {
  ***

  if (other is ProjectileComponent) {
    other.removeFromParent();
    life -= other.damage;
    if (life <= 0) {
      removeFromParent();
    }
  }

  super.onCollision(intersectionPoints, other);
}
```

Stop the Zombie in Collision with the Plants

As in the original game, when the zombie comes into contact with the plants, it starts attacking them; therefore, the zombie must stop for the duration of the attack:

```
***
class ZombieComponent extends SpriteAnimationComponent with
CollisionCallbacks {
  ***
  bool isAttacking = false;
  ***

  @override
  void update(double dt) {
    if (!isAttacking) position.add(Vector2(-dt * speed, 0));
    ***
  }

 @override
  void onCollision(Set<Vector2> intersectionPoints, PositionComponent
  other) {
    ***
```

```
//if (other is PeashooterComponent || other is CactusComponent) {
if (other is PlantComponent) {
  isAttacking = true;
}

super.onCollision(intersectionPoints, other);
}
***
}
```

The implementation is very simple. With the zombie coming into contact (collision) with the plants, the zombie can attack the plants and, with this, enter attack mode whose implementation is shown in the following section; for now, it's enough for the zombie to stop walking. For the section on collisions between the zombie and the plants, you can also compare it this way:

```
@override
void onCollision(Set<Vector2> intersectionPoints, PositionComponent
other) {
  ***

  if (other is PlantComponent) {
    isAttacking = true;
  }

  super.onCollision(intersectionPoints, other);
}
```

This is how we handle it in the book.

The Zombie Attacks the Plants

From the zombie component, we can also manage the collision with the plants and reduce their lives; with this, all collision implementations are handled in one place.

When detecting the collision between the zombie and the plant, the life is reduced from time to time until the plant is lifeless and is removed from the map:

```
***
class ZombieComponent extends SpriteAnimationComponent with
CollisionCallbacks {
  ***

  bool isAttacking = false;
  bool attack = false;
  double elapsedTimeAttacking = 0;
  ***

  @override
  void update(double dt) {
    if (!isAttacking) position.add(Vector2(-dt * speed, 0));

    ***

    if (elapsedTimeAttacking > 2) {
      elapsedTimeAttacking = 0.0;
      attack = true;
    }

    elapsedTimeAttacking += dt;

    super.update(dt);
  }

  @override
  void onCollision(Set<Vector2> intersectionPoints, PositionComponent
  other) {
    if (other is SeedComponent) _setChannel(true);

    if (other is ProjectileComponent) {
      other.removeFromParent();
      life -= other.damage;
      if (life <= 0) {
        removeFromParent();
      }
    }
```

```
    if (other is CactusComponent) {
      isAttacking = true;
      if (attack) {
        attack = false;
        other.life -= damage;
        if (other.life <= 0) {
          other.removeFromParent();
        }
      }
    }

    ***

    super.onCollision(intersectionPoints, other);
  }

  @override
  void onCollisionEnd(PositionComponent other) {
    if (other is PeashooterComponent || other is CactusComponent) {
      isAttacking = false;
      attack = false;
    }
    super.onCollisionEnd(other);
  }

  ***
}
```

In the preceding implementation, we see that from time to time, the life of the plant is reduced while the collision between the zombie and the plant is maintained; we use the same principle of adding zombies from time to time, but applied in the attack together with the collisions. We use the **attack** property to indicate an attack against the plant when it is set to true, which happens every two seconds when it is set by the **elapsedTimeAttacking** counter.

One way to simplify the preceding code would be to ask only for the base component of the plant:

```
@override
void onCollision(Set<Vector2> intersectionPoints, PositionComponent
other) {
  ***

  if (other is PlantComponent) {
    isAttacking = true;
    if (attack) {
      other.life -= damage;
      if (other.life <= 0) {
        other.removeFromParent();
      }

      attack = false;
    }
  }

  super.onCollision(intersectionPoints, other);
}
```

Vary Zombie Animation in Attack Mode and When Wounded

For the zombie component, let's set a couple more animations:

1. An animation for when they are injured and walking

2. An animation for when the zombie is eating the plant (attacking)

For this, we create the pair of properties in the zombie's base class and implement the functionality when we show each of the available animations:

lib\components\zombies\zombie_component.dart

```
class ZombieComponent extends SpriteAnimationComponent with
CollisionCallbacks {
  late SpriteAnimation walkingAnimation, walkingHurtAnimation, eatingAnimation;

  ***

  @override
  void onCollisionStart(
      Set<Vector2> intersectionPoints, PositionComponent other) {
```

```
    if (other is CactusComponent || other is PeashooterComponent) {
      animation = eatingAnimation;
    }

    super.onCollisionStart(intersectionPoints, other);
  }
@override
void onCollision(Set<Vector2> intersectionPoints, PositionComponent
other) {
    if (other is SeedComponent) _setChannel(true);

    if (other is ProjectileComponent) {
      other.removeFromParent();
      life -= other.damage;
      if (life <= 50) {
        animation = walkingHurtAnimation;
      }
      if (life <= 0) {
        removeFromParent();
      }
    }
    ***
    super.onCollision(intersectionPoints, other);
  }

@override
void onCollisionEnd(PositionComponent other) {
    if (other is PeashooterComponent || other is CactusComponent) {
      isAttacking = false;
      attack = false;
      if (life <= 50) {
        animation = walkingHurtAnimation;
      } else {
        animation = walkingAnimation;
      }
    }
```

```
    super.onCollisionEnd(other);
  }
}
```

For the animation of the zombie being wounded, we put a condition that indicates that, when the zombie's life is 50 or less, we show the said animation (you can use another type of logic – remember that it is possible to customize the amount of life for each zombie; therefore, if you want to use this animation for when the zombie loses half of its life, you must register in a constant the total amount of life of the zombie and do the calculation from said constant). To do this, the **onCollision()** function is used when the zombie is colliding with a projectile.

For the eating animation, the **onCollisionStart()** function is used so that when the zombie collides with a plant, it switches to the eating animation and when it finishes eating (and with this having killed a plant), it switches to the walking animation or injured depending on the standard of living; for this, the **onCollisionEnd()** function is used.

In the zombie component classes, we load the new animations. In the case of the female zombie, it does not have the frames for the eating state in the sprite sheet; therefore, the current one to walk is duplicated:

lib\components\zombies\zombie_male_component.dart

```
eatingAnimation = spriteSheet.createAnimationByLimit(
    xInit: 0, yInit: 12, step: 6, sizeX: 19, stepTime: .2);
walkingHurtAnimation = spriteSheet.createAnimationByLimit(
    xInit: 1, yInit: 5, step: 6, sizeX: 19, stepTime: .2);
```

lib\components\zombies\zombie_female_component.dart

```
eatingAnimation = spriteSheet.createAnimationByLimit(
    xInit: 0, yInit: 0, step: 6, sizeX: 19, stepTime: .2);
walkingHurtAnimation = spriteSheet.createAnimationByLimit(
    xInit: 2, yInit: 4, step: 6, sizeX: 19, stepTime: .2);
```

It is important to mention that these animations cause problems when playing them and it is due to the size that is variable in each of the frames and different from the size used for the walking animation; to solve the mentioned problem, you must edit the sprite sheets and indicate the same size for each frame.

Prevent Zombies from Colliding with Other Channels

Currently, zombies can collide with the attached channels; to avoid this behavior, all we have to do is specify some dimensions with which the zombie's hitbox is contained within the corresponding channel and not in both channels (remember that the height of the zombie is greater than the size of the tile). For this, you can make multiple adjustments, but, in the book, we will do the following:

lib/components/zombies/zombie_male_component.dart

lib/components/zombies/zombie_female_component.dart

```
body = RectangleHitbox(
    size: Vector2(size.x, size.y - alignZombie),
    position: Vector2(0, alignZombie))
  ..collisionType = CollisionType.active;
add(body);
```

And with this, the previous problem should not happen.

Block the Tile/Seed Occupied by a Zombie and Release the Seeded Channel

If there is a busy channel (through which the zombie is passing), the logical thing to do is to block it; with this, it is avoided that if a plant dies being attacked by the zombie, the user can quickly place another one and thus retain the zombie. With this, we add an additional level of difficulty. For this, we are going to create a property to check if the tile is busy or not. In our application, the tile is being the **SeedComponent**:

lib\maps\seed_component.dart

```
class SeedComponent extends PositionComponent with TapCallbacks {
  ***
  bool busy = false;
  ***
  @override
  void onTapDown(TapDownEvent event) {
    if (!sown & !busy) {
      Vector2 auxPos = position;
```

```
      auxPos += size / 2;
      if (game.addPlant(position, size)) {
        sown = true;
      }
    }
    super.onTapDown(event);
  }
}
```

And from the zombie, when colliding with the **SeedComponent**, the preceding property is marked as occupied, and it will be released when the collision ends:

lib\components\zombies\zombie_component.dart

```
class ZombieComponent *** {
  @override
  void onCollision(Set<Vector2> intersectionPoints, PositionComponent
  other) {
    if (other is SeedComponent) {
      other.busy = true;
      _setChannel(true);
    }
    ***
  }
  @override
  void onCollisionEnd(PositionComponent other) {
    if (other is SeedComponent) {
      other.busy = false;
      other.sown = false;
    }
    ***
  }
}
```

It is important to note that when the collision with the seed is finished, it also indicates that there are no seeded plants:

other.sown = false;

The reason is simple: if the zombie passed through the seed where a plant was planted, it means that it eliminated the plant.

Chapter source code:

```
https://github.com/libredesarrollo/flame-curso-libro-plantvszombie05/
releases/tag/v0.1
```

CHAPTER 12

Game 4: Many Experiments

In this chapter, we will implement several extra developments that are not part of the basic gameplay of the game, such as a sun counter to add the plants based on a counter, generation of suns to register in the counter, pause, restart, and changing the size of the screen.

Plant Overlay

In this section we will create the overlay to select a plant and establish it on the map. We will use one of the sprite sheet states used before, and we will generate an independent image and import it into the project:

pubspec.yaml

```
assets:
  - assets/images/cactus.png
  - assets/images/peashooter.png
```

We are going to need to manage the types of plants to know which one is selected and, with this, to be able to add it to the map; to do this, we will use an enum:

lib/components/plants/plant_component.dart

```
enum Plants { peashooter, cactus }
class PlantComponent extends SpriteAnimationComponent {***}
```

We use **StatefulWidget** as always and define a couple of buttons that refer to the selected plant:

lib/overlay/plant_overlay.dart

```dart
import 'package:flutter/material.dart';

import 'package:plantvszombie05/main.dart';
import 'package:plantvszombie05/components/plants/plant_component.dart'
    as pc;

class PlantOverlay extends StatefulWidget {
  final MyGame game;
  const PlantOverlay({super.key, required this.game});

  @override
  State<PlantOverlay> createState() => _PlantOverlayState();
}

class _PlantOverlayState extends State<PlantOverlay> {
  @override
  Widget build(BuildContext context) {
    return Padding(
      padding: const EdgeInsets.all(8.0),
      child: Column(mainAxisAlignment: MainAxisAlignment.end, children: [
        Row(
          crossAxisAlignment: CrossAxisAlignment.end,
          children: [
            GestureDetector(
              onTap: () {
                widget.game.setPlantSelected(pc.Plants.peashooter);
              },
              child: Image.asset(
                'assets/images/peashooter.png',
                width: 50,
              ),
            ),
```

```
        GestureDetector(
          onTap: () {
            widget.game.setPlantSelected(pc.Plants.cactus);
          },
          child: Image.asset(
            'assets/images/cactus.png',
            width: 50,
          ),
        ),
      ],
    )
  ]),
  );
  }
}
```

An alias "**pc**" is placed when importing the **PlantComponent**, a double import between

```
package:flutter/src/widgets/framework.dart
```

and

```
package:plantvszombie05/components/plants/plant_component.dart
```

For example:

```
The name 'State' is defined in the libraries 'package:flutter/src/widgets/
framework.dart' and 'package:plantvszombie05/components/plants/plant_
component.dart'.
Try using 'as prefix' for one of the import directives, or hiding the name
from all but one of the imports.
```

In main, we define the overlay created earlier and define the property and function to handle the selected plant:

lib/main.dart

***

```dart
class MyGame extends FlameGame
    with HasCollisionDetection /*TapDetector*/ {
  ***
  Plants plantSelected = Plants.peashooter;

  bool addPlant(Vector2 position, Vector2 sizeSeed) {
    late PlantComponent p;

    if (plantSelected == Plants.peashooter) {
      p = PeashooterComponent(sizeMap: background.tiledMap.size)
        ..position = Vector2(position.x, position.y);
    } else {
      p = CactusComponent(sizeMap: background.tiledMap.size)
        ..position = Vector2(position.x, position.y);
    }

    var fac = sizeSeed.y / p.size.y;
    p.size *= fac;
    add(p);

    return true;
  }

  setPlantSelected(Plants plant) {
    plantSelected = plant;
  }
  ***
}

void main() {
  runApp(GameWidget(
    game: MyGame(),
    overlayBuilderMap: {
      'Plant': (context, MyGame game) {
        return PlantOverlay(game: game);
      }
    },
```

```
initialActiveOverlays: const ['Plant'],
  ));
}
```

In the **addPlant()** function, we place a conditional and add a plant based on the selected type.

And we will have the following.

Figure 12-1. *Overlay of plants*

Mark the Selected Option

Continuing working on the plant overlay, now, we are going to place a frame or border around the selected image; to do this, we will place a **Container** with a border decorator for each of the images, which we will activate if the image corresponds to the selected plant:

lib/overlay/plant_overlay.dart

```
Row(
  crossAxisAlignment: CrossAxisAlignment.end,
  children: [
    GestureDetector(
        onTap: () {
          //widget.game.paused = !widget.game.paused;
          setState(() {
            widget.game
                .setPlantSelected(pc.Plants.peashooter);
          });
        },
```

```
              child: Container(
                decoration: BoxDecoration(
                    border: Border.all(
                        width: widget.game.plantSelected ==
                                pc.Plants.peashooter
                            ? 5
                            : 0,
                        color: Colors.blueGrey)),
                child: Image.asset(
                  'assets/images/peashooter.png',
                  width: 50,
                ),
              )),
          const SizedBox(
            width: 5,
          ),
          Container(
            decoration: BoxDecoration(
                border: Border.all(
                    width: widget.game.plantSelected ==
                            pc.Plants.cactus
                        ? 5
                        : 0,
                    color: Colors.blueGrey)),
            child: GestureDetector(
                onTap: () {
                  widget.game
                      .setPlantSelected(pc.Plants.cactus);
                },
                child: Image.asset(
                  'assets/images/cactus.png',
                  width: 50,
                )),
          ),
        ],
      )
```

From main, we update the overlay when the user selects a plant:

lib/main.dart

```
setPlantSelected(Plants plant) {
  plantSelected = plant;
  _refreshOverlayPlant();
}

_refreshOverlayPlant() {
  overlays.remove('Plant');
  overlays.add('Plant');
}
```

And we will have the selected plant in a box.

Figure 12-2. *Overlay of plants with borders around the selected option*

Suns

Being able to add plants without any limit does not offer any level of difficulty. Following the logic of the original game, it is necessary to have "suns" to be able to spend them on plants, where the plants can have different costs.

In this section, we are going to implement the functionality of the suns, where the suns are going to fall and the user can click to add a sun and, with this, increase a counter that is later consumed when we add plants; if there are no suns that can afford a plant, then the user will not be able to add the plant.

The sprite of the sun will be the following:

www.freepik.com/free-vector/yellow-sunny-icons_813343.htm#query=sun%20 spritesheet&position=15&from_view=search&track=ais

The image was edited to look like the following.

Figure 12-3. *Sprite sheet for the suns*

And we import the image:

pubspec.yaml

```
assets:
  - assets/images/Sun.png
  ***
```

The implementation will be pretty much the same as used in game 3 for the logic implemented for meteorites, but changing the image to the preceding one:

lib/components/plants/ sun_component.dart

```
import 'dart:async';
import 'dart:math';

import 'package:flame/flame.dart';
import 'package:flame/components.dart';
import 'package:flame/sprite.dart';
import 'package:flutter/material.dart';

import 'package:plantvszombie05/utils/create_animation_by_limit.dart';

class SunComponent extends SpriteAnimationComponent with HasGameReference{
  SunComponent() : super(size: Vector2.all(30)))) {
    debugMode = true;   }

  static const int circleSpeed = 50;
  static const double circleWidth = 26, circleHeight = 26;
```

```
Random random = Random();

late double screenWidth, screenHeight;

@override
void onLoad() async {
  screenWidth = game.size.x;
  screenHeight = game.size.y;

  position =
      Vector2(random.nextDouble() * screenWidth - circleWidth,
      -circleHeight);

  final spriteImage = await Flame.images.load('Sun.png');
  final spriteSheet = SpriteSheet(
      image: spriteImage, srcSize: Vector2(circleWidth, circleHeight));

  animation = spriteSheet.createAnimationByLimit(
      xInit: 0, yInit: 0, step: 2, sizeX: 2, stepTime: .8);
}

@override
void update(double dt) {
  position.y += circleSpeed * dt;
  if (position.y > screenHeight) {
    removeFromParent();
  }

  super.update(dt);
}
}
```

Another important point is that there is no need to handle collisions as in the case of meteors. From the main, we are adding the suns from time to time:

lib/ main.dart

```
class MyGame extends *** {
  ***
  double elapsedTimeSun = 0.0;
```

```
@override
void update(double dt) {
  if (elapsedTimeSun > 1.0) {
    add(SunComponent());
    elapsedTimeSun = 0.0;
  }

  elapsedTimeSun += dt;
  ***

}
}
```

And we will have the following.

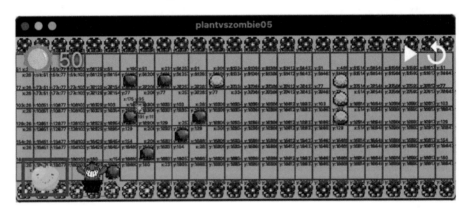

Figure 12-4. *Suns generated on the map*

Moving Suns in a Wavy Way

Not only can we move the suns from top to bottom as if they were falling but we can also move a little to the sides, on the X axis, in the form of a wave; this is a detail that we follow from the original game and that we can replicate with relative ease.

The function that we will use to make the wave movement is the sine function, which has the desired behavior.

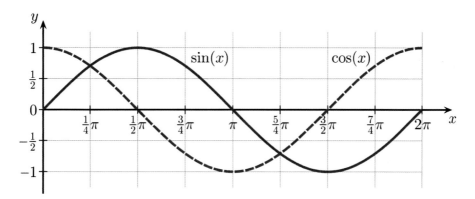

Figure 12-5. *Sine and cosine functions on a coordinate axis (`https://en.`*
`wikipedia.org/wiki/Sine_and_cosine`*)*

As you can see, its behavior is constant and easy to predict. We can make the wave
bigger or smaller by multiplying the value by a constant number, which, if greater than
one, then the wave would be more pronounced; otherwise, the wave would be smaller.

Of course, you can use other functions such as cosine.

In Dart, we have access to the sine function by

```
import 'dart:math';
sin(VALUE)
```

To calculate the value and make the wave movement, we could take any increasing
number, such as the position on Y:

```
position.y
```

However, the generated number can vary from one iteration to another in a not
entirely constant way; if you print the position at the time of the update, you will see that
the values do not have a homogeneous behavior other than being only incremental, like

- –3

- 17

- 25

- 49

- 60

Therefore, if we use this value for the sine function, the wave motion would be somewhat turbulent, which is not what we want. Therefore, we will use a number that is constant when incrementing it. Keeping the aforementioned in mind, the function looks like

`lib/components/plants/ sun_component.dart`

```
class SunComponent extends SpriteAnimationComponent with
CollisionCallbacks {
  ***
  double countSin = 0;
  @override
  @override
  void update(double dt) {
    countSin += 0.05;

    // position.y += circleSpeed * dt;
    position += Vector2(sin(countSin) * 60 * dt, circleSpeed * dt);
    if (position.y > screenHeight) {
      removeFromParent();
    }

    super.update(dt);
  }
}
```

As an exercise, try values other than 60 to increase the radius of the wave and 0.05 and evaluate their behavior.

Sun Counter

With the suns already being generated, now, it is necessary to be able to add them to a counter when the user taps/clicks them. We will place this counter in the Game-type class, and we will call it as **suns**, which will have a default value so that the user can add some plants initially:

lib/main.dart

```dart
class MyGame extends FlameGame *** {
  int suns = 50;
  ***

  @override
  void update(double dt) {
    if (elapsedTimeSun > 5.0) {
      add(SunComponent(game: this));
      elapsedTimeSun = 0.0;
    }

    elapsedTimeSun += dt;
    ***

    }

    elapsedTime += dt;
    super.update(dt);
  }

  addSuns(int sun) {
    suns += sun;
  }

  bool removeSuns(int sun) {
    if (suns - sun >= 0) {
      suns -= sun;
      return true;
    }
    return false;
  }
  ***
}
***
}
```

We also created a couple of functions called **addSuns()** and **removeSuns()** to add and remove suns to and from the counter. From the sun component, we call the **addSuns()** function when the user taps the sun sprites:

lib/components/plants/sun_component.dart

```
class SunComponent extends SpriteAnimationComponent with TapCallbacks {
  MyGame game;

  SunComponent({required this.game}) : super() {
    debugMode = true;
  }

  ***

  @override
  void onTapDown(TapDownEvent event) {
    removeFromParent();
    game.addSun(5);
    super.onTapDown(event);
  }
}
```

The false return of the **onTapDown()** function is very important to prevent the event from propagating to the rest of the components that also listen to the tap, that is, the **SeedComponent** (since this component is behind the sun component), and with this avoid adding a plant by mistake, apart from adding suns to the counter.

Another important detail is that the function **removeSuns()** first checks if the suns to be removed exist in order to discount them, and that is why it returns a bool **true** if a sun was removed and the transaction was completed successfully and **false** if the transaction could not be completed.

Suns Overlay

In this section, we are going to show the sun counter on the screen in an overlay; for the overlay's sun image, we'll use the following:

```
    www.flaticon.es/download/icon/landing/6126439?format=png&size=512&
type=standard
```

And we import it:

`pubspec.yaml`

```
assets:
  - lib/overlay/sun_overlay.dart
  ***
```

For the overlay, we use the image of the sun and a text that prints the **suns** property:

`lib/overlay/sun_overlay.dart`

```dart
import 'package:flutter/material.dart';
import 'package:plantsvszombie/main.dart';
import 'package:plantsvszombie/components/plants/plant_component.dart'
    as PlantComponent;

class SunOverlay extends StatefulWidget {
  final MyGame game;
  SunOverlay({Key? key, required this.game}) : super(key: key);
  @override
  State<SunOverlay> createState() => _SunOverlayState();
}

class _SunOverlayState extends State<SunOverlay> {
  @override
  Widget build(BuildContext context) {
    return Padding(
      padding: const EdgeInsets.all(8.0),
      child: Column(
        mainAxisAlignment: MainAxisAlignment.start,
        children: [
          Row(
            crossAxisAlignment: CrossAxisAlignment.center,
            children: [
              Container(
                child: Image.asset(
                  'assets/images/SunOverlay.png',
                  width: 50,
```

```
              ),
            ),
            const SizedBox(
              width: 5,
            ),
            Text(
              widget.game.suns.toString(),
              style: const TextStyle(
                  fontSize: 30,
                  color: Colors.amber,
                  shadows: [Shadow(color: Colors.black,
                   blurRadius: 5.0)]),
            )
          ],
        ),
      ],
    ),
  );
  }
}
```

From main, we import the overlay and implement the function to reload the overlay when removing and adding suns:

lib/main.dart

```
class MyGame *** {
  ***

  bool removeSuns(int sun) {
    if (suns - sun >= 0) {
      suns -= sun;
      _refreshOverlaySun();
      return true;
    }
    return false;
  }
```

```dart
  addSuns(int sun) {
    suns += sun;
    _refreshOverlaySun();
  }

  _refreshOverlaySun() {
    overlays.remove('Sun');
    overlays.add('Sun');
  }
}

void main() {
  runApp(GameWidget(
    game: MyGame(),
    overlayBuilderMap: {
      'Plant': (context, MyGame game) {
        return PlantOverlay(
          game: game,
        );
      },
      'Sun': (context, MyGame game) {
        return SunOverlay(
          game: game,
        );
      },
    },
    initialActiveOverlays: const ['Plant', 'Sun'],
  ));
}
```

And we will have the following.

Figure 12-6. *Sun counter overlay*

Cost per Plant

Once the sun counter has been created, with its overlay and the methods to add and remove suns to and from the counter, these suns need to be consumed. When the user wants to add a plant, we will verify if there are enough suns to pay for the plant. For that, let's first start by defining a cost for each plant:

lib/components/plants/plant_component.dart

```
class PlantCost {
  static const peashooter = 20;
  static const cactus = 30;

  static int cost(Plants plant) {
    switch (plant) {
      case Plants.peashooter:
        return peashooter;
      case Plants.cactus:
        return cactus;
    }
  }
}

class PlantComponent {***}
```

As you can see, the cost is defined in a separate class; this is useful since the cost is a check that is performed before creating the plant. Therefore, having the cost in a separate structure avoids having to create an instance of the component to ask if the plant can be added or not.

When adding a plant to the map, first, the suns are removed from the counter, and the necessary verifications are made to cancel the process of adding the plant when there are no suns available or discount the suns and add the plant on the map:

lib/main.dart

```
bool addPlant(Vector2 position, Vector2 size) {
  PlantComponent p;
```

```
if (!removeSuns(PlantCost.cost(plantSelected))) {
  return false;
}
if (plantSelected == Plants.peashooter) {
  p = PeashooterComponent(sizeMap: background.tiledMap.size)
    ..position = Vector2(position.x, position.y);
} else {
  p = CactusComponent(sizeMap: background.tiledMap.size)
    ..position = Vector2(position.x, position.y);
}
final fac = size.y / p.size.y; //25 50 = 2
p.size *= fac;
add(p);

return true;
}
```

Now, if there are suns available to add the plant, the user can add it; otherwise, the plants are not added.

Plant Overlay Transparency

A visual detail that we can define is to lower the opacity in the images of the plants

Figure 12-7. *Overlay of transparent plants when there are not enough suns to support the plants*

when there are no suns to pay for them. With this, the user will have a visual aid, and if the image has an opacity applied, then there are no suns to pay for the transaction; otherwise, the image is shown without opacity.

The **Opacity** widget is used on each of the images along with a check like

```
PlantCost.cost(pc.Plants.<TYPE>) <= widget.game.suns
```

With this, we verify if there are suns to pay for it; you can see how useful it is to place the cost outside of the plant instance, since we can place checks on the cost of the plants where we need. Finally, here's the complete code:

`lib/overlay/plant_overlay.dart`

```dart
***
class _PlantOverlayState extends State<PlantOverlay> {
  @override
  Widget build(BuildContext context) {
    return Padding(
      padding: const EdgeInsets.all(8.0),
      child: Column(
        mainAxisAlignment: MainAxisAlignment.end,
        children: [
          Row(
            crossAxisAlignment: CrossAxisAlignment.end,
            children: [
              Opacity(
                  opacity: pc.PlantCost.cost(pc.Plants.peashooter) <=
                          widget.game.suns
                      ? 1
                      : 0.5,
                  child: Container(***),
              )),
              const SizedBox(
                width: 5,
              ),
              Opacity(
                opacity: pc.PlantCost.cost(pc.Plants.cactus) <= widget.
                  game.suns
                    ? 1
                    : 0.5,
```

```
          child: Container(***),
        ),
      ],
    ),
  ],
),
);
}
}
```

Generate Suns on Map Space

As we did in previous projects, we will use the size of the map as a limit to generate the suns, leaving security zones at the ends to prevent them from disappearing from the window when the wave is formed:

lib/overlay/sun_overlay.dart

```
class SunComponent extends SpriteAnimationComponent with TapCallbacks {
  SunComponent({required this.game, required this.mapSize}) : super() {
    debugMode = true;
    size = Vector2(circleWidth, circleHeight);
  }

  MyGame game;
  Vector2 mapSize;

  static const int circleSpeed = 50;
  final int limitX = 80;
  static const double circleWidth = 26, circleHeight = 26;
  double countSin = 0;

  Random random = Random();

  final ShapeHitbox hitbox = CircleHitbox();
```

```
  @override
  void onLoad() async {
    var posX = random.nextDouble() * mapSize.x - circleWidth;

    if (posX < limitX) {
      posX += limitX;
    } else if (posX > mapSize.x - limitX) {
      posX -= limitX;
    }

    position = Vector2(posX, -circleHeight);

    ***

  }

  ***

}
```

And in main, we pass the size of the map:

lib/main.dart

```
@override
void update(double dt) {
  if (elapsepTimeSun > 2) {
    elapsepTimeSun = 0;
    add(SunComponent(game: this, mapSize: background.tiledMap.size));
  }
  ***
}
```

Plant Recharge

A feature that the original game has is that it is not possible to add the same plant consecutively, that is, once the plant is added, you have to wait a while to be able to add it again, regardless of whether or not you have the suns to pay. With this, we have an effect like the following.

Figure 12-8. *Image loading*

In this, a translucent white box appears on the image that in turn serves as a counter; as long as the frame is held over the image, the plant will remain locked and cannot be added.

Base Configuration

Let's start by creating the animation; since it is an animation that will require having complete control over it to start it and placing a listener for when it ends, among others, we are going to use an **AnimationController** in conjunction with an **AnimatedBuilder**. For this we must use the mixin class **SingleTickerProviderStateMixin**.

SingleTickerProviderStateMixin is a mixin class in Flutter that provides a controller for animations and can be used in conjunction with the **State** class to perform simple animations. Generally, when we want to perform animations in Flutter that we need to have controlled, it is enough to use a configuration like the following:

```
class MyWidget extends StatefulWidget {
  @override
  _MyWidgetState createState() => _MyWidgetState();
}

class _MyWidgetState extends State<MyWidget> with
SingleTickerProviderStateMixin {
  late final AnimationController _controller = AnimationController(
    duration: const Duration(seconds: 1),
    vsync: this,
  );

  @override
  void dispose() {
    _controller.dispose();
```

```
    super.dispose();
  }

  @override
  Widget build(BuildContext context) {
    return Container(
      ***
    );
  }
}
```

With this clarified, we are going to adapt it to the overlay of the plants, in which we will create a translucent **Container** that overlaps the image of the plant. For this, we will use a **Stack** widget and be able to stack or overlap the widgets:

lib/overlay/plant_overlay.dart

```
***
class _PlantOverlayState extends State<PlantOverlay>
    with SingleTickerProviderStateMixin {
  late AnimationController _controller;

  @override
  void initState() {
    _controller =
        AnimationController(duration: const Duration(seconds: 2),
        vsync: this);

    _controller.addListener(() {
      if (_controller.isCompleted) {
        _controller.reset();
      }
    });

    super.initState();
  }
```

```
@override
void dispose() {
  _controller.dispose();
  super.dispose();
}

@override
Widget build(BuildContext context) {
  return Padding(
    padding: const EdgeInsets.all(8.0),
    child: Column(mainAxisAlignment: MainAxisAlignment.end, children: [
      Row(
        crossAxisAlignment: CrossAxisAlignment.end,
        children: [
          Stack(
            alignment: Alignment.bottomCenter,
            children: [
              Opacity(
                opacity: pc.PlantCost.cost(pc.Plants.peashooter) <=
                        widget.game.suns
                    ? 1
                    : 0.5,
                child: Container(
                  decoration: BoxDecoration(
                      border: Border.all(
                          width: widget.game.plantSelected ==
                                  pc.Plants.peashooter
                              ? 5
                              : 0,
                          color: Colors.blueGrey)),
                  child: GestureDetector(
                    onTap: () {
                      widget.game.setPlantSelected(pc.Plants.peashooter);
                      _controller.forward();
                    },
```

```
                      child: Image.asset(
                        'assets/images/peashooter.png',
                        width: 50,
                      ),
                    ),
                  ),
                ),
              AnimatedBuilder(
                animation: _controller,
                builder: (context, child) {
                  return Container(
                    width: 60,
                    height: 55 * _controller.value,
                    color: const Color.fromARGB(125, 255, 255, 255),
                  );
                },
              )
            ],
          ),
          const SizedBox(
            width: 5,
          ),
          ***
        ],
      )
    ]),
  );
  }
}
```

In this first implementation, we adapt the animation to only one of the images; we see that tapping it starts the animation, which consists of a translucent rectangle.

Another important point is that, for the moment, the animation is activated when tapping/clicking the overlay of the plant and not when adding the plant to the map, which would be the purpose of this effect; this change is made later when finishing the application.

Reuse the Animation Widget

The next step is to be able to easily reuse the animation widget we created earlier. For this, an additional class will be created, and through arguments, the overlay of the plants is customized:

lib/overlay/plant_overlay.dart

***

```dart
class _PlantOverlayState extends State<PlantOverlay> {
  @override
  Widget build(BuildContext context) {
    return Padding(
      padding: const EdgeInsets.all(8.0),
      child: Column(mainAxisAlignment: MainAxisAlignment.end, children: [
        Row(
          crossAxisAlignment: CrossAxisAlignment.end,
          children: [
            _Plant(
              game: widget.game,
              selected: widget.game.plantSelected == pc.Plants.peashooter,
              plant: pc.Plants.peashooter,
              imageAsset: 'assets/images/peashooter.png',
            ),
            const SizedBox(
              width: 5,
            ),
            _Plant(
              game: widget.game,
              selected: widget.game.plantSelected == pc.Plants.cactus,
              plant: pc.Plants.cactus,
              imageAsset: 'assets/images/cactus.png',
            ),
          ],
        )
      ]),
```

```dart
      );
    }
}

class _Plant extends StatefulWidget {
  final MyGame game;
  final pc.Plants plant;
  final bool selected;
  final String imageAsset;

  const _Plant(
      {super.key,
      required this.game,
      required this.plant,
      required this.imageAsset,
      required this.selected});

  @override
  State<_Plant> createState() => __PlantState();
}

class __PlantState extends State<_Plant> with
SingleTickerProviderStateMixin {
  late AnimationController _controller;

  @override
  void initState() {
    _controller =
        AnimationController(duration: const Duration(seconds: 2),
            vsync: this);

    _controller.addListener(() {
      if (_controller.isCompleted) {
        _controller.reset();
      }
    });

    super.initState();
  }
```

```
@override
void dispose() {
  _controller.dispose();
  super.dispose();
}

@override
Widget build(BuildContext context) {
  return Stack(
    alignment: Alignment.bottomCenter,
    children: [
      Opacity(
        opacity:
            pc.PlantCost.cost(widget.plant) <= widget.game.suns ? 1 : 0.5,
        child: Container(
          decoration: BoxDecoration(
            border: Border.all(
              width: widget.selected ? 5 : 0, color: Colors.
              blueGrey)),
          child: GestureDetector(
            onTap: () {
              widget.game.setPlantSelected(widget.plant);
              _controller.forward();
            },
            child: Image.asset(
              widget.imageAsset,
              width: 50,
            ),
          ),
        ),
      ),
      AnimatedBuilder(
        animation: _controller,
        builder: (context, child) {
          return Container(
            width: 60,
```

```
            height: 55 * _controller.value,
            color: const Color.fromARGB(125, 255, 255, 255),
          );
        },
      )
    ],
  );
  }
}
```

Show Animation When Adding the Plant on the Map

Now, we're going to want to use the animation created earlier using the Animated
Container widget used for the plant overlay when adding a plant to the map. Since this
action is carried out in another component, specifically in the main, this is where the
control must be carried out. We will create an additional property with which it will be
known which plant we want to add to the map; the property is null in case a plant has
not been selected to add to the map:

lib/main.dart

```
class MyGame extends *** {
  ***

  Plants? plantAddedInMap;
}
```

From the function of adding plants, the plant to be added to the map is assigned:

lib/main.dart

```
class MyGame extends *** {
  ***

  bool addPlant(Vector2 position, Vector2 sizeSeed) {
    late PlantComponent p;

    if (!removeSuns(PlantCost.cost(plantSelected))) {
      return false;
    }
```

```
    plantAddedInMap = plantSelected;
    ***

  }

}
```

The overlay component, when building the widget (remember that the plant overlay widget is built from main every time the **_refreshOverlayPlant()** function is called), checks if there is an assigned plant to the property **plantAddedInMap** defined in class Game; if the plant matches the one used in the overlay, we start the animation:

lib/overlay/plant_overlay.dart

***

```
class __PlantState extends State<_Plant> with
SingleTickerProviderStateMixin {
  late AnimationController _controller;

  ***

  @override
  void initState() {
    _controller =
        AnimationController(duration: const Duration(seconds: 2),
        vsync: this);

    _controller.addListener(() {
      if (_controller.isCompleted) {
        _controller.reset();
        widget.game.plantAddedInMap = null;
      }
    });

    super.initState();
  }

  @override
  Widget build(BuildContext context) {
    if (widget.game.plantAddedInMap == widget.plant) {
```

```
    _controller.forward();
  }

return Stack(
  alignment: Alignment.bottomCenter,
  children: [
    Opacity(
      opacity:
          pc.PlantCost.cost(widget.plant) <= widget.game.suns ? 1 : 0.5,
      child: Container(
        decoration: BoxDecoration(
            border: Border.all(
                width: widget.selected ? 5 : 0, color: Colors.
                blueGrey)),
        child: GestureDetector(
          onTap: () {
            widget.game.setPlantSelected(widget.plant);
            // _controller.forward();
          },
          child: Image.asset(
            widget.imageAsset,
            width: 50,
          ),
        ),
      ),
    ),
    ***
  ],
);
}
}
```

Remember to remove the start of the animation from the **GestureDetector** as shown in the preceding code; we also reset the property of **plantAddedInMap** when the animation ends.

Avoid Adding a Plant When an Animation Is in Progress

The previously implemented animation will serve as a blocker so that no more plants can be added to the map while the block is in effect. So the only thing to do is verify that, when adding the plant, it is null; if it is not null, no plant will be added:

lib\main.dart

```
bool addPlant(Vector2 position, Vector2 sizeSeed) {
  late PlantComponent p;

  if (plantAddedInMap != null) {
    // do not add the selected plant
    return false;
  }
  ***
}
```

This blocking could be done in a very easy way since the property used to know which plant is going to be added (**plantAddedInMap**) has a non-null value while the blocking animation is running according to the implementation made previously.

This implementation blocks any access to add a plant to the map as long as any of the plants is in a loading state.

Lock Plants Individually

The traditional way of the game is that each plant is blocked individually and not as a group as we currently have. For this, we will create a list that will have as many positions as there are plants in the overlay; this list will be of type Boolean:

- True if the plant is available to add to the map

- False otherwise.

Here's the Game-type class for this new implementation:

lib\main.dart

```
class MyGame *** {
  ***
  //Plants? plantAddedInMap;
  final List<bool> plantsAddedInMap = [false, false];
```

421

```dart
bool addPlant(Vector2 position, Vector2 sizeSeed) {
    late PlantComponent p;

    if (plantsAddedInMap[plantSelected.index]) {
    ***

    plantsAddedInMap[plantSelected.index] = true;
  }
}
```

And we also make the same changes in the overlay of the plants:

lib/overlay/plant_overlay.dart

```dart
class __PlantState extends State<_Plant> *** {
  @override
  void initState() {
    _controller =
        AnimationController(duration: const Duration(seconds: 20),
        vsync: this);

    _controller.addListener(() {
      if (_controller.isCompleted) {
        _controller.reset();
        widget.game.plantsAddedInMap[widget.plant.index] = false;
      }
    });

    super.initState();
  }

  @override
  Widget build(BuildContext context) {
    if (widget.game.plantsAddedInMap[widget.plant.index]) {
      _controller.forward();
    }
  }
}
```

Customize Blocking Time of Plants

The more powerful the plant, the more suns it costs and the longer it takes to regenerate; therefore, we are going to make a time constant, as follows:

lib/overlay/plant_overlay.dart

```
class _PlantOverlayState extends State<PlantOverlay> {
  @override
  Widget build(BuildContext context) {
    return Padding(
      padding: const EdgeInsets.all(8.0),
      child: Column(mainAxisAlignment: MainAxisAlignment.end, children: [
        Row(
          crossAxisAlignment: CrossAxisAlignment.end,
            ***
            const SizedBox(
              width: 5,
            ),
            _Plant(
              game: widget.game,
              duration: const Duration(seconds: 4),
              selected: widget.game.plantSelected == pc.Plants.cactus,
              plant: pc.Plants.cactus,
              imageAsset: 'assets/images/cactus.png',
            ),
        ],
      )
    ]),
  );
  }
}
***

class _Plant extends StatefulWidget {
  ***
  const _Plant(
```

```
    {super.key,
    required this.game,
    this.duration = const Duration(milliseconds: 1500),
    required this.plant,
    required this.imageAsset,
    required this.selected});
  ***
}

class __PlantState extends State<_Plant> with
SingleTickerProviderStateMixin {
  late AnimationController _controller;

  @override
  void initState() {
    _controller = AnimationController(duration: widget.duration,
    vsync: this);
}
```

Relocate Widgets from the Edge of the Plants in the Overlay

Currently, if the loading process appears in one of the plants that are not selected, the transparent container is broken. To fix this, we can move the **Stack** so that it is inside the **Container** that defines the border of the selection, and with this, whether or not it is selected will not change the size of the plant widget:

lib/overlay/plant_overlay.dart

```
class __PlantState extends State<_Plant> with
SingleTickerProviderStateMixin {
  late AnimationController _controller;

  @override
  void initState() {
    _controller = AnimationController(duration: widget.duration,
        vsync: this);
```

```
  _controller.addListener(() {
    if (_controller.isCompleted) {
      _controller.reset();
      widget.game.plantsAddedInMap[widget.plant.index] = false;
    }
  });

  super.initState();
}

@override
void dispose() {
  _controller.dispose();
  super.dispose();
}

@override
Widget build(BuildContext context) {
  if (widget.game.plantsAddedInMap[widget.plant.index]) {
    _controller.forward();
  }

  return Opacity(
    opacity: pc.PlantCost.cost(widget.plant) <= widget.game.suns ? 1 : 0.5,
    child: Container(
      decoration: BoxDecoration(
          border: Border.all(
              width: widget.selected ? 5 : 0, color: Colors.blueGrey)),
      child: GestureDetector(
        onTap: () {
          widget.game.setPlantSelected(widget.plant);
        },
        child: Stack(
          alignment: Alignment.bottomCenter,
          children: [
            Image.asset(
              widget.imageAsset,
```

```
              width: 50,
            ),
            AnimatedBuilder(
              animation: _controller,
              builder: (context, child) {
                return Container(
                  width: 50,
                  height: 55 * _controller.value,
                  color: const Color.fromARGB(125, 255, 255, 255),
                );
              },
            )
          ],
        ),
      ),
    ),
  );
  }
}
```

Pause

Another function is to pause the game as was done in previous projects; for this, an overlay will be created:

lib/overlay/option_overlay.dart

```
import 'package:flutter/material.dart';
import 'package:plantvszombie05/main.dart';

class OptionOverlay extends StatefulWidget {
  final MyGame game;

  const OptionOverlay({super.key, required this.game});

  @override
  State<OptionOverlay> createState() => _OptionOverlayState();
}
```

```dart
class _OptionOverlayState extends State<OptionOverlay> {
  @override
  Widget build(BuildContext context) {
    return Padding(
      padding: const EdgeInsets.all(8.0),
      child: Column(
        children: [
          Row(
            crossAxisAlignment: CrossAxisAlignment.end,
            children: [
              const Expanded(
                  child: SizedBox(
                height: 10,
              )),
              GestureDetector(
                onTap: () {
                  widget.game.paused = !widget.game.paused;
                },
                child: Icon(
                  widget.game.paused ? Icons.play_arrow : Icons.pause,
                  size: 40,
                  color: Colors.white,
                ),
              )
            ],
          ),
        ],
      ),
    );
  }
}
```

Reset

In this section we are going to enable a button through an overlay with which we can restart the level.

For main, we are going to create a Boolean property called **resetGame** that indicates if the game is to be reset (**true**) or not (**false**).

A couple of additional functions are also created, one to reset the values of the properties used to control different aspects of the game, such as the sun counter and the iterable for zombies, and finally the **reset()** function to **restart** the game:

lib/main.dart

```
import 'dart:async';
***
class MyGame *** {

  ***

  bool resetGame = false;
  reset() {
    resetGame = true;
    Timer(const Duration(milliseconds: 300), () {
      init();
    });
  }
  init() {
    suns = 50;
    zombieI = 0;
    resetGame = false;
    _refreshOverlaySun();
    _refreshOverlayPlant();
  }
}
void main() {
  runApp(GameWidget(
    game: MyGame(),
    overlayBuilderMap: {
```

```
    ***
    'Statistics': (context, MyGame game) {
      return StatisticsOverlay(
        game: game,
      );
    },
  },
  initialActiveOverlays: const [
    ***
    'Statistics'
  ],
));
}
```

The strangest part of the preceding code may be the timer:

```
Timer(const Duration(milliseconds: 300), () {
    init();
  });
```

The **resetGame** property indicates that the game is going to be restarted; this property will be used by all the components created by us (zombie, plant, and sun components) in the **update()** function to remove their instances when it is set to **true**. Therefore, let's remember that the **update()** function is not called directly, but is called from time to time (several times per second) in a loop as we explained when we introduced the game loop concept of the game. Therefore, to give the components time to do the revision before resetting the **resetGame** property, the timer is set.

In the components, since the base components of the zombie and the plant do not have the instance of the Game-type class, to avoid changing the definition of these components, we are going to make use of the mixin **HasGameReference**, which provides access to the global instance of the game, that is, the class of type Game; the mixin **HasGameReference** is a generic that receives as a parameter the reference to the Game-type class.

Finally, the plant and zombie base components are left as follows:

lib/components/plants/plant_component.dart

```
class PlantComponent extends SpriteAnimationComponent
    with *** HasGameReference<MyGame> {

  @override
  void update(double dt) async {
   if (game.resetGame) {
     removeFromParent();
   }
    ***
  }
}
```

and

lib/components/zombies/zombie_component.dart

```
class ZombieComponent extends SpriteAnimationComponent
    with *** HasGameReference<MyGame> {

  @override
  void update(double dt) async {
    if (game.resetGame) {
      removeFromParent();
    }
    ***
  }
}
```

In the sun component, since we already have the instance, we can do two things: keep the instance

lib/components/plants/ sun_component.dart

```
class SunComponent extends SpriteAnimationComponent
    with TapCallbacks {
    MyGame game;
```

```dart
  @override
  void update(double dt) async {
    if (game.resetGame) {
      removeFromParent();
    }
    ***

  }
}
```

or

```dart
class SunComponent extends SpriteAnimationComponent
    with *** HasGameReference<MyGame> {

    // MyGame game;

  @override
  void update(double dt) async {
    if (game.resetGame) {
      removeFromParent();
    }
    ***

  }
}
```

The common operation that occurs in all cases is to remove the instance of the game components (zombies, plants, and suns) if the game reset is activated, an operation that is done from the Game-type class using the **resetGame** flag.

And in the overlay we have

lib/overlay/option_overlay.dart

***

```dart
class _OptionOverlayState extends State<OptionOverlay> {
  @override
  Widget build(BuildContext context) {
    return Padding(
      padding: const EdgeInsets.all(8.0),
```

```
    child: Column(
      children: [
        Row(
          crossAxisAlignment: CrossAxisAlignment.end,
          children: [
            ***
            GestureDetector(
              onTap: () {
                widget.game.reset();
              },
              child: const Icon(
                Icons.replay,
                size: 40,
                color: Colors.white,
              ),
            )
          ],
        ),
      ],
    ),
  );
}
}
```

And we will have the following.

Figure 12-9. *Pause/play and restart options*

Move the Camera Using the Drag Event

One problem that the game currently has is that on small screens, the map may not be completely visible; therefore, the application must be adapted so that the user can scroll the screen. It is important to note that, in this opportunity, there is no player like in the dinosaur game that the camera can follow to move around the world. Instead, we have to give the user total freedom so that they can move to an area that is not viewable by gestures. In Flame, we have an event that is very suitable for this need, the Drag event:

```
@override
void onDragUpdate(DragUpdateEvent event) {
    print('canvasPosition--' + event.canvasPosition.toString());
    print('devicePosition--' + event.devicePosition.toString());
    print('localPosition--' + event.localPosition.toString());
    print('event--' + event.localDelta.toString());

    super.onDragUpdate(event);
}
```

This is one of the methods that we have available when using the Drag event in Flame, along with the following:

- **onDragStart** is executed only once, when starting the Drag event.

- **onDragEnd** is executed only once, at the end of the Drag event.

The **onDragUpdate** method is executed during the Drag event, so using the event supplied as an argument, we have access to several properties to get the user's dragging on the screen:

- event.localPosition

- event.parentPosition

- event.devicePosition

The property that best adapts what we need is

```
event.localDelta
```

This property returns the displacement made by each iteration of the method, and with this, we can change the position of the camera viewer to be able to move the viewing area exactly where the user wants. With this clarified, we can make the following implementation.

Implementation

Let's start by adding the camera component along with the world component and make the necessary adaptations; specifically, we will now add the plants, zombies, and other game components inside world and not directly in the Game class:

`lib/main.dart`

```
class MyGame extends FlameGame
    with
        HasCollisionDetection {

  ***
  final World world = World();
  late final CameraComponent cameraComponent;

  @override
  void onLoad() {
    add(world);

    background = TileMapComponent(game: this);

    world.add(background);

    cameraComponent = CameraComponent(world: world);
    cameraComponent.viewfinder.anchor = Anchor.topLeft;

    add(cameraComponent);
  }
}
```

Now, the problem we have is that it is not a good idea to add the Drag event to the **TileMapComponent**, since Flame can confuse the Drag event with the tap event and place a plant where we don't want it. So we'll implement the Drag event on a rectangle that is equal to the size of the window:

`lib/map/background_component.dart`

```
import 'dart:async';

import 'package:flame/components.dart';
import 'package:flame/events.dart';
```

```dart
import 'package:flutter/material.dart';
import 'package:plantvszombie05/main.dart';

class BackgroundComponent extends PositionComponent
    with HasGameReference<MyGame>, DragCallbacks {
  late RectangleComponent _rectangleComponent;

  @override
  FutureOr<void> onLoad() {
    size = game.size;
    // scale = Vector2.all(1);

    _rectangleComponent = RectangleComponent(
        position: Vector2.all(0),
        size: game.size,
        paint: Paint()..color = Colors.purple);

    add(_rectangleComponent);
  }

  @override
  void onGameResize(Vector2 size) {
    // print(size.toSize());
    _rectangleComponent.size = size;
    this.size = size;
    super.onGameResize(size);
  }

  @override
  void onDragUpdate(DragUpdateEvent event) {
    final camera =
        game.firstChild<CameraComponent>()!; // game.cameraComponent;
    // camera.moveBy(event.localDelta);
    camera.viewfinder.position += event.localDelta / camera.viewfinder.zoom;

    position = camera.viewfinder.position;

    super.onDragUpdate(event);
  }
```

```
// @override
// void onDragStart(DragStartEvent event) {
//    print("event.canvasPosition" + event.canvasPosition.toString());
//    print("event.devicePosition" + event.devicePosition.toString());
//    print("event.localPosition" + event.localPosition.toString());
//    print("event.parentPosition" + event.parentPosition.toString());

//    super.onDragStart(event);
// }

// @override
// void onDragEnd(DragEndEvent event) {
//    print("DragEndEvent");
//    super.onDragEnd(event);
// }
}
```

The strangest thing is the reference to the camera:

`game.firstChild<CameraComponent>()!`

In order to reference the camera component, we make it return the first occurrence (and the only one we have based on the preceding implementation) of a camera component in the Game-type class:

`final camera = game.firstChild<CameraComponent>()!;`

However, you can also use the traditional approach of referencing at the property level:

`final camera = game.cameraComponent // game.firstChild<CameraComponent>()!;`

With the **moveBy()** function, we can move the viewport. It is the same as if we do the following operation:

`camera.viewport.position += (event.localDelta / camera.viewfinder.zoom)`

If there is zoom applied to the camera, so that it does not influence the displacement, the zoom is removed by division:

`event.localDelta / camera.viewfinder.zoom`

When the window is resized, the size of the rectangle is updated so that it occupies all the visible space on the screen through the **onGameResize()** function that we will discuss a little later.

We also update the position of the component that automatically updates the position of the rectangle based on the visible area defined in the viewport:

```
position = camera.viewfinder.position;
```

In order to use the Drag event, there is no need to register it from the main event, as is the case with other events. We add the new component from the main instance:

lib\main.dart

```
class MyGame extends FlameGame {
  @override
  void onLoad() {
    ***

    world.add(BackgroundComponent());
    background = TileMapComponent(game2: this);
    world.add(background!);
    ***

  }
}
```

It is essential that this new **BackgroundComponent** is added before the **TileMapComponent**, to avoid overlapping the map with the new component.

With this implementation, by dragging your finger in the area that does not correspond to the TileMap (**TileMapComponent**), we can scroll through the map.

Finally, we will place the color of the rectangle equal to that of the background defined in the Game-type class:

lib\map\background_component.dart

```
_rectangleComponent = RectangleComponent(
    position: Vector2.all(0),
    size: game.size,
    paint: Paint()..color = Colors.purple);
```

With this scheme, this type of applications can be used more easily regardless of the device's screen size. This behavior is common in various types of games where the world (or map in our case) is larger than the device's screen and there is no main character that the camera should follow and it is necessary that the user can have a complete vision of the world.

Scale Components to Window Size

How the game currently works is that the map size does not adapt to the device window size if the device window is smaller than the map.

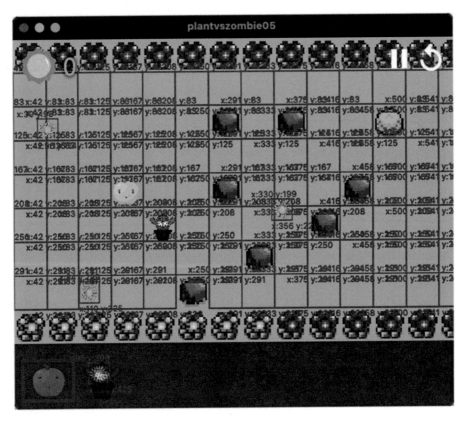

Figure 12-10. *Window without scaling the components*

Then the map along with all the components should be scaled to make it visible.

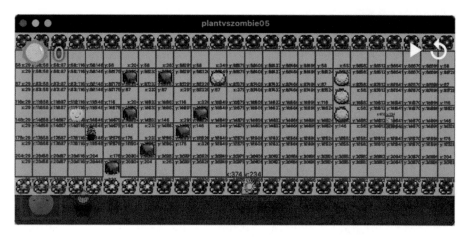

Figure 12-11. *Window with scaling the components*

And if the window exceeds the size of the map, the game components could be left without resizing, but, for the implementation that we are going to do, we are always going to scale the map and all the components to the size of the window, an operation that may seem complicated to perform, but is really very simple to implement.

To understand the implementation, suppose the following example.

We have a variable that records the size of our map, both in width and height:

```
sizeMap = Vector2(500,200)
```

This means the map is 500 in width (X axis) and 200 in height (Y axis).

The window would have the following size:

```
sizeWindow = Vector2(800,400)
```

So the idea is that the size of the map should be equal to the size of the window, in order to use all the available space; specifically, in order not to distort the image, we are going to scale only on one axis, for example, on X. Therefore, we need to know what the factor is so that we can scale the map on the X axis to the size of the window:

```
sizeMap.x * fact = sizeWindow.x
```

In our case, we have the size of the map and the window; therefore, we need to know the factor (called **fact** for this example):

```
sizeMap.x * fact / sizeMap.x = sizeWindow.x / sizeMap.x (remember that the
order of the factors does not alter the product)
```

Therefore, the simplified formula is

```
fact = sizeWindow.x / sizeMap.x
```

With this cleared up, we can easily calculate the factor by resizing the window and scaling all game components; in Flame, we have access to a function that is executed every time the window is resized (which we used earlier to scale the rectangle):

```
@override
void onGameResize(Vector2 size) {
}
```

We can use this function both at the component level and in the Game class of Flame. From the Game class, we make the following change:

```
lib\main.dart
```

```
class MyGame extends *** {
  TileMapComponent? Background;

  ***

  @override
  void onLoad() {
    add(world);

    background = TileMapComponent(game: this);
    world.add(BackgroundComponent());
    world.add(background!);

    ***

  }

  @override
  void onGameResize(Vector2 size) {
    background?.loaded.then((value) {
      factScale = size.x / background!.tiledMap.size.x;
      print(factScale);
      background!.tiledMap.scale = Vector2.all(factScale);
    });

    super.onGameResize(size);
  }
```

440

```
bool addPlant(Vector2 position, Vector2 sizeSeed) {
  ***

  plantsAddedInMap[plantSelected.index] = true;

  if (plantSelected == Plants.peashooter) {
    p = PeashooterComponent(sizeMap: background!.tiledMap.size)
      ..position = Vector2(position.x, position.y);
  } else {
    p = CactusComponent(sizeMap: background!.tiledMap.size)
      ..position = Vector2(position.x, position.y);
  }

  var fac = sizeSeed.y / p.size.y;
  p.size *= fac;
  world.add(p);

  return true;
}
***
}
```

As you can see, we indicate that the background component can be null **TileMapComponent?**, and we remove the **late**. Each time the window is resized, the **onGameResize()** method is executed whose argument corresponds to the size of the window, and with it, the factor is calculated based on the size of the map (**background!. tiledMap**) and the window that is then used to scale ALL components that make up our game, such as the suns, zombies, plants, and of course the map. However, since the user can do the scaling at any time, this factor must be used internally in each of the components when detecting the scaling.

There are special components whose scaling is not as simple as in the case of the suns. One of them is the plants whose implementation looks like the following:

lib\components\plants\plant_component.dart

```
class PlantComponent extends SpriteAnimationComponent {
  PlantComponent(this.sizeMap, position) : super(position: position)

  ***
```

```
Vector2 positionOriginal = Vector2(0, 0);

PlantComponent(this.sizeMap, position) : super(position: position) {
  debugMode = true;
  positionOriginal = position;
}

@override
void update(double dt) async {
    ***
    if (enemiesInChannel[(positionOriginal.y / sizeTileMap).
    toInt() - 1]) {
      ***
}

@override
void onGameResize(Vector2 size) {
  position = positionOriginal * game.factScale;
  scale = Vector2.all(game.factScale);
  super.onGameResize(size);
  }
}
```

lib\components\plants\cactus_component.dart

```
class CactusComponent extends PlantComponent {
  CactusComponent({required sizeMap, required position})
      : super(sizeMap, position)
    ***
```

lib\components\plants\peashooter_component.dart

```
class PeashooterComponent extends PlantComponent {
  PeashooterComponent({required sizeMap, required position})
      : super(sizeMap, position) {
```

It is important to note that for the plants the constructor was changed so that it receives the position at the beginning of its creation (the base without scaling), and a copy of the original position of the plant can be created for subsequent calculations at the time of scaling the window.

For the zombies, it is a bit more complex in calculation since the position in X changes over time, but it follows the same principle as for the plants in which a position must be kept before rescaling:

lib\components\zombies\zombie_component.dart

```
class ZombieComponent extends *** {
  Vector2 positionCopy = Vector2(0, 0);

  ZombieComponent(position) : super(position: position) {
    debugMode = true;
    positionCopy = position;
  }
  @override
  void update(double dt) {
    ***
    if (!isAttacking) {
      position.add(Vector2(-dt * speed, 0));
      positionCopy.add(Vector2(-dt * speed, 0));
    }
    ***
  }
  @override
  void onGameResize(Vector2 size) {
    scale = Vector2.all(game.factScale);
    position = positionCopy * game.factScale;
    super.onGameResize(size);
  }

_setChannel(bool value) {
    if (positionCopy.y + alignZombie == 48) {
      enemiesInChannel[0] = value;
    } else if (positionCopy.y + alignZombie == 96) {
      enemiesInChannel[1] = value;
    } else if (positionCopy.y + alignZombie == 144) {
      enemiesInChannel[2] = value;
    } else if (positionCopy.y + alignZombie == 192) {
      enemiesInChannel[3] = value;
```

```
    } else if (positionCopy.y + alignZombie == 240) {
      enemiesInChannel[4] = value;
    } else if (positionCopy.y + alignZombie == 288) {
      enemiesInChannel[5] = value;
    } else if (positionCopy.y + alignZombie == 336) {
      enemiesInChannel[6] = value;
    }
    // print(enemiesInChannel.toString());
  }
}
```

The idea in both implementations (zombies and plants) is to preserve the original position (or the one before the rescaling) factor so that when recalculating, it operates with the position before scaling.

One more component is missing that corresponds to the **SeedComponent** that is used internally from the **TileMapComponent**; therefore, we cannot scale it directly from the Game class. Apart from that, this component requires special treatment, since, to build itself, the sizes and positions defined in the **ObjectGroup** of the tmx (map) are used. For this reason, at the level of this component, we place another method **onGameResize()** that recalculates the position and size based on the scale:

lib\maps\seed_component.dart

```
class SeedComponent extends *** {
  ***
  Vector2 positionOriginal = Vector2(0, 0);

  SeedComponent({required size, required position, required this.game})
      : super(size: size, position: position) {
    ***
    positionOriginal = position;
    add(RectangleHitbox()..collisionType = CollisionType.active);
  }

  @override
  void onGameResize(Vector2 size) {
    position = positionOriginal * game.factScale;
    scale = Vector2.all(game.factScale);
```

```
    super.onGameResize(size);
  }
}
```

The logic for the position is simple: if we have that a seed must be located in the 20 × 20 space and we double the window, that is, twice its size, the position is not 20 × 20 but double, that is, 40 × 40, and this is to prevent the seeds from overlapping each other.

With this, we can rescale the window, and the map along with all the components will be scaled as well.

Chapter source code:

```
https://github.com/libredesarrollo/flame-curso-libro-plantvszombie05/
releases/tag/v0.2
```

CHAPTER 13

Game 5: Parallax Backgrounds

In this chapter, we will work with parallax backgrounds in a new project; we will create a project called **parallax06**.

Parallax backgrounds are a technique used in the development of applications, as well as web, mobile and including games, of course, which with the superposition of several fragments of an image, create the illusion of depth and together with all these layers, we generate the bottom; but, to give the sensation of depth, each one of these layers moves at different speeds and with this, the outermost layers seem to be closer and the innermost layers seem to be further away. This is what ultimately creates a sense of depth resulting in a very interesting experience for game creation.

Configure the Project

To create the parallax effect on a background, it is necessary to use a set of images from which the background is assembled in pieces. You can search in your browser the following:

2D parallax background free download

And you will find multiple resources. In this chapter we will use the following

```
https://craftpix.net/freebies/free-cartoon-parallax-2d-backgrounds/
```

whose images we will copy in the project and reference:

pubspec.yaml

```
assets:
  - assets/images/layer01_ground.png
  - assets/images/layer02_cake.png
  - assets/images/layer03_trees.png
```

A. Cruz Yoris, *Flame Game Development*, https://doi.org/10.1007/979-8-8688-0063-4_13

- assets/images/layer04_clouds.png
- assets/images/layer05_rocks.png
- assets/images/layer06_sky.png

These images are layers that we will use to generate the parallax background as we discussed previously. The next step is to create the base structure for the project:

lib/main.dart

```
import 'package:flutter/material.dart';

import 'package:flame/components.dart';
import 'package:flame/game.dart';

class MyGame extends FlameGame with HasKeyboardHandlerComponents,
HasCollisionDetection {

  @override
  void onLoad() async {
    super.onLoad();

  }
}
void main() {
  runApp(GameWidget(game: MyGame()));
}
```

Create the Parallax Effect

In Flame, we have a component called **ParallaxComponent** that makes the process of creating a parallax effect very easy. We will define the images to use as a list:

lib/main.dart

```
class MyGame extends FlameGame with HasKeyboardHandlerComponents,
HasCollisionDetection {
  @override
  void onLoad() async {
    super.onLoad();
    add(await bgParallax());
  }
```

```
Future<ParallaxComponent> bgParallax() async {
    ParallaxComponent parallaxComponent = await loadParallaxComponent([
      ParallaxImageData('layer06_sky.png'),
      ParallaxImageData('layer05_rocks.png'),
      ParallaxImageData('layer04_clouds.png'),
      ParallaxImageData('layer03_trees.png'),
      ParallaxImageData('layer02_cake.png'),
      ParallaxImageData('layer01_ground.png'),
    ],
        baseVelocity: Vector2(10, 0));

        return parallaxComponent;
  }
}
```

You will see that we have almost gotten the parallax effect. For now, all the layers move at the same speed. The **baseVelocity** argument allows you to define the movement of the backgrounds. Usually you want the movement to occur on the X axis and not on the Y axis, as follows:

```
baseVelocity: Vector2(10, 0)
```

As homework, try different values when defining the vector and using different images (comment out and uncomment some of the **ParallaxImageData** defined previously or change the order of layers) and evaluate their behavior. However, in essence, if you use high values, such as

```
baseVelocity: Vector2(100, 0)
```

you will see a rapid movement in the backgrounds. If you place lower values

```
baseVelocity: Vector2(5, 0)
```

the scroll will be slower. And if you define the scroll on the Y

```
baseVelocity: Vector2(5, 10)
```

the layers will move on the X and Y axes.

When you run the application, you should see output like the following.

Figure 13-1. *Parallax background*

Vary Speed in Layers

At the moment we get a somewhat boring parallax background since, although we have a background that moves, everything moves at the same speed. To customize this aspect, that is, the backgrounds move at different speeds, we can use the **velocityMultiplierDelta** parameter, which allows moving the background images (layers) with a faster speed the closer the image is:

lib/main.dart

```
Future<ParallaxComponent> bgParallax() async {
    ParallaxComponent parallaxComponent = await loadParallaxComponent([
    ***
    baseVelocity: Vector2(10, 0),
    velocityMultiplierDelta: Vector2(1.1, 0));
}
```

With this, we will have the same effect, but now the layers move at different speeds. So that you understand how this argument works, try placing higher values, and you will see that the closer the layer is, the faster it will move.

Create a Component Class for the Parallax

We can create the parallax equivalent with a component class looking like the following:

lib\background\candy_background.dart

```
import 'dart:async';

import 'package:flame/components.dart';
import 'package:flame/parallax.dart';

import 'package:parallax06/main.dart';

class CandyBackground extends ParallaxComponent {
  @override
  void onLoad() async {
    parallax = await game.loadParallax([
      ParallaxImageData('layer06_sky.png'),
      ParallaxImageData('layer05_rocks.png'),
      ParallaxImageData('layer04_clouds.png'),
      ParallaxImageData('layer03_trees.png'),
      ParallaxImageData('layer02_cake.png'),
      ParallaxImageData('layer01_ground.png'),
    ],
        baseVelocity: Vector2(10, 0),
        velocityMultiplierDelta: Vector2(1.1, 1.1));
  }
}
```

The **game** allows you to get a reference to the game (the **MyGame** class defined in main). As for the main, we have

lib/main.dart

```
import 'package:flutter/material.dart';
import 'package:flame/game.dart';
import 'package:parallax06/background/candy_background.dart';
```

451

```
class MyGame extends FlameGame with HasKeyboardHandlerComponents,
HasCollisionDetection {
  @override
  void onLoad() async {
    super.onLoad();
    add(CandyBackground());
}
```

And with this we have the same result as before.

Player

In this section, we will create the basic functionalities for the player. Let's start by defining the sprite sheet to use, which you can download from the following link:

```
https://github.com/libredesarrollo/flame-curso-libro-parallax06/blob/
main/assets/images/player.png
```

This image was edited and created by the writer and can be freely used in any type of project.

We copy and reference the image from the project:

```
pubspec.yaml
```

```
  assets:
    ***
    - assets/images/player.png
```

We create the base class for the player:

```
lib\components\character.dart
```

```
import 'package:flame/collisions.dart';
import 'package:flame/components.dart';

class Character extends SpriteAnimationComponent
    with KeyboardHandler, CollisionCallbacks {
  double speed = 160;

  final double spriteSheetWidth = 231;
  final double spriteSheetHeight = 230;
```

```
  late SpriteAnimation idleAnimation, chewAnimation;

  late RectangleHitbox body;
}
```

And here's the implementation or component of the player:

lib\components\player_component.dart

```
import 'dart:async';

import 'package:flame/collisions.dart';
import 'package:flame/flame.dart';
import 'package:flame/components.dart';
import 'package:flame/sprite.dart';
import 'package:flutter/src/services/keyboard_key.g.dart';
import 'package:flutter/src/services/raw_keyboard.dart';

import 'package:parallax06/components/character.dart';
import 'package:parallax06/utils/create_animation_by_limit.dart';

class PlayerComponent extends Character {
  PlayerComponent() : super() {
    anchor = Anchor.center;
    debugMode = true;
    position = Vector2(spriteSheetWidth, spriteSheetHeight);
    size = Vector2(spriteSheetWidth, spriteSheetHeight);
  }

  @override
  void update(double dt) {
    super.update(dt);

    _movePlayer(dt);
  }

  @override
  bool onKeyEvent(RawKeyEvent event, Set<LogicalKeyboardKey> keysPressed) {
    if (keysPressed.isEmpty) {
      movementType = MovementType.idle;
    }
```

```
  // movement
  if (keysPressed.contains(LogicalKeyboardKey.arrowRight) ||
      keysPressed.contains(LogicalKeyboardKey.keyD)) {
    movementType = MovementType.right;
  } else if (keysPressed.contains(LogicalKeyboardKey.arrowLeft) ||
      keysPressed.contains(LogicalKeyboardKey.keyA)) {
    movementType = MovementType.left;
  } else if (keysPressed.contains(LogicalKeyboardKey.arrowUp) ||
      keysPressed.contains(LogicalKeyboardKey.keyW)) {
    movementType = MovementType.up;
  } else if (keysPressed.contains(LogicalKeyboardKey.arrowDown) ||
      keysPressed.contains(LogicalKeyboardKey.keyS)) {
    movementType = MovementType.down;
  }

  return super.onKeyEvent(event, keysPressed);
}

@override
void onLoad() async {
  final spriteImage = await Flame.images.load('player.png');
  final spriteSheet = SpriteSheet(
      image: spriteImage,
      srcSize: Vector2(spriteSheetWidth, spriteSheetHeight));

  chewAnimation = spriteSheet.createAnimationByLimit(
      xInit: 0, yInit: 0, step: 4, sizeX: 2, stepTime: .08);

  idleAnimation = spriteSheet.createAnimationByLimit(
      xInit: 1, yInit: 0, step: 1, sizeX: 2, stepTime: .08);

  animation = idleAnimation;

  body = RectangleHitbox();
  add(body);
}

void _movePlayer(double dt) {
  switch (movementType) {
```

```
          case MovementType.right:
          case MovementType.left:
            position.add(Vector2(
                dt * speed * (movementType == MovementType.left ? -1 : 1), 0));
            break;
          case MovementType.up:
          case MovementType.down:
            position.add(Vector2(
                0, dt * speed * (movementType == MovementType.up ? -1 : 1)));
            break;
          case MovementType.idle:
            break;
      }
    }
}
```

This implementation is similar to other projects in which we define

- The animations section:
  - Idle state, to show the open mouth, in which no animation is running
  - Chewing state, in which we use all the states of the sprite sheet
- Basic mobility, not including gravity
  - Left, right, up, and down movements by defining the **enum** type, updating the **enum** on keypress, and using the **update()** function with the delta parameter to update the position for smooth changes
- The full body hitbox

We add the component from the main after the background:

lib\main.dart

```
void onLoad() async {
  super.onLoad();
  add(CandyBackground());
  add(PlayerComponent());
}
```

And with this, we will have an output like the following.

Figure 13-2. *Player included in the Flame game*

You can use the arrow keys or the WASD keys to move the player around the screen.

Rotation

Another feature that the game will have is the ability to rotate the player by pressing a key; to rotate a component, the **angle** property is used, which is expressed in radians, where one full turn is equivalent to two PI. With this in mind, each time a key is pressed (R key), we will apply an abrupt rotation at 90-degree angles (1/2 PI). Let's start by defining the enumerated type to control the rotation:

lib\utils\helper.dart

```
enum SideType { right, left, up, down }

class Character extends SpriteAnimationComponent
    with KeyboardHandler, CollisionCallbacks {
  ***
  SideType sideType = SideType.left;
}
```

And we implement the rotation on keypress to be an abrupt change, and therefore when the player presses the R key, the rotation is instantaneous:

lib\components\player_component.dart

```dart
import 'dart:math' as math;
***
class PlayerComponent extends Character {
  ***
  @override
  bool onKeyEvent(RawKeyEvent event, Set<LogicalKeyboardKey> keysPressed) {
    if (keysPressed.isEmpty) {
      movementType = MovementType.idle;
    }

    // movement
    ***

      // rotation
    if (keysPressed.contains(LogicalKeyboardKey.keyR)) {
      _rotate();
    }

    return super.onKeyEvent(event, keysPressed);
  }

  void _rotate() {
    switch (sideType) {
      case SideType.right:
        sideType = SideType.down;
        break;
      case SideType.down:
        sideType = SideType.left;
        break;
      case SideType.left:
        sideType = SideType.up;
        break;
      case SideType.up:
```

```
        sideType = SideType.right;
        break;
   }

   if (sideType == SideType.left || sideType == SideType.right) {
     flipVertically();
   }

   angle += math.pi * 0.5;
 }
 ***
}
```

If you wanted it to be progressive, the update would have to be done in the **update()** function using the delta time.

In the preceding implementation, we see that we use an enum to know in which direction the player is rotated, in addition to being able to use it to implement additional logic, specifically the use of the **flipVertically()** function, which prevents the player from appearing upside down in some rotations. Finally, with this we have the following:

Up

Figure 13-3. *Player looking up*

Right

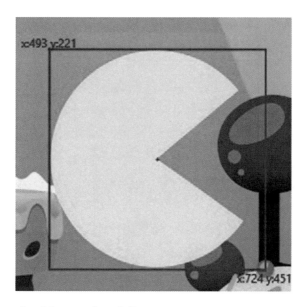

Figure 13-4. *Player looking to the right*

Down

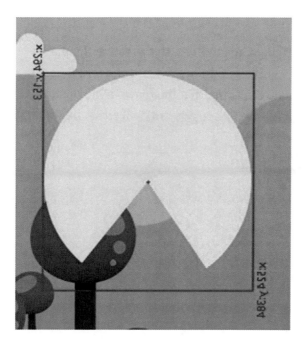

Figure 13-5. *Player looking down*

Left

Figure 13-6. *Player looking to the left*

Foods (Sweets)

It is time to implement the consumables. In the game, the player must eat the sweets that appear on the screen. In this section, we will use the terms *sweets*, *food*, and *consumables* as equivalents to indicate the sprite that the player will consume.

The sweets can appear on either side and will cross the screen from end to end, that is, the sweets can appear

1. Right to left

2. Left to right

3. Top to bottom

4. Bottom to top

With this, we will be able to implement various types of gameplay based on the fact that the player must devour the sweets that can appear on any of the sides. Some game ideas can be as follows:

1. The player loses when a piece of candy (or a certain number of pieces of candy) crosses the screen from one end to the other.

2. The player loses when consuming certain types of sweets.

3. The player must consume a certain amount of sweets in a certain time.

4. The player must consume certain types of food (sweets, breads, fruits, etc.).

This is just to mention some ideas for the game, but there are many other variants that you could implement.

The images used are available at

www.flaticon.es/icono-gratis/cup-cake_1888907

www.flaticon.es/icono-gratis/piruli_2697811

www.flaticon.es/icono-gratis/piruleta_1953854

www.flaticon.es/icono-gratis/dulce_1065299

www.flaticon.es/icono-gratis/cup-cake_1784121

www.flaticon.es/icono-gratis/pastel_2443037

www.flaticon.es/icono-gratis/pastel_2388066

www.flaticon.es/icono-gratis/chupete_983352

And the images were converted to a sprite sheet using TexturePacker and imported into the project (you can download the sprite sheet used in this project from the GitHub repository associated with this project; the link is at the end of the chapter):

pubspec.yaml

```
assets:
  ***
  - assets/images/candies.png
```

Help Functions and Base Structure

We will create a help file in which functions and structures are defined to manage the consumables. Although the game is based on sweets, to refer to sweets, we will use *food*, in case you want to implement another type of food as well:

lib\components\food.dart

```
import 'package:flame/components.dart';
import 'package:flame/flame.dart';
import 'package:flame/sprite.dart';
import 'package:parallax06/utils/helper.dart';

/*
types of foods that could be on the sprite sheet, in the
example sprite sheet only sweets and cakes appear
*/
enum TypeFood { bread, fruit, meat, candy, cake }

/* class with the properties to define a food/sprite per screen */
class Food {
  TypeFood typeFood;
  double chewed;
  Sprite sprite;
  Food({required this.typeFood, required this.chewed, required this.
  sprite});
}

/*
class used by the levels to define the time of appearance on the screen
The name of FoodPreSprite is that this class is used for (before/pre)
to generate the food sprite
*/
class FoodPreSprite {
  Food food;
  double speed;
  SideType sideType;
  double timeToOtherFood;
```

```dart
    FoodPreSprite(
        {required this.food,
        required this.speed,
        required this.sideType,
        this.timeToOtherFood = 3});
}

// food available
List<Food> foods = [];
// each position in the list is equivalent to a sprite in the sprite sheet
List<FoodPreSprite> foodLeve1 = [];

init() async {
  final spriteImage = await Flame.images.load('candies.png');
  final spriteSheet =
      SpriteSheet(image: spriteImage, srcSize: Vector2.all(512));

  foods = [
    Food(
        typeFood: TypeFood.cake,
        chewed: 1,
        sprite: spriteSheet.getSprite(0, 0)),

    Food(
        typeFood: TypeFood.candy,
        chewed: 3,
        sprite: spriteSheet.getSprite(0, 1)),
    Food(
        typeFood: TypeFood.cake,
        chewed: 5,
        sprite: spriteSheet.getSprite(0, 2)),

    Food(
        typeFood: TypeFood.cake,
        chewed: 2.5,
        sprite: spriteSheet.getSprite(0, 3)),
```

```
    Food(
        typeFood: TypeFood.cake,
        chewed: 5,
        sprite: spriteSheet.getSprite(1, 0)),
    Food(
        typeFood: TypeFood.candy,
        chewed: 5,
        sprite: spriteSheet.getSprite(1, 1)),
    Food(
        typeFood: TypeFood.candy,
        chewed: 5,
        sprite: spriteSheet.getSprite(1, 2)),
    Food(
        typeFood: TypeFood.candy,
        chewed: 5,
        sprite: spriteSheet.getSprite(1, 3)),
    ];

    foodLevel1 = [
      FoodPreSprite(food: foods[0], sideType: SideType.up, speed: 50),
      FoodPreSprite(food: foods[0], sideType: SideType.down, speed: 60),
      FoodPreSprite(food: foods[2], sideType: SideType.left, speed: 100),
      FoodPreSprite(food: foods[4], sideType: SideType.right, speed: 50),
      FoodPreSprite(food: foods[0], sideType: SideType.up, speed: 50),
      FoodPreSprite(food: foods[1], sideType: SideType.down, speed: 40),
      FoodPreSprite(food: foods[3], sideType: SideType.left, speed: 45),
      FoodPreSprite(food: foods[3], sideType: SideType.right, speed: 25),
    ];
}

// amount of sprite in the sprite sheet
int foodLevel1Size = foodLevel1.length;
```

In the preceding file, a class called **Food** is defined with all the characteristics/ properties that food has, such as

1. The type of food (sweets in this implementation).

2. The chewing time, in which the chewing animation will be shown and the player (chewing the food) will not be able to consume another food

3. The sprite used from the sprite sheet

The **FoodPreSprite** class is used by the food component (introduced later) to build a candy with the following characteristics/properties:

1. An instance of the **Food** class to indicate the food

2. A factor called **speed** that will be used to vary the speed of movement of the candy on the screen

3. A factor called **timeToOtherFood** that is used to indicate when the next sweet is added

4. The direction of movement

With the **init()** function, a list with all the foods/sweets defined in the sprite sheet is initialized. With this list, lists are created to indicate each of the levels of the game, such as the **foodLevel1** list; the sprite sheet is also processed into individual sprites.

This is a possible implementation that allows solving the problem of generating sweets on any side of the screen, but, of course, there are other possible implementations to solve the same situation.

Food Component (Sweet)

In this section, we are going to start generating the consumables, which are the sprites of the sweets that are defined in the sprite sheet.

Spawn the Candy in Random Positions

Let's start by creating a new component to handle the candy (the consumables) with the following body:

lib\components\food_component.dart

```
import 'dart:async';
import 'dart:math';
```

```dart
import 'package:flame/collisions.dart';
import 'package:flame/components.dart';
import 'package:flutter/widgets.dart';

import 'package:parallax06/components/food.dart';
import 'package:parallax06/utils/helper.dart';

class FoodComponent extends SpriteComponent with CollisionCallbacks,
HasGameReference {
  FoodPreSprite foodPreSprite;

  int factX = 0, factY = 0;

  late double screenWidth, screenHeight;

  CircleHitbox hitbox = CircleHitbox();

  FoodComponent({required this.foodPreSprite}) : super() {
    debugMode = true;
    size = Vector2.all(50);
  }

  @override
  void onLoad() {
    _initPosition();

    sprite = foodPreSprite.food.sprite;

    hitbox.collisionType = CollisionType.passive;
    add(hitbox);
  }

  _initPosition() {
    screenWidth = game.size.x;
    screenHeight = game.size.y;

    Random random = Random();

    // check incident side
    if (foodPreSprite.sideType == SideType.up) {
      factY = 1;
```

```
  } else if (foodPreSprite.sideType == SideType.down) {
    factY = -1;
  } else if (foodPreSprite.sideType == SideType.left) {
    factX = 1;
  } else if (foodPreSprite.sideType == SideType.right) {
    factX = -1;
  }

  // init position
  if (foodPreSprite.sideType == SideType.up ||
      foodPreSprite.sideType == SideType.down) {
    // Y
    position = Vector2(
        random.nextDouble() * screenWidth, factY == 1 ? 0 :
        screenHeight);
  } else {
    // X
    position = Vector2(
        factX == 1 ? 0 : screenWidth, random.nextDouble() *
        screenHeight);
  }
}

@override
void update(double dt) {
  position.add(Vector2(
      foodPreSprite.speed * dt * factX, foodPreSprite.speed * dt *
      factY));
  super.update(dt);
}
}
```

Code explanation

The objective of the preceding component is to generate and manage a single food (sweet depending on the sprite sheet used) in a random position on one of the sides of the screen (up, down, right, or left) and move the food around the screen in the opposite direction, that is to say:

- If the candy is generated on the right side, the candy will cross to the other end of the screen until it reaches the left side and vice versa.

- If the candy is generated at the top, the candy will cross to the other end of the screen until it reaches the bottom and vice versa.

It is also important to mention that the movement of the candy occurs on the X axis or on the Y axis, but not on both axes at the same time.

To implement this logic, we use two factors:

```
int factX = 0, factY = 0;
```

These factors are initialized according to the movement that the candy has to have:

```
if (foodPreSprite.sideType == SideType.up) {
  factY = 1;
} else if (foodPreSprite.sideType == SideType.down) {
  factY = -1;
} else if (foodPreSprite.sideType == SideType.left) {
  factX = 1;
} else if (foodPreSprite.sideType == SideType.right) {
  factX = -1;
}
```

They are then used to make the movement of the sweet, taking the preceding factors to make the movement in the function **update()**:

```
position.add(Vector2(
    foodPreSprite.speed * dt * factX, foodPreSprite.speed * dt * factY));
```

Again, this process is done for each piece of candy individually. For each candy, one of the factors will always be zero, that is to say:

```
factX = 1 o -1;
factY = 0;
```

468

or

```
factX = 0;
factY = 1 o -1;
```

This indicates that the movement of the candy occurs either on the X axis or on the Y axis, but not on both axes.

From the main, we add the sweets from time to time; it is a similar process to the one used in game 1 to generate the meteorites, only this time the meteorites are food that spawns from all sides of the screen:

lib\main.dart

```
class MyGame extends FlameGame with HasKeyboardHandlerComponents,
HasCollisionDetection {
  double foodTimer = 0.0;
  int foodIndex = 0;

  ***

  @override
  void onLoad() async {
    await food.init();
    add(CandyBackground());
    add(PlayerComponent());
  }

  @override
  void update(double dt) {
    _addSpriteFoodToWindow(dt);
    super.update(dt);
  }

  _addSpriteFoodToWindow(double dt) {
    if (foodIndex < food.foodLevel1Size) {
      if (foodTimer > food.foodLevel1[foodIndex].timeToOtherFood) {
        add(FoodComponent(foodPreSprite: food.foodLevel1[foodIndex]));
        foodTimer = 0.0;
        foodIndex++;
      }
```

```
        foodTimer += dt;
      }
    }
}
```

As key points, the property called **foodTimer** is used as a counter to generate the next sweet according to the time specified in **timeToOtherFood** and **foodIndex** to move within the array called **foodLevel1**.

Also initialize the food listing **await food.init()** in the **onLoad()** before performing any operations on the food array.

Remove Sweets When They Are No Longer Visible on the Screen

One optimization issue we currently have is that the candy is not removed when it leaves the screen, that is, when they are not consumed by the player.

The verification to be used is different depending on the side on which the candy appears; for example:

If a candy appears on the right side, it must be removed from the screen when its position is equal to the width of the screen.

If the candy appears on the left side, then it must be removed when its position equals zero.

In both cases, the sprite size must be added to prevent the sprite from disappearing in the visible area of the window; leaving us to implement it as:

lib\components\food_component.dart

```
@override
void update(double dt) {

  position.add(Vector2(
      foodPreSprite.speed * dt * factX, foodPreSprite.speed * dt * factY));

  if (foodPreSprite.sideType == SideType.up && position.y > screenHeight) {
    removeFromParent();
  } else if (foodPreSprite.sideType == SideType.down &&
      position.y < -size.y) {
    removeFromParent();
  } else if (foodPreSprite.sideType == SideType.left &&
      position.x > screenWidth) {
```

```
    removeFromParent();
  } else if (foodPreSprite.sideType == SideType.right &&
      position.x < -size.x) {
    removeFromParent();
  }

  super.update(dt);
}
```

Avoid Generating Sweets at the Ends of the Screen

Another common problem is spawning candy at the edges of the screen, like the following.

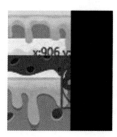

Figure 13-7. *Hidden candy on the edge of the screen*

That is, part or all of the sweet is hidden on the edge of the window. For this, once the position of the sweet is generated, it is verified that the position of the sprite of the sweet is in a safe position, that is, completely visible on the screen:

lib\components\food_component.dart

```
_initPosition() {
  screenWidth = game.size.x;
  screenHeight = game.size.y;

  Random random = Random();

  // check incident side
  if (foodPreSprite.sideType == SideType.up) {
    factY = 1;
  } else if (foodPreSprite.sideType == SideType.down) {
    factY = -1;
  } else if (foodPreSprite.sideType == SideType.left) {
```

```
    factX = 1;
  } else if (foodPreSprite.sideType == SideType.right) {
    factX = -1;
  }

  // init position
  if (foodPreSprite.sideType == SideType.up ||
      foodPreSprite.sideType == SideType.down) {
    // Y
    // position = Vector2(
    //     screenWidth * 0.99 /* 0 */ , factY == 1 ? 0 : screenHeight);
    // TEXT EXTREMOS
    position = Vector2(
        random.nextDouble() * screenWidth, factY == 1 ? 0 : screenHeight);

    if (position.x > (screenWidth - size.x / 2)) {
      // very close to the right, it is not visible correctly
      position.x = screenWidth - size.x;
    }
  } else {
    // X
    // position = Vector2(
    // factX == 1 ? 0 : screenWidth, /*0*/ screenHeight); // TEST EXTREMOS
    position = Vector2(
        factX == 1 ? 0 : screenWidth, random.nextDouble() * screenHeight);
    if (position.y > (screenHeight - size.y / 2)) {
      // too close down, not visible correctly
      position.y = screenHeight - size.y;
    }
  }
}
```

You can test values to test for extremes, for example, to the right and left sides, with

lib\components\food_component.dart

```
_initPosition() {
  screenWidth = game.size.x;
  screenHeight = game.size.y;
```

```
  if (foodPreSprite.sideType == SideType.up ||
      foodPreSprite.sideType == SideType.down) {
   position = Vector2(/*screenWidth*/ 0, factY == 1 ? 1 : screenHeight);
   ***

  }
}
```

And you'll see that they always appear on a visible side, so there's no need to add additional validations.

In the case of the top and bottom, on the top, it would not be necessary to add a check. If we try with

lib\components\food_component.dart

```
_initPosition() {
   ***
   } else {
//      position = Vector2(
  //        factX == 1 ? 1 : screenWidth, random.nextDouble() *
            screenHeight);
      position = Vector2(factX == 1 ? 1 : screenWidth, 0);
  }
}
```

we will see that the candy is still visible, but when it is a value close to or equal to the height (or width) of the window

lib\components\food_component.dart

```
_initPosition() {
   ***
   } else {
      position = Vector2(factX == 1 ? 1 : screenWidth, screenHeight);
  }
}
```

the sweet is not visible, and therefore the player could not consume it. Here's how to avoid this:

```
_initPosition() {
    ***
    } else {
       position = Vector2(
           factX == 1 ? 1 : screenWidth, random.nextDouble() *
           screenHeight);
       if (position.y > (screenHeight - size.y / 2)) {
         position.y = screenHeight - size.y;
       }
    }
  }
}
```

These are additional checks where if the candy sprite passes a certain threshold, it is relocated.

Eat Food

In this section, we are going to implement the function of consuming sweets. Let's start by defining a hitbox that spans just the mouth space:

lib\components\character.dart

```
late RectangleHitbox body, mouth;
```

And here's the implementation:

lib\components\player_component.dart

```
f
class PlayerComponent extends Character {
  MyGame game;

  @override
  void onLoad() async {
    ***
```

```
mouth = RectangleHitbox(size: Vector2(100, 80), position:
Vector2(110, 70))
    ..collisionType = CollisionType.active;

add(body);
add(mouth);
}

@override
void onCollisionStart(
    Set<Vector2> intersectionPoints, PositionComponent other) {
  if (mouth.isColliding) {
    other.removeFromParent();
  }
  super.onCollisionStart(intersectionPoints, other);
}
}
```

With the preceding code, we initialize the hitbox for the mouth and implement the collision (for the mouth only) in which, if it is a candy, then remove the component; the process shown here is similar to the one implemented in game 1 for the dinosaur's feet. With this, we will have the following.

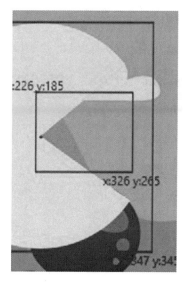

Figure 13-8. *Player's mouth*

In the preceding implementation, several more functionalities need to be defined:

- When colliding with a candy, play the chewing animation for the specified amount of time on the candy.

- You can only consume sweets where the player has the same angle as the sweet, that is, if a sweet comes from above, the player has to be rotated upward.

- Candy can only be consumed if the player's animation state is idle.

- There should be a counter for devoured and lost sweets.

Play the Chewing Animation

Another fundamental detail of the game is that the chewing animation will be played when devouring food for the time specified in **food.chewed**. To do this, we will create three additional properties:

1. *changeAnimationTimer*: A counter to keep the time of the player chewing

2. *timeToChangeAnimation*: Records the time that the player should be chewing

3. *chewing*: Indicates if the player is chewing

Its implementation is similar to the one used in the main to generate the sweets:

lib\components\player_component.dart

```
class PlayerComponent extends Character {

  double changeAnimationTimer = 0;
  double timeToChangeAnimation = 0;
  bool chewing = false;

@override
  void update(double dt) {
    super.update(dt);
```

```
    if (chewing) {
      changeAnimationTimer += dt;
      if (changeAnimationTimer >= timeToChangeAnimation) {
        timeToChangeAnimation = 0;
        changeAnimationTimer = 0;
        chewing = false;
        animation = idleAnimation;
      }
    }

    movePlayer(dt);
  }

  @override
  void onCollisionStart(
      Set<Vector2> intersectionPoints, PositionComponent other) {
    if (mouth.isColliding && other is FoodComponent) {
      timeToChangeAnimation = other.foodPreSprite.food.chewed;
      chewing = true;
      animation = chewAnimation;

      other.removeFromParent();
    }
    super.onCollisionStart(intersectionPoints, other);
  }
}
```

Do Not Eat Food While Chewing

If the player is in the chewing state (**chewing = true**), it means that they can't eat another sweet until the chewing animation finishes executing according to the implementation of the previous section. Performing this functionality is as easy as placing one more condition at the moment of colliding:

lib\components\player_component.dart

```
@override
void onCollisionStart(
    Set<Vector2> intersectionPoints, PositionComponent other) {
  if (mouth.isColliding && other is FoodComponent && !chewing) {
    ***
  }
  super.onCollisionStart(intersectionPoints, other);
}
```

Eating Food in One Position

Another characteristic that we must implement is that the player can only devour the sweets if both have the same angle, that is, if a sweet comes from above, the player has to be looking up to be able to consume the sweet. This functionality is as easy to do as verifying that the player and the candy to be devoured are at the same angle (**SideType**) at the moment of the collision:

lib\components\player_component.dart

```
@override
void onCollisionStart(
    Set<Vector2> intersectionPoints, PositionComponent other) {
  if (mouth.isColliding &&
      other is FoodComponent &&
      !chewing &&
      rotateType == other.foodPreSprite.sideType) {
    ***
  }
  super.onCollisionStart(intersectionPoints, other);
}
```

Show Statistics in an Overlay

In this section, we are going to implement an overlay to display

- A score per candy eaten

- How many candies the player has devoured

- How many sweets have not been devoured

Let's start by importing a reference image for the overlay:

www.flaticon.es/icono-gratis/piruli_2697811?term=candy&page=1&position=7
1&origin=search&related_id=2697811

pubspec.yaml

```
  assets:
    ***
    - assets/images/food.png
```

In the **Food** class, we will create a new property to indicate the points for sweets and update the list with the scores that you consider:

```
class Food {
  TypeFood typeFood;
  double chewed;
  Sprite sprite;
  int point;

  Food(
      {required this.typeFood,
      required this.chewed,
      required this.sprite,
      this.point = 1});
}

init() async {
  final spriteImage = await Flame.images.load('candies.png');
  final spriteSheet =
      SpriteSheet(image: spriteImage, srcSize: Vector2.all(512));
```

```
foods = [
  Food(
      typeFood: TypeFood.cake,
      chewed: 2,
      point: 5,
      sprite: spriteSheet.getSprite(0, 0)),
    ***

  ]
}
```

We created an overlay showing the statistics, similar to the one implemented in other games:

lib\overlay\statistics_overlay.dart

```
import 'package:flutter/material.dart';
import 'package:parallax06/main.dart';

class StatisticsOverlay extends StatefulWidget {
  final MyGame game;

  StatisticsOverlay({Key? key, required this.game}) : super(key: key);

  @override
  State<StatisticsOverlay> createState() => _StatisticsOverlayState();
}

class _StatisticsOverlayState extends State<StatisticsOverlay> {
  @override
  Widget build(BuildContext context) {
    return Padding(
      padding: const EdgeInsets.all(8.0),
      child: Column(mainAxisAlignment: MainAxisAlignment.start, children: [
        Row(
          crossAxisAlignment: CrossAxisAlignment.end,
          children: [
            Image.asset(
              'assets/images/food.png',
              width: 50,
```

```
      ),
      const SizedBox(
        width: 5,
      ),
      Text(
        widget.game.points.toString(),
        style: const TextStyle(
            fontSize: 30,
            color: Colors.amber,
            shadows: [Shadow(color: Colors.black, blurRadius: 5.0)]),
      )
    ],
  ),
),
Row(
  crossAxisAlignment: CrossAxisAlignment.end,
  children: [
    const Text(
      "E",
      style: TextStyle(
          fontSize: 15,
          color: Colors.amber,
          shadows: [Shadow(color: Colors.black, blurRadius: 5.0)]),
    ),
    const SizedBox(
      width: 5,
    ),
    Text(
      widget.game.eatenFood.toString(),
      style: const TextStyle(
          fontSize: 15,
          color: Colors.amber,
          shadows: [Shadow(color: Colors.black, blurRadius: 5.0)]),
    )
  ],
),
```

```
      Row(
        crossAxisAlignment: CrossAxisAlignment.end,
        children: [
          const Text(
            "L",
            style: TextStyle(
                fontSize: 15,
                color: Colors.amber,
                shadows: [Shadow(color: Colors.black, blurRadius: 5.0)]),
          ),
          const SizedBox(
            width: 5,
          ),
          Text(
            widget.game.lostFood.toString(),
            style: const TextStyle(
                fontSize: 15,
                color: Colors.amber,
                shadows: [Shadow(color: Colors.black, blurRadius: 5.0)]),
          )
        ],
      )
    ]),
  );
  }
}
```

From the main, we create three properties to handle the score and candy eaten and lost, respectively, plus a function to reload the overlay and define the overlay in the **GameWidget**:

```
class MyGame extends FlameGame
    with HasKeyboardHandlerComponents, HasCollisionDetection {

  int points = 0;
  int eatenFood = 0;
  int lostFood = 0;
```

```
  refreshStatistics(bool isEaten) {
    overlays.remove('Statistics');
    overlays.add('Statistics');
  }
}

void main() {
  runApp(GameWidget(
    game: MyGame(),
    overlayBuilderMap: {
      'Statistics': (context, MyGame game) {
        return StatisticsOverlay(game: game);
      },
    },
    initialActiveOverlays: const ['Statistics'],
  ));
}
```

The **isEaten** argument allows us to know if the food was eaten (true) or left the screen (false).

From the food component, we increase the candy lost counter by one for when the component is destroyed by not being visible and therefore not being consumed by the player:

lib\components\food_component.dart

```
class FoodComponent extends SpriteComponent
    with CollisionCallbacks, HasGameReference<MyGame> {
***
  @override
  void update(double dt) {
    position.add(Vector2(
        foodPreSprite.speed * dt * factX, foodPreSprite.speed * dt *
        factY));

    if (foodPreSprite.sideType == SideType.up && position.y >
    screenHeight) {
      removeFromParent();
```

```
        game.lostFood++;
        game.refreshStatistics(false);
      } else if (foodPreSprite.sideType == SideType.down &&
          position.y < -size.y) {
        removeFromParent();
        game.lostFood++;
        game.refreshStatistics(false);
      } else if (foodPreSprite.sideType == SideType.left &&
          position.x > screenWidth) {
        removeFromParent();
        game.lostFood++;
        game.refreshStatistics(false);
      }
      if (foodPreSprite.sideType == SideType.right && position.x < -size.x) {
        removeFromParent();
        game.lostFood++;
        game.refreshStatistics(false);
      }

      super.update(dt);
    }
}
```

From the player component, the consumed candy counters are increased when there is a collision between the player's mouth and the candy:

lib\components\player_component.dart

```
class PlayerComponent extends Character with HasGameReference<MyGame> {
  ***
  @override
  void onCollisionStart(
      Set<Vector2> intersectionPoints, PositionComponent other) {
    if (mouth.isColliding &&
        other is FoodComponent &&
        !chewing &&
```

```
    sideType == other.foodPreSprite.sideType) {
  other.removeFromParent();

  chewing = true;
  animation = chewAnimation;
  timeToChangeAnimation = other.foodPreSprite.food.chewed;

  // Statistics
  game.points += other.foodPreSprite.food.point;
  game.eatenFood++;
  game.refreshStatistics(true);
  }

  super.onCollisionStart(intersectionPoints, other);
  }

}
```

With this, we will have the following.

Figure 13-9. *Statistics*

Implement Ways of Gameplay

As we mentioned before, for this type of games, we can have different implementations to play, for example:

1. The player loses when a piece of candy (or a certain number of pieces of candy) crosses the screen from one end to the other.

2. The player loses when they consume a certain type of candy.

3. The player must consume a certain amount of sweets in a certain time.

4. The player can only consume a certain type of candy.

In this section we are going to start by implementing the logic for each of these possible ways of playing the game previously implemented. Let's start by defining the game state:

1. The player won.

2. The player lost.

3. The game is still running.

With this in mind, we create the following enumerated type to know the state at all times:

lib\utils\type_game.dart

```
enum StateGame { running, win, lose }
```

Based on the cases explained previously, we will have the following functions:

lib\utils\type_game.dart

```
import 'package:parallax06/components/food.dart';

enum StateGame { running, win, lose }

// type of game that ends when the player loses a piece of candy
StateGame oneLost(List<FoodPreSprite> levelN, int eatenFood, int lostFood,
bool isEaten) {
  return StateGame.running;
}

// points per level
List<int> levelsMinPoints = [50, 80, 100];
// type of game that ends when the player gets a certain number of points
StateGame byPoints(List<FoodPreSprite> levelN, int points, int index, int
currentLevel, bool isEaten) {
  return StateGame.running;
}
```

```
// type of sweets not to eat
List<TypeFood> levelsOnlyTypeFood = [TypeFood.candy, TypeFood.cake,
TypeFood.cake];
// type of game in which only one type of food can be consumed
StateGame onlyTypeFood(
    List<FoodPreSprite> levelN, int index, int currentLevel, bool
    isEaten) {
  return StateGame.running;
}

// type of sweets you can eat
List<TypeFood> levelsNotEatenThisFood = [TypeFood.candy, TypeFood.cake];
// type of game in which only one type of food can be consumed
StateGame notEatenThisFood(
    List<FoodPreSprite> levelN, int index, int currentLevel, bool
    isEaten) {
  return StateGame.running;
}
```

- The **levelN** argument indicates the current list of candies.

- The **index** argument indicates the index of the current candy.

- The **points** argument indicates the current points.

- The **eatenFood** argument indicates the food consumed.

- The **lostFood** argument indicates the lost food.

- The **currentLevel** argument indicates the current level.

- The **isEaten** argument is a Boolean indicating the status of the candy, whether it was eaten or lost.

Now, let's define the body of each of these functions.

1: Losing a Candy

This is the simplest type of game, in which the player loses when a candy is not consumed (**lostFood == 1**), so thinking about this, we will have

```
if (lostFood >= 1) return StateGame.lose;
```

The player wins when all the candies that appear are consumed:

```
if (levelN.length == eatenFood) return StateGame.win;
```

```
lib\utils\type_game.dart
```

```
// type of game that ends when the player loses a piece of candy
StateGame oneLost(List<FoodPreSprite> levelN, int eatenFood,
    int lostFood /*, bool isEaten*/) {
  // if (!isEaten) return StateGame.lose;
  if (lostFood >= 1) return StateGame.lose;
  if (levelN.length == eatenFood) return StateGame.win;

  return StateGame.running;
}
```

You could also check the status of **isEaten**. If it is false, it means that the player lost the candy and therefore lost:

```
if (!isEaten) return StateGame.lose;
```

2: Get a Minimum of Points

This is the type of game where the player wins when the number of points obtained is equal to or greater than that configured in the level:

```
if (points >= levelsMinPoints[currentLevel-1]) return StateGame.win;
```

One unit is subtracted from the level

```
currentLevel-1
```

since from the **main.dart**, we will use the value of one to reference level zero in the list of **levelsMinPoints**.

The player loses when all the candies appear but not enough points are reached:

```
if (levelN.length <= (eatenFood + lostFood)) return StateGame.lose;
```

This condition applies with the sum of sweets lost and eaten

```
(eatenFood + lostFood)
```

instead of using the index of the list (**foodIndex**) because the **foodIndex** is updated based on the sweets added on the screen and not on the sweet with which it interacted.

The function looks like the following:

```
lib\utils\type_game.dart
```

```
// points per level
List<int> levelsMinPoints = [50, 80, 100];
// type of game that ends when the player gets a certain number of points
StateGame byPoints(List<FoodPreSprite> levelN, int points, int eatenFood,
    int lostFood, int currentLevel /*, bool isEaten*/) {
  if (points >= levelsMinPoints[currentLevel-1]) return StateGame.win;
  if (levelN.length <= (eatenFood + lostFood)) return StateGame.lose;

  return StateGame.running;
}
```

3: Only Consume One Type of Sweet

This is the type of game where the player can only consume one type of candy:

```
if (levelN[(lostFood + eatenFood) - 1].food.typeFood !=
        levelsOnlyTypeFood[currentLevel - 1] &&
    isEaten) return StateGame.lose;
```

And the player wins when all the sweets have already appeared on the screen and the preceding condition is not met:

```
if (levelN.length <= (eatenFood + lostFood)) return StateGame.win;
```

The function looks like the following:

`lib\utils\type_game.dart`

```
// type of sweets not to eat
List<TypeFood> levelsOnlyTypeFood = [
  TypeFood.candy,
  TypeFood.cake,
  TypeFood.candy,
];
// type of game in which only one type of food can be consumed
StateGame onlyTypeFood(List<FoodPreSprite> levelN, int index, int
currentLevel,
    int eatenFood, int lostFood, bool isEaten) {
  if (levelN[(lostFood + eatenFood) - 1].food.typeFood !=
        levelsOnlyTypeFood[currentLevel - 1] &&
      isEaten) return StateGame.lose;

  if (levelN.length <= (eatenFood + lostFood)) return StateGame.win;

  return StateGame.running;
}
```

4: Cannot Consume a Type of Sweet

This is the type of game where the player loses when consuming the wrong candy:

```
if (levelN[(lostFood + eatenFood) - 1].food.typeFood ==
      levelsOnlyTypeFood[currentLevel - 1] &&
    isEaten) return StateGame.lose;
```

And the player wins when all the sweets have already appeared on the screen and the preceding condition is not met:

```
if (levelN.length <= (lostFood + eatenFood)) return StateGame.win;
```

The function looks like the following:

```
// type of sweets that can not consume
List<TypeFood> levelsNotEatenThisFood = [
  TypeFood.candy,
  TypeFood.cake,
  TypeFood.cake
];

// type of game in which only one type of food can be consumed
StateGame notEatenThisFood(List<FoodPreSprite> levelN, int index,
    int currentLevel, int eatenFood, int lostFood, bool isEaten) {
  if (levelN[(lostFood + eatenFood) - 1].food.typeFood ==
        levelsOnlyTypeFood[currentLevel - 1] &&
      isEaten) return StateGame.lose;

  if (levelN.length <= (lostFood + eatenFood)) return StateGame.win;
  return StateGame.running;
}
```

Test Previous Implementations

It's time to test the previous implementations. To do this, we'll create a function in **main. dart**, that is, in the main instance of Flame, which we will call every time an update occurs with the sweets (whether they are eaten or escape the screen). For this, we can use the same **refreshStatistics()** function called from the components to generate the sweet or the player when an update with candy occurs:

```
refreshStatistics(bool isEaten) {
  overlays.remove('Statistics');
  overlays.add('Statistics');

  _checkEndGame(isEaten);
}
  _checkEndGame(bool isEaten) {}
}
```

Here's the implementation for each of the game forms, starting with the first implementation:

```
void _checkEndGame() {
  switch (
      oneLost(food.foodLevel1, points, eatenCandy, lostCandy, foodIndex)) {
    case StateGame.lose:
      print("losing");
      paused = true;
      break;
    case StateGame.win:
      print("win");
      paused = true;
      break;
    default:
      break;
  }
}
```

Second:

```
void _checkEndGame(bool isEaten) {
  switch (typegame.byPoints(food.foodLeve1, points, eatenFood,
  lostFood, 1)) {
    case typegame.StateGame.lose:
      paused = true;
      print("losing");
      break;
    case typegame.StateGame.win:
      paused = true;
      print("win");
      break;
    default:
      break;
  }
}
```

Third:

```
void _checkEndGame(bool isEaten) {
    switch (typegame.onlyTypeFood(
        food.foodLevel1, foodIndex, 1, eatenFood, lostFood, isEaten)) {
     case typegame.StateGame.lose:
       paused = true;
       print("losing");
       break;
     case typegame.StateGame.win:
       paused = true;
       print("win");
       break;
     default:
       break;
  }
}
```

And fourth:

```
void _checkEndGame(bool isEaten) {
  switch (typegame.notEatenThisFood(
      food.foodLevel1, foodIndex, 1, eatenFood, lostFood, isEaten)) {
    case typegame.StateGame.lose:
      paused = true;
      print("losing");
      break;
    case typegame.StateGame.win:
      paused = true;
      print("win");
      break;
    default:
      break;
  }
}
```

Define Multiple Levels

We are going to implement a more scalable format in order to implement more levels for the game. From the previously implemented help file, we will create a function that, given the level, returns the list with the candies that should appear. We will define at least six levels:

lib\components\food.dart

```
// levels
List<FoodPreSprite> getCurrentLevel({int level = 1}) {
  switch (level) {
    case 2:
      return [
        FoodPreSprite(food: foods[0], sideType: SideType.up, speed: 50),
        FoodPreSprite(food: foods[0], sideType: SideType.down, speed: 60),
        FoodPreSprite(food: foods[2], sideType: SideType.left, speed: 100),
        FoodPreSprite(food: foods[4], sideType: SideType.right, speed: 50),
        FoodPreSprite(food: foods[5], sideType: SideType.up, speed: 50),
        FoodPreSprite(food: foods[1], sideType: SideType.down, speed: 40),
        FoodPreSprite(food: foods[3], sideType: SideType.left, speed: 45),
        FoodPreSprite(food: foods[7], sideType: SideType.right, speed: 25),
        FoodPreSprite(food: foods[2], sideType: SideType.left, speed: 100),
        FoodPreSprite(food: foods[4], sideType: SideType.right, speed: 50),
      ];
    case 3:
      return [
        FoodPreSprite(food: foods[0], sideType: SideType.up, speed: 50),
        FoodPreSprite(food: foods[0], sideType: SideType.down, speed: 60),
        FoodPreSprite(food: foods[2], sideType: SideType.left, speed: 100),
        FoodPreSprite(food: foods[4], sideType: SideType.right, speed: 50),
        FoodPreSprite(food: foods[0], sideType: SideType.up, speed: 50),
        FoodPreSprite(food: foods[1], sideType: SideType.down, speed: 40),
        FoodPreSprite(food: foods[7], sideType: SideType.left, speed: 45),
        FoodPreSprite(food: foods[3], sideType: SideType.right, speed: 25),
```

```
    FoodPreSprite(food: foods[3], sideType: SideType.left, speed: 45),
    FoodPreSprite(food: foods[8], sideType: SideType.right, speed: 25),
  ];
case 4:
  return [
    FoodPreSprite(food: foods[2], sideType: SideType.left, speed: 100),
    FoodPreSprite(food: foods[4], sideType: SideType.right, speed: 50),
    FoodPreSprite(food: foods[0], sideType: SideType.up, speed: 50),
    FoodPreSprite(food: foods[2], sideType: SideType.down, speed: 60),
    FoodPreSprite(food: foods[0], sideType: SideType.up, speed: 50)
  ];
case 5:
  return [
    FoodPreSprite(food: foods[0], sideType: SideType.down, speed: 60),
    FoodPreSprite(food: foods[3], sideType: SideType.right, speed: 25),
    FoodPreSprite(food: foods[0], sideType: SideType.up, speed: 50),
    FoodPreSprite(food: foods[4], sideType: SideType.right, speed: 50),
    FoodPreSprite(food: foods[0], sideType: SideType.up, speed: 50),
    FoodPreSprite(food: foods[1], sideType: SideType.down, speed: 40),
    FoodPreSprite(food: foods[2], sideType: SideType.left, speed: 100),
    FoodPreSprite(food: foods[3], sideType: SideType.left, speed: 45),
  ];
case 6:
  return [
    FoodPreSprite(food: foods[0], sideType: SideType.up, speed: 50),
    FoodPreSprite(food: foods[1], sideType: SideType.down, speed: 60),
    FoodPreSprite(food: foods[2], sideType: SideType.left, speed: 100),
    FoodPreSprite(food: foods[4], sideType: SideType.right, speed: 50),
    FoodPreSprite(food: foods[0], sideType: SideType.up, speed: 50),
    FoodPreSprite(food: foods[1], sideType: SideType.down, speed: 40),
    FoodPreSprite(food: foods[3], sideType: SideType.left, speed: 45),
    FoodPreSprite(food: foods[3], sideType: SideType.right, speed: 25),
  ];
```

```
    default: // 1
      return [
        FoodPreSprite(food: foods[0], sideType: SideType.up, speed: 50),
        FoodPreSprite(food: foods[1], sideType: SideType.down, speed: 60),
        FoodPreSprite(food: foods[2], sideType: SideType.left, speed: 100)
      ];
  }
}
```

This function is the one we will use instead of the variables

```
foodLevel1Size = ***
foodLevel1 = ***
```

which we remove and replace in the rest of the application. It is important to note the creation of a property to handle the current level (**currentLevel**):

```
lib\main.dart
```

```
class MyGame extends FlameGame
    with HasKeyboardHandlerComponents, HasCollisionDetection {
  ***

  int currentLevel = 1;

  void _checkEndGame(bool isEaten) {
    switch (typegame.notEatenThisFood(
        food.getCurrentLevel(level: currentLevel),
        ***
    }
  }

  ***

  _addSpriteFoodToWindow(double dt) {
    if (foodIndex < food.getCurrentLevel(level: currentLevel).length) {
      if (foodTimer >=
          food
              .getCurrentLevel(level: currentLevel)[foodIndex]
              .timeToOtherFood) {
```

```
        add(FoodComponent(
            foodPreSprite:
                food.getCurrentLevel(level: currentLevel)[foodIndex]));
        foodIndex++;
        foodTimer = 0;
      }
      foodTimer += dt;
    }
  }
}
```

With this, we have a simpler scheme with which to go from one level to another.

Function to Load Game Levels

We will need a function to load the levels and, with this, also to reset the game. Let's start by creating a function with which we initialize and do a reset from the player:

lib\components\player_component.dart

```
class PlayerComponent extends *** {
  PlayerComponent() : super() {
    _init();
  }
  _init() {
    anchor = Anchor.center;
    debugMode = true;
    position = Vector2(spriteSheetWidth, spriteSheetHeight);
    size = Vector2(spriteSheetWidth, spriteSheetHeight);
  }

  reset() {
    _init();
    changeAnimationTimer = 0;
    timeToChangeAnimation = 0;
    chewing = false;
```

```
    animation = idleAnimation;
  }
  ***
}
```

As you can see, the main properties of the player are reinitialized with the exception of the rotation, which would require additional logic other than just doing the flip that the reader (you) could implement (if they (you) deem it necessary). From main, we create a property to manage the player and a function to reset the game; we also define a property to specify the type of game and another function to advance to the next level; finally, we also use a property called **resetGame** to indicate that the game is going to be reset and we can delete the consumables, just like we did with game 3:

lib\main.dart

```
class MyGame extends *** {
  int currentLevel = 1;
  TypeGame typeGame = TypeGame.byPoints;
  bool resetGame = false;
  ***
  void loadLevel(
      {bool dead = false,
      int currentLevel = 1,
      typegame.TypeGame typeGame = typegame.TypeGame.byPoints}) {
    paused = false;

    resetGame = true;

    Timer(const Duration(milliseconds: 300), () {
      resetGame = false;
    });

    foodTimer = 0;
    foodIndex = 0;

    points = 0;
    eatenFood = 0;
    lostFood = 0;
```

```
    this.currentLevel = currentLevel;
    this.typeGame = typeGame;

    _playerComponent.reset();

    overlays.remove('GameOver');
    overlays.remove('Statistics');
    overlays.add('Statistics');
  }
}
```

And here's the enumerated type used:

lib\utils\type_game.dart

```
enum TypeGame { oneLost, byPoints, onlyTypeFood, notEatenThisFood }
```

We use the **resetGame** property to check if the instances need to be removed:

lib\components\food_component.dart

```
@override
void update(double dt) {
  if (game.resetGame) {
    removeFromParent();
  }
  ***
}
```

Overlays

In this section, we will create various overlays for the game, such as overlays to define the end of the game, level selection, and actions, among others.

Game Over

We will create an overlay that will be displayed when the user wins or loses:

lib\overlay\game_over_overlay.dart

```
import 'package:flutter/material.dart';
import 'package:parallax06/main.dart';

class GameOverOverlay extends StatefulWidget {
  MyGame game;
  GameOverOverlay({Key? key, required this.game}) : super(key: key);

  @override
  State<GameOverOverlay> createState() => _GameOverOverlayState();
}

class _GameOverOverlayState extends State<GameOverOverlay> {
  @override
  Widget build(BuildContext context) {
    return Center(
      child: Container(
        padding: const EdgeInsets.all(4),
        height: 200,
        width: 300,
        decoration: const BoxDecoration(
            color: Colors.black,
            borderRadius: BorderRadius.all(Radius.circular(20))),
        child: Column(children: [
          const Text(
            'Game Over',
            style: TextStyle(color: Colors.white, fontSize: 24),
          ),
          const SizedBox(
            height: 40,
          ),
```

```
            SizedBox(
              width: 200,
              height: 75,
              child: ElevatedButton(
                onPressed: () {
                  widget.game.overlays.remove('GameOver');
                  widget.game.loadLevel();
                },
                style: ElevatedButton.styleFrom(backgroundColor: Colors.white),
                child: const Text(
                  'Play Again',
                  style: TextStyle(fontSize: 28, color: Colors.black),
                ),
              ),
            )
          ]),
        ),
      );
    }
}
```

And we configure the overlay from the main; also, we add the overlay to the screen when winning/losing the game:

lib\main.dart

```
class MyGame extends *** {
***
  checkEndGame() {
    switch (oneLost(
        food.getCurrentLevel(level: currentLevel), eatenCandy,
        lostCandy)) {
      case StateGame.lose:
        print("losing");
        overlays.add('GameOver');
```

```
      paused = true;
      break;
    case StateGame.win:
      print("win");
      overlays.add('GameOver');
      paused = true;
      break;
    default:
      break;
    }
  }
}

void main() {
  runApp(GameWidget(
    game: MyGame(),
    overlayBuilderMap: {
      'Statistics': (context, MyGame game) {
        return StatisticsOverlay(game: game);
      },
      'GameOver': (context, MyGame game) {
        return GameOverOverlay(
          game: game,
        );
      }
    },
    initialActiveOverlays: const ['Statistics'],
  ));
}
```

Game Actions

We will update the statistics overlay to include the game pause and reset options on the right side of the screen:

```
class _StatisticsOverlayState extends State<StatisticsOverlay> {
  @override
  Widget build(BuildContext context) {
    return Padding(
      padding: const EdgeInsets.all(8.0),
      child: Column(
        mainAxisAlignment: MainAxisAlignment.start,
        children: [
          Row(
            crossAxisAlignment: CrossAxisAlignment.end,
            children: [
              Container(
                child: Image.asset(
                  'assets/images/candy.png',
                  width: 50,
                ),
              ),
              const SizedBox(
                width: 5,
              ),
              Text(
                widget.game.points.toString(),
                style: const TextStyle(
                    fontSize: 30,
                    color: Colors.amber,
                    shadows: [Shadow(color: Colors.black,
                    blurRadius: 5.0)]),
              ),
              const Expanded(
                child: SizedBox(),
              ),
              GestureDetector(
                onTap: () {
```

```
            setState(() {
              widget.game.paused = !widget.game.paused;
            });
          },
          child: Icon(
            widget.game.paused ? Icons.play_arrow : Icons.pause,
            color: Colors.white,
            size: 40,
          ),
        ),
        GestureDetector(
          onTap: () {
            setState(() {
              widget.game.reset();
            });
          },
          child: const Icon(
            Icons.replay,
            color: Colors.white,
            size: 40,
          ),
        ),
      ],
    ),
***

}
```

Select a Level

The following overlay allows you to select the level in which to play; in this example, we only have six levels. For the following overlay, we use a **GridView** with a **Container** that represents each of the levels:

lib\overlay\level_selection_overlay.dart

```
import 'package:flutter/material.dart';
import 'package:parallax06/main.dart';
```

```
class LevelSelectionOverlay extends StatefulWidget {
  MyGame game;
  LevelSelectionOverlay({Key? key, required this.game}) : super(key: key);

  @override
  State<LevelSelectionOverlay> createState() => _
LevelSelectionOverlayState();
}

class _LevelSelectionOverlayState extends State<LevelSelectionOverlay> {
  late double screenWidth, screenHeight;

  @override
  Widget build(BuildContext context) {
    screenWidth = MediaQueryData.fromView(View.of(context)).size.width;
    screenHeight = MediaQueryData.fromView(View.of(context)).size.height;

    return Container(
      color: Colors.black45,
      width: screenWidth,
      height: screenHeight,
      child: Center(
          child: Container(
        padding: const EdgeInsets.all(150),
        decoration: BoxDecoration(
          color: Colors.white,
          borderRadius: BorderRadius.circular(15),
        ),
        child: Column(
          children: [
            const Text(
              "Level Selection",
              style: TextStyle(fontSize: 40, color: Colors.black),
            ),
            Expanded(
              child: GridView.count(
                crossAxisCount: screenWidth > 900 ? 6 : 3,
```

```dart
                children: List.generate(6, (index) {
                  return _getLevel(index + 1);
                }),
              ),
            ),
          ],
        ),
      )),
    );
  }

  Widget _getLevel(int level) {
    return GestureDetector(
      onTap: () {
        widget.game.loadLevel(currentLevel: level);
        widget.game.overlays.remove('LevelSelection');
      },
      child: Container(
        width: 100,
        height: 100,
        alignment: Alignment.center,
        decoration: BoxDecoration(
            border: Border.all(color: Colors.blueAccent, width: 4)),
        child: Text(
          level.toString(),
          style: const TextStyle(
              fontSize: 40, fontWeight: FontWeight.w900, color:
              Colors.black),
        ),
      ),
    );
  }
}
```

Using the **Expanded** widget allows you to expand the **GridView** widget contained within the **Column**. Finally, a conditional is used:

```
crossAxisCount: screenWidth > 900 ? 6 : 3
```

For when the screens are of small dimensions (900 pixels), change the number of cells aligned in a row.

We enable the overlay in the main:

lib\main.dart

```
void main() {
  runApp(GameWidget(
    game: MyGame(),
    overlayBuilderMap: {
      'Statistics': (context, MyGame game) {
        return StatisticsOverlay(game: game);
      },
      'GameOver': (context, MyGame game) {
        return GameOverOverlay(
          game: game,
        );
      },
      'LevelSelection': (context, MyGame game) {
        return LevelSelectionOverlay(
          game: game,
        );
      }
    },
    initialActiveOverlays: const ['Statistics', 'LevelSelection'],
  ));
}
```

We put the option to show the preceding overlay from the statistics overlay:

```
class _StatisticsOverlayState extends State<StatisticsOverlay> {
  @override
  Widget build(BuildContext context) {
    return Padding(
      padding: const EdgeInsets.all(8.0),
      child: Column(
        mainAxisAlignment: MainAxisAlignment.start,
        children: [
          Row(
            crossAxisAlignment: CrossAxisAlignment.end,
            children: [
              ***
              GestureDetector(
                onTap: () {
                  setState(() {
                    widget.game.reset();
                  });
                },
                child: const Icon(
                  Icons.replay,
                  color: Colors.white,
                  size: 40,
                ),
              ),
              GestureDetector(
                onTap: () {
                  setState(() {
                    widget.game.overlays.add("LevelSelection");
                  });
                },
                child: const Icon(
                  Icons.grid_on,
                  color: Colors.white,
```

```
        size: 40,
      ),
    ),
  ],
),
```
***

Finally: we will have the following.

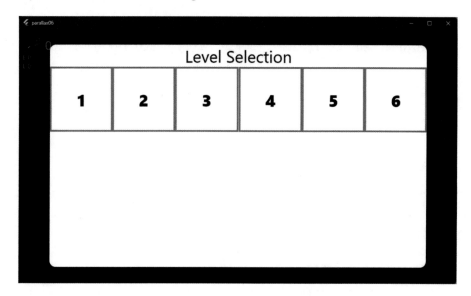

Figure 13-10. *Level selection*

Select a Gameplay

We are going to create an overlay to select the four types of gameplay available; for this, we will use a design similar to the previous overlay:

lib\overlay\type_game_overlay.dart

```
import 'package:flutter/material.dart';
import 'package:parallax06/main.dart';
import 'package:parallax06/utils/type_game.dart';

class TypeGameOverlay extends StatefulWidget {
  MyGame game;
  TypeGameOverlay({Key? key, required this.game}) : super(key: key);
```

```dart
  @override
  State<TypeGameOverlay> createState() => _TypeGameOverlayState();
}

class _TypeGameOverlayState extends State<TypeGameOverlay> {
  late double screenWidth;
  late double screenHeight;

  @override
  Widget build(BuildContext context) {
    screenWidth = MediaQueryData.fromView(View.of(context)).size.width;
    screenHeight = MediaQueryData.fromView(View.of(context)).size.height;

    return Container(
      color: Colors.black45,
      width: screenWidth,
      height: screenHeight,
      child: Center(
          child: Container(
        padding: const EdgeInsets.all(150),
        decoration: BoxDecoration(
          color: Colors.white,
          borderRadius: BorderRadius.circular(15),
        ),
        child: Column(
          children: [
            const Text(
              "Type Game Selection",
              style: TextStyle(fontSize: 40, color: Colors.black),
            ),
            Expanded(
              child: GridView.count(
                crossAxisCount: 2,
                crossAxisSpacing: 10,
                mainAxisSpacing: 10,
                childAspectRatio: 2.5,
```

```
            children: List.generate(4, (index) {
              return _getTypeGame(index);
            }),
          ),
        ),
      ],
    ),
  )),
  );
}

Widget _getTypeGame(int index) {
  return GestureDetector(
    onTap: () {
      widget.game.loadLevel(typeGame: TypeGame.values[index]);
      widget.game.overlays.remove('TypeGame');
    },
    child: Container(
      alignment: Alignment.center,
      decoration: BoxDecoration(border: Border.all(color: Colors.black)),
      child: Text(TypeGame.values[index].name,
          style: const TextStyle(
              fontSize: 40,
              fontWeight: FontWeight.w900,
              color: Colors.black)),
    ),
  );
}
}
```

An important change we have is the printing of the types listed by the index:

`TypeGame.values[index].name`

And we use the **childAspectRatio** property to change the aspect ratio on top:

`childAspectRatio: 2.5,`

We specify the separation in the X and Y for the cells:

```
crossAxisSpacing: 10,
mainAxisSpacing: 10,
```

We add the overlay in the main:

`lib\main.dart`

```
void main() {
  runApp(GameWidget(
    game: MyGame(),
    overlayBuilderMap: {
      ***
      'TypeGameOverlay': (context, MyGame game) {
        return TypeGameOverlay(
          game: game,
        );
      }
    },
    initialActiveOverlays: const ['Statistics'],
  ));
}
```

And we have a new icon on the statistics overlay:

`lib\overlay\statistics_overlay.dart`

```
class _StatisticsOverlayState extends State<StatisticsOverlay> {
  @override
  Widget build(BuildContext context) {
    return Padding(
      padding: const EdgeInsets.all(8.0),
      child: Column(
        mainAxisAlignment: MainAxisAlignment.start,
        children: [
          Row(
            crossAxisAlignment: CrossAxisAlignment.end,
```

```
children: [
  ***
  GestureDetector(
    onTap: () {
      setState(() {
        widget.game.overlays.add("LevelSelection");
      });
    },
    child: const Icon(
      Icons.grid_on,
      color: Colors.white,
      size: 40,
    ),
  ),
  GestureDetector(
    onTap: () {
      setState(() {
        widget.game.overlays.add("TypeGameOverlay");
      });
    },
    child: const Icon(
      Icons.gamepad,
      color: Colors.white,
      size: 40,
    ),
  ),
```

And by clicking the option, we obtain the following.

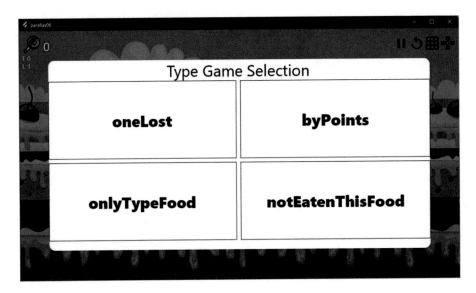

Figure 13-11. *Type of game*

Information About the Type of Game and Level

We will place two texts to present the type of game established and the level:

lib\overlay\type_game_overlay.dart

```
class _StatisticsOverlayState extends State<StatisticsOverlay> {
  @override
  Widget build(BuildContext context) {
    return Padding(
      padding: const EdgeInsets.all(8.0),
      child: Column(
        crossAxisAlignment: CrossAxisAlignment.start,
        mainAxisAlignment: MainAxisAlignment.start,
        children: [
          ***
          const Expanded(
              child: SizedBox(
            height: 50,
          )),
```

```
        Text(widget.game.typeGame.toString()),
        Text("Level: ${widget.game.currentLevel}")
      ],
    ),
  );
  }
}
```

And we will have the following.

Figure 13-12. *Type of game and level, overlay*

Additional Details About the Type of Game

In the impression about the type of game, additional details that the player must know are missing. For example, if they choose the points play, the player must know how many points they must get. The same is true for all other types of games. So we'll create additional functions that return this detail for each type of game:

lib\utils\type_game.dart

```
***
String oneLostMetadata() {
  return "";
}

String byPointsMetadata(int currentLevel) {
  return levelsMinPoints[currentLevel].toString();
}

String onlyTypeFoodMetadata(int currentLevel) {
  return levelsOnlyTypeFood[currentLevel].toString();
}
```

```
String notEatenThisFoodMetadata(int currentLevel) {
  return levelsNotEatenThisFood[currentLevel].toString();
}
```

We will create a function that checks the game type and calls the corresponding detail function:

lib\main.dart

```
class MyGame extends FlameGame *** {
***
    String typeGameDetail() {
    String meta = '';

    switch (typeGame) {
      case typegame.TypeGame.oneLost:
        meta = typegame.oneLostMetadata();
        break;
      case typegame.TypeGame.byPoints:
        meta = typegame.byPointsMetadata(currentLevel);
        break;
      case typegame.TypeGame.notEatenThisFood:
        meta = typegame.notEatenThisFoodMetadata(currentLevel);
        break;
      case typegame.TypeGame.onlyTypeFood:
        meta = typegame.onlyTypeFoodMetadata(currentLevel);
        break;
    }

    return "$typeGame $meta";
  }
}
```

And now, we use this new function instead of printing the game type from the overlay:

```
lib\overlay\statistics_overlay.dart
```

```
***
Text(widget.game.typeGameDetail()),
Text("Level: ${widget.game.currentLevel}")
***
```

GameOver: Implement Game Types

By having the entire implementation ready with the types of games and levels, the next step is to configure the end of the game in the function that is responsible for evaluating the type of game established. For this, the **checkEndGame()** function looks like the following:

```
lib\main.dart
```

```
void _checkEndGame(bool isEaten) {
  typegame.StateGame stateGame = typegame.StateGame.running;

  switch (typeGame) {
    case typegame.TypeGame.oneLost:
      stateGame = typegame.oneLost(
          food.getCurrentLevel(level: currentLevel), eatenFood, lostFood);
      break;
    case typegame.TypeGame.byPoints:
      stateGame = typegame.byPoints(food.getCurrentLevel(level:
      currentLevel),
          points, eatenFood, lostFood, 1);
      break;
    case typegame.TypeGame.onlyTypeFood:
      stateGame = typegame.onlyTypeFood(
          food.getCurrentLevel(level: currentLevel),
          foodIndex,
          currentLevel,
          eatenFood,
```

```
            lostFood,
            isEaten);
      break;
    case typegame.TypeGame.notEatenThisFood:
      stateGame = typegame.notEatenThisFood(
            food.getCurrentLevel(level: currentLevel),
            foodIndex,
            currentLevel,
            eatenFood,
            lostFood,
            isEaten);
      break;
  }

  switch (stateGame) {
    case typegame.StateGame.lose:
      paused = true;
      print("losing");
      overlays.add('GameOver');
      break;
    case typegame.StateGame.win:
      paused = true;
      print("win");
      overlays.add('GameOver');
      break;
    default:
      break;
  }
}
```

An additional **switch** is implemented in which the type of game selected by the user is asked and the corresponding function is executed; then the **stateGame** variable is evaluated to know the state of the game.

Next Level

The next functionality to be implemented is to go to the next level once the current one has been passed; to do this, you just have to add some additional logic in the _ **checkEndGame()** function:

lib\main.dart

```
void _checkEndGame(bool isEaten) {
  ***

  switch (stateGame) {
    case typegame.StateGame.lose:
      paused = true;
      print("losing");
      loadLevel(
          /*currentLevel: currentLevel , */ typeGame: typeGame,
          dead: true);
      overlays.add('GameOver');
      break;
    case typegame.StateGame.win:
      paused = true;
      print("win");
      loadLevel(currentLevel: currentLevel + 1, typeGame: typeGame);
      overlays.add('GameOver');
      break;
    default:
      break;
  }
}
```

When losing the game, we also implement additional logic, and it goes back to level 1. You can adapt the handling of the levels as you prefer. For example, currently the GameOver overlay appears both for when the player wins and loses and returns to level one. You could supply in the GameOver function the next level if the player wins or use different overlays for when the player wins and loses among other possible implementations.

Virtual Joystick

Until now, we have used the keyboard as the main element to interact with the game, but with this, it is only possible to play the game on devices that have a keyboard, such as a PC or Mac, leaving the application unusable on other devices such as Android and iOS phones. For this type of application, in which it is necessary to move the player on all axes (or only from left to right and vice versa, as in the case of the dinosaur game), we can implement a virtual joystick. Flame has these types of components ready to use in our application.

A virtual joystick looks like the following.

Figure 13-13. *Example virtual joystick*

In short, you can see that it consists of two components:

1. The translucent circle that indicates the area of movement of the stick/knob

2. The solid color circle that is contained in the previous one that indicates the control so that the user can move the virtual joystick – this corresponds to the lever or control.

Let's start by implementing a joystick class like the following:

lib\components\hud\joystick.dart

```
import 'package:flame/components.dart';
import 'package:flutter/material.dart';
```

```
class Joystick extends JoystickComponent {
  Joystick(
      {required PositionComponent knob,
      required PositionComponent background,
      required EdgeInsets margin})
      : super(knob: knob, background: background, margin: margin);
}
```

The **JoystickComponent** class exists in the Flame API, and to implement it, we have to define two fundamental properties:

1. **knob**, which refers to the command

2. **background**, which is the area in which the controller can be hovered

Both are **PositionComponent**, so they can be a sprite or a geometric figure like a circle.

There are other properties to customize the joystick as you can see in the official documentation, but these are the main.

Finally, we create another file and class, with which we will implement the previously defined custom Joystick class and which we will call Hud for heads-up display, which is a common term in video games to refer to the section of icons, maps, life, etc. In this class we implement the **knob** and **background** properties of the joystick as a pair of colored circles, in addition to positioning it on the screen using the margin:

lib\components\hud\hud.dart

```
import 'dart:async';
import 'package:flame/components.dart';
import 'package:flame/palette.dart';
import 'package:flutter/widgets.dart';
import 'package:parallax06/hud/joystick.dart';

class HudComponent extends PositionComponent {
  late Joystick joystick;
```

```
  @override
  void onLoad() {
    final joystickKnobPaint = BasicPalette.red.withAlpha(200).paint();
    final joystickBackgroundPaint = BasicPalette.black.withAlpha(100).
    paint();

    joystick = Joystick(
        knob: CircleComponent(radius: 30.0, paint: joystickKnobPaint),
        background:
            CircleComponent(radius: 100, paint: joystickBackgroundPaint),
        margin: const EdgeInsets.only(left: 40, top: 100));

    add(joystick);
  }
}
```

Finally, from main, we add an instance of the preceding class:

lib\main.dart

```
import 'package:parallax06/hud/hud_component.dart';
***
class MyGame extends FlameGame
    with HasKeyboardHandlerComponents, HasCollisionDetection {
  ***
  late HudComponent hudComponent;

  @override
  void onLoad() async {
    ***
    hudComponent = HudComponent();
    add(hudComponent);
  }
  ***
}
```

The Flame joystick component has everything necessary to implement mobility in our components. Using the enumerated type

```
joystick.direction
```

we know the status of the knob:

```
enum JoystickDirection {
  up,
  upLeft,
  upRight,
  right,
  down,
  downRight,
  downLeft,
  left,
  idle,
}
```

We also have other options that we can use to determine the movement of the knob. That is, the higher the user takes the knob

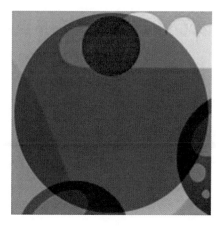

Figure 13-14. *Example virtual joystick, up*

the higher the vector will be:

[-1.0,-67.0] (joystick.delta)

And the closer the knob is to the center

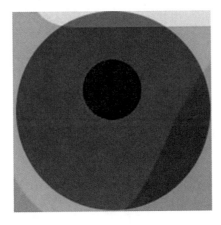

Figure 13-15. *Example virtual joystick, below*

the lesser it moves:

> [-1.0,-21.0] (joystick.delta)

With this vector we also have the angle. That is to say, if we move the knob upward, we will have a negative value in Y

> [X,-72.0] (joystick.delta)

and positive if we move it down:

> [X,72.0] (joystick.delta)

And the same logic applies to the X axis. With this, we can directly use this property to move the player without the need for additional comparisons. Finally, here's the movement of the player using the joystick:

lib\components\player_component.dart

```
class PlayerComponent extends Character with HasGameReference<MyGame> {
  ***
  final double maxVelocity = 10;

  @override
  void update(double dt) {
    ***
    movePlayerJoystick(dt);
  }
```

```
void movePlayerJoystick(double delta) {
  if (game.hudComponent.joystick.direction != JoystickDirection.idle) {
    position.add(game.hudComponent.joystick.delta * maxVelocity * delta);
  }
 }
}
```

It is important to mention that we can have enabled (as is the case for our application) two or more functions for moving; in our project it would be moving by keyboard and also by joystick.

Finally, when executing the application, we will have the following.

Figure 13-16. *Virtual joystick in the application*

Of course, you can implement the joystick in previous games to use the game on other devices that do not have keyboards.

Button to Rotate the Player

So that the game does not require any interaction with the keyboard, we must implement another parallel solution that allows the player to rotate not only by pressing the "R" key but also by interacting with the touch screen, just as we did before with movement of the player through the virtual joystick. For this we will implement a **HudButtonComponent**

A **HudButtonComponent** is a button that can be defined with margins for easy alignment in the viewport; its implementation is very simple and similar to the joystick but this time based on a button. This component takes two **PositionComponents**:

- **button**, displayed when the button is inactive
- **buttonDown**, displayed when the button is pressed

With this cleared up, let's implement a new component:

lib\components\hud\rotate_button.dart

```dart
import 'package:flame/components.dart';
import 'package:flame/input.dart';
import 'package:flutter/material.dart';

class RotateButton extends HudButtonComponent {
  RotateButton({
    required button,
    buttonDown,
    EdgeInsets? margin,
    Vector2? size,
    Anchor anchor = Anchor.center,
    onPressed,
  }) : super(
          button: button,
          buttonDown: buttonDown,
          margin: margin,
          size: size ?? button.size,
          anchor: anchor,
          onPressed: onPressed);

  // @override
  // void onTapDown(TapDownEvent event) {
  //   super.onTapDown(event);
  // }

  // @override
  // void onTapUp(TapUpEvent event) {
```

```
//    super.onTapUp(event);
// }

// @override
// void onTapCancel(TapCancelEvent event) {
//    super.onTapCancel(event);
// }
}
```

Being a button you can implement functions such as **onTapDown()** if you consider it necessary. It is important to note the **onPressed** parameter, which is the function that is executed when the button is pressed and whose behavior will be implemented in the player component to rotate it.

Similar to the joystick, a **HudButtonComponent** is implemented as a hub:

lib\components\hud\hud.dart

```
import 'dart:async';

import 'package:flame/components.dart';
import 'package:flame/palette.dart';
import 'package:flutter/widgets.dart';
import 'package:parallax06/hud/joystick.dart';
import 'package:parallax06/hud/rotate_button.dart';

class HudComponent extends PositionComponent {
  late Joystick joystick;
  late RotateButton rotateButton;

  @override
  void onLoad() {
    final joystickKnobPaint = BasicPalette.red.withAlpha(200).paint();
    final joystickBackgroundPaint = BasicPalette.black.withAlpha(100).
    paint();
    final buttonBackgroundPaint = BasicPalette.blue.withAlpha(200).paint();
    final buttonDownBackgroundPaint = BasicPalette.blue.withAlpha(100).
    paint();
```

```
    joystick = Joystick(
        knob: CircleComponent(radius: 30.0, paint: joystickKnobPaint),
        background:
            CircleComponent(radius: 100, paint: joystickBackgroundPaint),
        margin: const EdgeInsets.only(left: 40, top: 100));
    rotateButton = RotateButton(
        button: CircleComponent(radius: 25, paint: buttonBackgroundPaint),
        buttonDown:
            CircleComponent(radius: 25, paint: buttonDownBackgroundPaint),
        margin: const EdgeInsets.only(right: 20, bottom: 20),
        onPressed: () => {});

    add(joystick);
    add(rotateButton);
  }
}
```

As you can see in the preceding code, a **CircleComponent** is again implemented just like for the joystick, but you can place any other shape or a sprite; finally, the **onPressed** function is implemented from the player so that, when the button is pressed, the player is rotated as it happened when the "R" key was pressed:

lib\components\player_component.dart

```
@override
Future<void>? onLoad() async {
  ***
  // game.hudComponent.rotateButton.onPressed = _rotate;
  game.hudComponent.rotateButton.onPressed = () {
    _rotate();
  };

  return super.onLoad();
}
```

Gamepad

The gamepad is the input device used to interact with a video game and one of the first elements that come to mind when we hear the word "video game" or "video game console." Using these types of controls for our games is not impossible; however, in Flame, we don't have many options. In the official documentation, we will see that at the time these words were written, there is a very short section that mentions the use of the gamepad in Flame:

```
https://docs.flame-engine.org/latest/flame/inputs/other_inputs.html
```

The problem with the package that the Flame team mentions

```
https://github.com/flame-engine/flame_gamepad
```

is that at the time these words were written, it has not been updated for more than three years, and in software development, which includes video game development, it is a considerably long time. Therefore, I personally would not recommend its use since there may be package version problems with the current project, which would cause problems in the implementation.

In Flutter (not directly Flame, but the framework known as Flutter), there are a few plugins that we can use, for example:

```
https://pub.dev/packages/gamepads
```

At the time these words were written, the package is under development; therefore, its documentation is very scarce and its implementation is not entirely friendly as we will see in the following section. However, it is a package that has potential and is in constant development; therefore, it is the one we are going to use. It is important to mention that this package is not designed specifically for Flame like the SharedPreferences package, but it is maintained by the same team that created Flame, and we can use it without problems in a project with Flutter and Flame. This package is currently not available for web or mobile, only for Linux, MacOS, and Windows.

First Steps with the gamepads Plugin

Let's start by adding the dependency for the preceding package:

pubspec.yaml

```
dependencies:
  flutter:
    sdk: flutter
***
  gamepads:
```

It has two main classes:

1. ***GamepadController:*** Represents a single currently connected gamepad.

2. ***GamepadEvent:*** It is an event that is built when an input from a gamepad occurs; in other words, when a key is pressed, an event of this type is built.

The **GamepadEvent** class contains the following properties:

```
class GamepadEvent {
  // The id of the gamepad controller that fired the event.
  final String gamepadId;

  // The timestamp in which the event was fired, in milliseconds
  since epoch.
  final int timestamp;

  // The [KeyType] of the key that was triggered.
  final KeyType type;

  // A platform-dependent identifier for the key that was triggered.
  final String key;

  // The current value of the key.
  final double value;
}
```

The most important would be the key, which indicates the key pressed, and the value, with which, depending on the type of button pressed, we can know the angle or if the button was pressed or released.

The input can be of two types that is represented by an enumerated type called **KeyType**:

1. **analog**: Analog inputs have a range of possible values depending on how far/hard they are pressed (they represent analog sticks, back triggers, some kinds of d-pads, etc.).

2. **button**: Buttons have only two states, pressed (1.0) or not (0.0).

Define a Listener to Detect Keys Pressed

For this plugin, we have two main uses. We can know the number of connected controls:

```
gamepads = await Gamepads.list()
```

Or we can create a listener that allows us to listen to the keys pressed on all connected gamepads:

```
Gamepads.events.listen((GamepadEvent event) { });
```

As you can see, here we have the **GamepadEvent** that has the structure mentioned before. The use of the package is extremely simple, since it does not require establishing a connected control or something similar. We automatically have a listener of all the controls connected to the device. From the player component, we place the listener for the gamepad:

```
import 'package:gamepads/gamepads.dart';
***

@override
Future<void>? onLoad() async {
  // final gamepads = await Gamepads.list();
  // print('Gamepads' + gamepads.toString());
  Gamepads.events.listen((GamepadEvent event) {
    print("gamepadId" + event.gamepadId);
    print("timestamp" + event.timestamp.toString());
    print("type    " + event.type.toString());
```

```
    print("key    " + event.key.toString());
    print("value    " + event.value.toString());
  });
}
```

As a recommendation, connect a device to your PC/Mac, by Bluetooth or its USB cable. Start the application and start pressing some buttons on the gamepad, including its joystick and d-pad. And analyze the response. You will see that some are actually "button" and others are "analog" based on the type classification mentioned previously. In the case of buttons, you will see that the preceding listener is executed when the button is pressed and released.

Based on tests performed from a Windows 11 device with an Xbox S/X controller, we have the following implementation to detect the "A" button:

```
import 'package:gamepads/gamepads.dart';
***
@override
Future<void>? onLoad() async {
  Gamepads.events.listen((GamepadEvent event) {

    if (event.key == 'button-0' && event.value == 1.0) {
      print('rotate');
    }
  });
}
```

And for the d-pad, we detect the movement:

```
import 'package:gamepads/gamepads.dart';
***
@override
Future<void>? onLoad() async {
  Gamepads.events.listen((GamepadEvent event) {

    if (event.key == 'button-0' && event.value == 1.0) {
      print('jump');
    } else if (event.key == 'pov' && event.value == 0.0) {
      // up
      print('up');
```

```
    } else if (event.key == 'pov' && event.value == 4500.0) {
      // up - right
      print('up - right');
    } else if (event.key == 'pov' && event.value == 9000.0) {
      // right
      print('right');
    } else if (event.key == 'pov' && event.value == 13500.0) {
      // buttom right
      print('buttom right');
    } else if (event.key == 'pov' && event.value == 18000.0) {
      // buttom
      print('buttom');
    } else if (event.key == 'pov' && event.value == 22500.0) {
      // buttom left
      print('buttom left');
    } else if (event.key == 'pov' && event.value == 27000.0) {
      // left
      print('left');
    } else if (event.key == 'pov' && event.value == 31500.0) {
      // top left
      print('top left');
    }
  });
}
```

The case of the d-pad is interesting since, depending on the plugin used, it corresponds to the same button. Therefore, when pressing the "up arrow," we have a value of 0.0; when pressing the "down arrow," we have a value of 18000. As you can see, they are values that correspond to a space of 360 degrees; therefore, we can customize the experience however we want. Finally, the implementation using the d-pad looks like the following:

```
import 'package:gamepads/gamepads.dart';
***

@override
FutureOr<void> onLoad() async {
```

```
// var gamepads = await Gamepads.list();
// print('*******');
// print(gamepads.toString());

Gamepads.events.listen(((GamepadEvent event) {

  if (event.key == 'button-0' && event.value == 1.0) {
    // print('Rotate');
    _rotate();
  } else if (event.key == 'pov' && event.value == 0) {
    // up
    // print('up');
    movementType = MovementType.up;
  } else if (event.key == 'pov' && event.value == 4500) {
    // up right
    // print('up right');
  } else if (event.key == 'pov' && event.value == 9000) {
    // right
    // print('right');
    movementType = MovementType.right;
  } else if (event.key == 'pov' && event.value == 13500) {
    // bottom right
    // print('buttom right');
  } else if (event.key == 'pov' && event.value == 18000) {
    //bottom
    // print('bottom');
    movementType = MovementType.down;
  } else if (event.key == 'pov' && event.value == 22500) {
    // buttom left
    // print('buttom left');
  } else if (event.key == 'pov' && event.value == 27000) {
    // left
    // print('left');
    movementType = MovementType.left;
  } else if (event.key == 'pov' && event.value == 31500) {
    // top left
    // print('top left');
```

```
  } else {
    movementType = MovementType.idle;
    //
  }
});
***
}
```

Of course, it is possible that these values will change if you use another type of control or in future versions of the plugin; therefore, you are recommended to adapt the preceding script to your needs.

With this implementation, we have other inputs for the games that we have implemented in this book.

SharedPreferences: Set Game State

One of the problems that we have in all the previous games is that, when you close the application, all the progress is lost. If you implement a game with 20 or more levels in which to go to the next level, you must pass the previous one, saving the game registry, specifically the metadata, is a fundamental task. Flame, being nothing more than a plugin for Flutter, allows us to be able to use any other feature available to Flutter, such as a database, for example, SQFlite. In this example, we use shared preferences, which is nothing more than a plugin that allows us to save data persistently. You can get more information about the package at

```
https://pub.dev/packages/shared_preferences
```

However, if you are a Flutter developer, you probably already know it since it is the package used par excellence in the development of Flutter applications to save application metadata, such as user data, among others.

To install the package, we have

```
pubspec.yaml

dependencies:
  ***
  shared_preferences:
```

Its use is very simple. We have a scheme to save data

```
final prefs = await SharedPreferences.getInstance();
await prefs.setInt('counter', 10);
```

and to read data:

```
final prefs = await SharedPreferences.getInstance();
await prefs.getInt('counter');
```

We can save the data based on some supported types:

```
// Save an integer value to 'counter' key.
await prefs.setInt('counter', 10);
// Save a boolean value to 'repeat' key.
await prefs.setBool('repeat', true);
// Save a double value to 'decimal' key.
await prefs.setDouble('decimal', 1.5);
// Save a String value to 'action' key.
await prefs.setString('action', 'Start');
```

And with this in mind, let's query the data to load the player's game level and form at play time:

```
lib\main.dart
```

```
import 'package:shared_preferences/shared_preferences.dart';
***
class MyGame extends *** {
  @override
  void onLoad() async {
    ***

    final prefs = await SharedPreferences.getInstance();
    currentLevel = prefs.getInt('currentLevel') ?? 1;
    typeGame = TypeGame.values[prefs.getInt('typeGame') ?? 1];
  }
```

Then, when you select the level, the data is saved based on the current preferences:

```
void reset(
    {bool dead = false,
    int currentLevel = 1,
    TypeGame typeGame = TypeGame.byPoints}) async {
  ***

  this.currentLevel = currentLevel;
  this.typeGame = typeGame;

  final prefs = await SharedPreferences.getInstance();
  prefs.setInt('currentLevel', currentLevel);
  prefs.setInt('typeGame', typeGame.index);
  ***

  }
}
```

As a result, when entering the application, the last level will be loaded with the type of game the user played.

Of course, you can use this scheme to record more game metadata than you think is necessary and apply the same logic to previous projects.

Adapt to Small Screens

In this section, we are going to discuss how we could adapt the game on mobile devices. The joystick adaptation was a necessary element in this game so that the user can interact with the game directly from a mobile device such as a phone, but, in this type of devices, another problem arises, which is that these devices have screens of small dimensions. To detect the size of the screens, we can use any of the many ways in Flutter or Flame support, such as

```
MediaQueryData.fromView(View.of(context)).size
```

Or ask for the type of device, for example:

```
Platform.isAndroid
```

Regardless of the way that you prefer to use, when detecting a small screen, you can also detect the orientation of the screen, if it is portrait or landscape. From this, if you are in portrait mode

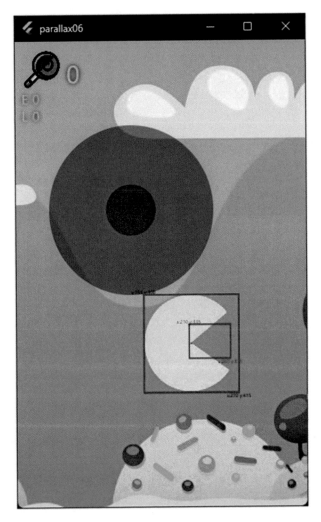

Figure 13-17. *Application in smaller window, portrait*

generate the candy (at least mostly) from below and above. If you are in landscape mode

Figure 13-18. *Application in smaller window, landscape*

generate the sweets from the right and left. This would be to prevent the sweets from escaping too quickly as they are the smallest part of the screen.

You could also scale the player (just like in the dinosaur game) to keep it from taking up too much space:

lib\components\player_component.dart

```
class PlayerComponent extends Character with HasGameReference<MyGame> {
  ***
  _init() {
    ***
    scale = Vector2.all(.5);
  }
}
```

You can do the same for sweets:

lib\components\food_component.dart

```
@override
Future<void>? onLoad() async {
    size = Vector2(50, 50);
    scale = Vector2.all(.5);
}
```

Chapter source code:

https://github.com/libredesarrollo/flame-curso-libro-parallax06/releases/tag/v0.2

CHAPTER 14

Audio

Sound is a crucial part in almost any game today. Background music and when the player or enemy walks, dies, attacks, or is injured are scenarios in which a chord sound is commonly played to enhance the experience. In Flame, to use sounds, we must install an additional extension to the Flame package:

```
flutter pub get flame_audio
```

The official documentation and use can be found at the following link:

https://pub.dev/packages/flame_audio

Its use is very simple. If you want to use background music, you use

```
FlameAudio.bgm.initialize();
FlameAudio.bgm.play('music/bg_music.ogg');
```

Or if you want a sound based on some action performed, you use

```
FlameAudio.play('sfx/fire_1.mp3');
```

When installing the package, you may get an error like the following when trying to run the application on Windows:

```
Please enable Developer Mode in your system settings. Run
  start ms-settings:developers
to open settings.
```

To correct the error, you must execute the following command:

```
$ start ms-settings:developers
```

© Andrés Cruz Yoris 2024
A. Cruz Yoris, *Flame Game Development*, https://doi.org/10.1007/979-8-8688-0063-4_14

Before implementing sounds in the application, it is important to comment on an exception that can occur if you use a web browser as a development device:

```
The process does not have access to the file because it is being used by
another process.
```

Although in all the implementations the disposal or release of the resources is done at the moment of destroying the components, the hot reload/restart mechanisms do not execute said methods, leaving undesired behaviors at the moment of the development of the applications.

Dino Jump Project

For this game, we are going to put in background music and sounds for walking, dying, jumping, and getting hit by the meteorite.

We will use the following audios:

1. *Background (file renamed to **background**):*
   https://freesound.org/people/szegvari/sounds/594223/

2. *Walk (file renamed to **step**):*
   https://freesound.org/people/_bepis/sounds/423196/

3. *Die (file renamed to **die**):*
   https://freesound.org/people/Jofae/sounds/364929/

4. *Jump (file renamed to **jump**):*
   https://freesound.org/people/jeremysykes/sounds/341247/

5. *Impact (file renamed to **explosion**):*
   https://freesound.org/people/InspectorJ/sounds/448226/

And we import them into the project:

pubspec.yaml

```
  assets:
    ***

    - assets/audio/explosion.wav
    - assets/audio/background.wav
```

```
- assets/audio/die.mp3
- assets/audio/jump.wav
- assets/audio/step.wav
```

You can customize the preceding sounds to your liking and use others of your choice.

Before moving on to the sound implementations, it is important to mention an exception that can happen if you use as a device when developing a web browser:

```
NotAllowedError: play() failed because the user didn't interact with the
document first
```

As the exception indicates, it occurs when an attempt is made to play a sound as soon as you enter the web without the user interacting with the web; this type of exception occurs in any conventional web development when an attempt is made to play an audio file as soon as the web is accessed for the first time.

Background Music

For the background music, we implement it from the Game class, as we showed before:

```
lib/main.dart
```

```dart
import 'package:audioplayers/audioplayers.dart';
import 'package:flame_audio/flame_audio.dart';
***
class MyGame extends FlameGame
    with HasKeyboardHandlerComponents, HasCollisionDetection {
  ***

  @override
  void onLoad() {
    ***
    startBgMusic();
  }

  @override
  void onRemove() {
    FlameAudio.bgm.stop();
    super.onRemove();
  }
```

```
void startBgMusic() {
  FlameAudio.bgm.initialize();
  FlameAudio.bgm.play('background.wav', volume: 0.1);
}
***
}
```

Also, we use the volume option, which can have a value between 0 for completely silent and 1 for maximum volume.

Audios for Actions

For the rest of the actions, they are applied to the player class, and the sound will be played based on the actions performed:

```
import 'package:flame_audio/flame_audio.dart';
***
class PlayerComponent extends Character {
  ******

  @override
  bool onKeyEvent(RawKeyEvent event, Set<LogicalKeyboardKey> keysPressed) {
    ******

    if (inGround) {
      // RIGHT
      if (keysPressed.contains(LogicalKeyboardKey.arrowRight) ||
          keysPressed.contains(LogicalKeyboardKey.keyD)) {
        // FlameAudio.play('step.wav');
        ***
      }
      // LEFT
      if (keysPressed.contains(LogicalKeyboardKey.arrowLeft) ||
          keysPressed.contains(LogicalKeyboardKey.keyA)) {
        // FlameAudio.play('step.wav');
        ***
      }
```

```
    ******
  *** @override
void onCollision(Set<Vector2> points, PositionComponent other) {
    ******

    if (other is Life && game.colisionMeteors > 0) {
      FlameAudio.play('explosion.wav');
      ***
    }
    ***
    if (game.colisionMeteors >= 3 && !invinciblePlayer) {
      ***
      FlameAudio.play('die.mp3');
    }

    super.onCollision(points, other);
  }   ***
}
```

In the preceding code, you can see the sections where the action sounds are used, which, unlike the background sound, are only played once, that is, they are not played in a loop; therefore, it is the ideal format to use when the player is hit, jumps, or dies.

The problem happens with the walking sound, where if we uncomment the references to

```
FlameAudio.play('step.wav');
```

you will see that the sound is saturated, that is, by leaving the arrow key pressed, the **onKeyEvent()** function is called more times before it finishes playing the previous sound, giving a bad result, apart from being very inefficient (since the function that plays the walking sound is called many times in a short period of time) and throwing some exceptions in the process.

Audio Loop

For the walking one, we will use another scheme in which we will repeat the sound in a loop when the player is walking/running and we will stop the sound reproduction when they stop walking. We'll look at a couple of implementations.

Implementation 1

For this first implementation, it looks like the following:

lib\components\player_component.dart

```
import 'package:flame_audio/flame_audio.dart';
import 'package:audioplayers/audioplayers.dart';
***

class PlayerComponent extends Character {
  ***

  late AudioPlayer audioPlayerRunning;

  void onLoad() async {
    ***

    FlameAudio.loop('step.wav', volume: 0).then((audioPlayer) {
      audioPlayerRunning = audioPlayer;
    });

    ***
  }

  @override
  bool onKeyEvent(RawKeyEvent event, Set<LogicalKeyboardKey> keysPressed) {
    ***
    if (keysPressed.isEmpty) {
      ***
      audioPlayerRunning.setVolume(0);
    } else {
      audioPlayerRunning.setVolume(1);
    }
  }
}
```

With the preceding code, first, we initialize the loop playback of the walking sound and set the volume to zero, so no walking sound is heard:

```
FlameAudio.loop('step.wav').then((audioPlayer) {

  audioPlayerRunning = audioPlayer;

});
```

When pressing any key, the volume is raised to the maximum:

```
audioPlayerRunning.setVolume(1);
```

And by not pressing any key, the volume is lowered:

```
audioPlayerRunning.setVolume(0);
```

In practice, if there is no player movement, the volume is set to zero; another important point is that, even if the player jumps, the sound of walking will be played.

Implementation 2

For this second implementation, it looks like the following:

lib\components\player_component.dart

```
***
import 'package:audioplayers/audioplayers.dart';
import 'package:flame_audio/flame_audio.dart';

class PlayerComponent extends Character {
  ***

  bool isMoving = false;
  late AudioPlayer audioPlayerRunning;

@override
  void onLoad() async {
    ***

    FlameAudio.loop('step.wav').then((audioPlayer) {
      audioPlayerRunning = audioPlayer;
      audioPlayerRunning.stop();
    });

    ***
  }
```

```
@override
bool onKeyEvent(RawKeyEvent event, Set<LogicalKeyboardKey> keysPressed) {
  ***

  if (keysPressed.isEmpty) {
    ***
    if (audioPlayerRunning.state == PlayerState.playing) {
      audioPlayerRunning.stop();
    }
  } else {
    if (!isMoving) {
      if (audioPlayerRunning.state == PlayerState.stopped) {
        audioPlayerRunning.resume();
      }
    }
  }

  ***

  return true;
  }
}
```

With the preceding code, first, we initialize the loop playback of the walking sound:

```
FlameAudio.loop('step.wav').then((audioPlayer) {
  audioPlayerRunning = audioPlayer;
  audioPlayerRunning.stop();
});
```

Also, it stops the walking sound since, by default, the sound starts playing once the audio is loaded; using the **audioPlayerRunning** property, we can get the audio playback status as well as handle the audio, for example, how to stop it

```
audioPlayerRunning.stop();
```

or play the audio:

```
audioPlayerRunning.resume();
```

It is important to note the conditions to evaluate the playback status and know if the audio is being played

```
if (audioPlayerRunning.state == PlayerState.playing) {
    ***
}
```

or if the audio is stopped:

```
if (audioPlayerRunning.state == PlayerState.stopped) {
    ***
}
```

It is important to do these checks before starting or stopping audio to avoid exceptions and strange behavior in the game.

Remember that you can combine the preceding two implementations to have the desired behavior.

Source code:

https://github.com/libredesarrollo/flame-curso-libro-dinojump03/releases/tag/v0.4

Plants vs. Zombies

For this game, we are going to put in background music and sounds for walking, dying, jumping, and getting hit by the meteorite.

Once the **flame_audio** package is installed in the project, we can start configuring our project.

Zombies: Base Sound

The zombie component when walking or attacking will play a sound; for this, we will use the following audios:

1. *Walk (file renamed to **zombie1.wav**):*
   https://freesound.org/people/silentbob530/sounds/214462/

2. *Walk (file renamed to **zombie2.wav**):*
   https://freesound.org/people/Slave2theLight/sounds/157027/
   (this file was converted from aiff to wav)

3. *Multiple zombies (file renamed to **zombies_many.wav**):*
   https://freesound.org/people/JossuTossu/sounds/483592/

We copy them into the project and reference them to be able to use them:

```
pubspec.yaml
  assets:

   ***

   - assets/audio/zombie1.wav

   - assets/audio/zombie2.wav

   - assets/audio/zombies_many.wav
```

The audio will be in loop, therefore the component of **FlameAudio.loop** is similar to the project implementation above:

```
lib\components\zombies\zombie_component.dart
import 'package:audioplayers/audioplayers.dart';
import 'package:flame_audio/flame_audio.dart';
***
class ZombieComponent extends *** {
  ***
  late AudioPlayer audioWalk;

  @override
  void onLoad() {
    FlameAudio.loop('zombie2.wav', volume: .4).then((audioPlayer) {
      audioWalk = audioPlayer;
```

```
    });
  }

  @override
  void onRemove() {
    _setChannel(false);
    audioWalk.dispose();
    super.onRemove();
  }
}
```

The only difference is that, since the zombie components can be removed, in the **onRemove()** method, the audio is disposed of to cancel it, which indicates that we are not going to use the audio anymore.

Customize Sound for Each Zombie Component

We can customize the sound for each component as we did previously with other properties via a property defined in the base component:

lib/components/zombies/zombie_component.dart

```
class ZombieComponent *** {
  ***
  String audioWalkSound = 'zombie1.wav';

  @override
  void onLoad() {
    FlameAudio.loop(
      audioWalkSound,
      volume: .5,
    ).then((audioPlayer) {
      audioWalk = audioPlayer;
    });
  }
  ***
}
```

The sound can be customized in any component, for example, in the one with the female:

lib/components/zombies/zombie_female_component.dart

```
class ZombieFemaleComponent extends ZombieComponent {
    ***
    audioWalkSound = 'zombie2.wav';
  ***
}
```

Detect Game Over

For the following implementation that we are going to carry out, it is necessary to know when the game ends. The game can end when

1. All the zombies were added on the map, and at least one crossed the map from end to end.

2. All the zombies were added and all were destroyed.

In both scenarios the game is over, and with this, there are no zombies in the channel. Therefore, we must detect when all the zombies were added and when there are no zombies in the channel. To know when all the zombies have been added, we can use the following operation:

```
if (zombieI >= enemiesMap1.length - 1) {
}
```

To know when there are no zombies in the channel, we have to verify the array:

enemiesInChannel

To avoid iterating the entire array and thus making a more expensive operation in terms of resources used, we are going to create a variable that will indicate how many zombies exist in the channel in real time:

lib/helpers/enemies/movements.dart

```
// the number of enemies on the map
int countEnemiesInMap = 0;
```

When a zombie is added, the preceding variable is incremented, and when the zombie is removed, it is subtracted:

lib/main.dart

```
class ZombieComponent *** {
  ***
  @override
  void onLoad() {
    countEnemiesInMap++;
    ***
  }

  @override
  void onRemove() {
    countEnemiesInMap--;
    ***
  }

   ***
}
```

From main, we create the function that checks when the game is over based on the preceding logic:

lib/main.dart

```
class MyGame *** {
  ***
  void checkEndGame() {
    if (zombieI >= enemiesMap1.length - 1) {
      // all the zombies were already added to the map
      if (countEnemiesInMap == 0) {
        // there are no enemies on the map
        print('game over');
        paused = true;
      }
    }
  }
}
```

We should see that, when all the zombies reach the goal or when all the zombies are destroyed, the message

> game over

appears on the console and immediately the game is paused.

Play a Single Sound for All Zombies

Another possible implementation to play an audio is to play a single sound when there are zombies on the map and not a sound for each component; to do this, from main, we play a sound in a loop when the first zombie enters.

We need to know when the game is over; for this, if these two conditions are met:

1. The channels are free (variable **countEnemiesInMap** at zero).

2. All zombies were added (**zombieI** property with the value of **enemiesMap1.length** - **1**).

This was the implementation made in the previous section.

When adding a zombie on the map, we play the sound:

```
lib/components/zombies/zombie_component.dart
class MyGame *** {
  late AudioPlayer audioWalk;

  _zombieWalkAudio() {
    FlameAudio.loop(
      'zombies_many',
      volume: .5,
    ).then((audioPlayer) {
      audioWalk = audioPlayer;
    });
  }

  @override
  void update(double dt) {
    ***
    if (elapsedTime > 3.0) {
      if (zombieI < enemiesMap1.length) {
```

```
    if (zombieI == 0) _zombieWalkAudio();
    ***

  }
 }
}
***
}
```

When detecting that there are no zombies in the channels, the audio playback is canceled:

lib/components/zombies/zombie_component.dart

```
class MyGame *** {
  l***
  void checkEndGame() {
    if (zombieI >= enemiesMap1.length - 1) {
      // we checked if all the zombies of the current map were loaded
        on the map
      if (countEnemiesInMap == 0) {
        // we check if all the zombies were defeated
        audioWalk.dispose()
      }
    }
  }
}
```

Remember to comment the zombie audio playback from the component:

lib/components/zombies/zombie_component.dart

```
class ZombieComponent *** {

  // late AudioPlayer audioWalk;
  // String audioWalkSound = 'zombie1.wav';

  // @override
  // void onLoad() {
  //   FlameAudio.loop(
  //     audioWalkSound,
```

```
//     volume: .5,
//   ).then((audioPlayer) {
//     audioWalk = audioPlayer;
//   });
//
// }

@override
void onRemove() {
  countEnemiesInMap--;
  _setChannel(false);
  // audioWalk.dispose();
  super.onRemove();
}
}
```

Chapter source:
https://github.com/libredesarrollo/flame-curso-libro-plantvszombie05/releases/tag/v0.3

Parallax

For this game, we are going to implement a sound for when a food collides with the player's mouth and another sound for when the player is chewing.

Once the **flame_audio** package is installed in the project, we can start configuring our project.

Basic Sounds

We are going to implement a sound when the food collides with the player's mouth and when chewing; for this reason, we use two audios:

1. *Eating (file renamed as **eating.mp3**)*:
   https://freesound.org/people/Jofae/sounds/353067/

2. *Chewing (file renamed as **chewing.wav**)*:
   https://freesound.org/people/Natymon/sounds/430251/

We copy them into the project and reference them to be able to use them:

pubspec.yaml

```
assets:
  ***
  - assets/audio/chewing.wav
  - assets/audio/eating.mp3
```

Implementation

The sound for when the candy collides with the player's mouth is executed only once, while the chewing sound is executed in a loop, following the same logic that we used in the dinosaur game when the player is walking:

```
import 'package:flame_audio/flame_audio.dart';
import 'package:audioplayers/audioplayers.dart';
***
class PlayerComponent extends Character with HasGameReference<MyGame> {
  ***
  late AudioPlayer audioPlayerChewing;

  PlayerComponent() : super() {
    FlameAudio.loop('chewing.wav', volume: 0).then((audioPlayer) {
      audioPlayerChewing = audioPlayer;
    });
    _init();
  }
  @override
  void update(double dt) {
    super.update(dt);

    if (chewing) {
      changeAnimationTimer += dt;
      if (changeAnimationTimer >= timeToChangeAnimation) {
        ***
        audioPlayerChewing.setVolume(0);
      }
```

```
    }
    ***
  }
  @override
  void onCollisionStart(
      Set<Vector2> intersectionPoints, PositionComponent other) {
    if (mouth.isColliding &&
        other is FoodComponent &&
        !chewing &&
        rotateType == other.foodPreSprite.sideType) {
      ***
      FlameAudio.play('eating.mp3');
      audioPlayerChewing.setVolume(1);
    }
    super.onCollisionStart(intersectionPoints, other);
  }
  @override
  void onRemove() {
    audioPlayerChewing.dispose();
    super.onRemove();
  }
}
```

Chapter source:
https://github.com/libredesarrollo/flame-curso-libro-parallax06/
releases/tag/v0.3

Index

Printed in the United States
by Baker & Taylor Publisher Services